WOODROW WILSON

World Statesman

TWAYNE'S TWENTIETH-CENTURY AMERICAN BIOGRAPHY SERIES

John Milton Cooper, Jr., General Editor

WOODROW WILSON

World Statesman

Kendrick A. Clements

TWAYNE PUBLISHERS • BOSTON
A Division of G.K. Hall & Co.

Copyright 1987 by G.K. Hall & Co.
All rights reserved.
Published by Twayne Publishers
A Division of G.K. Hall & Co.
70 Lincoln St., Boston, Massachusetts 02111

Twayne's Twentieth-Century
American Biography Series No. 7

Book production by Janet Zietowski
Copyediting supervised by Lewis DeSimone
Typeset in 11/13 Goudy by P&M Typesetting, Inc.

First Printing

Library of Congress Cataloging-in-Publication Data

Clements, Kendrick A., 1939–
Woodrow Wilson, world statesman /
Kendrick A. Clements.
p.   cm.—(Twayne's Twentieth-century
American biography series: no. 7)
Bibliography: p.
Includes index.
ISBN 0-8057-7756-3.   ISBN 0-8057-7779-2 (pbk.)
1. Wilson, Woodrow, 1856–1924.
2. Presidents—United States—Biography.
3. United States—Foreign relations—1913–1921.
I.Title.   II. Series.
E767.C63   1987
87-25390

To Linda, Wilson, and James

CONTENTS

FOREWORD

Woodrow Wilson is, arguably, the most interesting and important U.S. president since the Civil War, and he is almost certainly the most controversial president of the twentieth century.

In sharp contrast to the bulk of lawyers, generals, and career politicians who have taken up residence in the White House, Wilson—holder of a Ph.D. degree, professor of political science, and president of Princeton University—is the only academic to have done so. Unlike nearly all of those who have sought, much less attained, the presidency, Wilson had no lengthy political career behind him. Within three years he rose from private life, through the governorship of New Jersey, to the beginning of two terms in the White House. He stood as a candidate in just three elections, once for governor and twice for president. Moreover, Wilson's well-deserved reputations for social respectability, thanks to his association with Princeton, and as an intellectual, through his writing and teaching, were somewhat misleading. Alone among presidents since the 1830s, he did not have American-born grandparents; probably alone among all presidents, he suffered from a childhood reading disability. None of these circumstances would appear to bode well for success at the top job in American politics and government.

Yet, far from being ineffectual in the White House, Woodrow Wilson became a spectacular success during most of his two terms. No other career in American history, perhaps in any nation's history, has so handsomely justified the study of politics as preparation for the practice of politics. Wilson drew upon his analyses of modern democratic government to devise a strategy of presidential leadership that reaped rich rewards. During his first term, he pushed through Congress domestic reform legislation that responded to twenty years of previous agitation and set the agenda of social and economic policy for the next sixty years. In foreign affairs, he steered the country through treacherous conditions in Latin America, made an agonizing decision to enter World War I, prosecuted the war to swift victory, and negotiated an unprecedentedly liberal peace settlement that incorporated the first international peacekeeping organization, the League of Nations. Wilson's sole failure as president was his inability to overcome the bitter stalemate between himself and the Senate, which prevented the United States from ratifying the peace treaty and joining the League. Yet if Wilson had not suffered from deteriorating health during the controversy and a crippling stroke at a critical moment, he might have achieved his objectives. Even in defeat, his international outlook set the agenda for American foreign policy for the rest of this century.

This book is the first full-scale one-volume biography of Woodrow Wilson in fifty years. Kendrick Clements probes deeply into the traits and circumstances that made Wilson so unusual, so successful, and so significant as president. But Clements penetrates still further, into the most fascinating and disturbing aspect of Wilson's place in American history—his controversiality. Wilson combined the intellectual sophistication of Thomas Jefferson with the boldness of Theodore Roosevelt and at times echoed the spiritual elevation of Abraham Lincoln. Yet he has seldom shared in the adulation and affection that have come to surround most great presidents in retrospect. Why? Why has a leader who accomplished greater things than any but three or four other people in the nation's history and who had such a lasting influence remained for so long both an object of attack and an object lesson of how not to pursue public affairs at home and abroad? Why has a man who generally led a quiet, studious life before he belatedly entered politics and who pursued a personally unblemished public career nevertheless found himself subjected to far more pathological-psychological diagnoses than any other figure in American history? The answer lies, in part, in Wilson's inner contractions and conflicts, which Clements examines with sensitivity and sympathy. As a result, this biography provides the clearest and best balanced view of Woodrow Wilson yet written. This biography provides a superb way to come to terms with the president who is perhaps more important to understand than any other in the twentieth century.

John Milton Cooper, Jr.

INTRODUCTION

Woodrow Wilson's long-term influence on the United States justifies the claim that he is one of the most important presidents of the twentieth century. Historians and policymakers alike still commonly refer to policies, especially foreign policies, as "Wilsonian," although they often disagree violently about whether that adjective is complimentary or insulting.

A number of historians have pointed out that Wilson had a record of success in securing what he wanted from Congress that may be unparalleled. Beginning his term in a time of domestic tranquillity and international peace, he secured from Congress every major program he sought and enjoyed a long period of unusual harmony with the legislature. Other presidents notable for domestic achievements, such as Franklin Roosevelt or Lyndon Johnson, held office during times of domestic and/or foreign crisis, which rallied public support for their leadership. Wilson had no such advantage before the American entrance into World War I in 1917.

Except for the Federal Reserve System, Wilson's major reform achievements, tariff reduction and regulation of big business, have had little lasting importance and were, even when passed, conservative measures. Nevertheless, his role in reshaping the relationship among government, business, and organized labor helped to lay the foundation for redefinition of the federal role during the 1920s and 1930s. Critics on the left who charge that all progressive reforms, including Wilson's, were conservative attempts to deflect radical change oversimplify the subtle interplay among interests and government that gradually evolved during his presidency. In addition to providing a model for effective cooperation between president and Congress, Wilson thus contributed significantly to enlarging the functions of the federal government.

Wilson's foreign policy legacy is also controversial. He asserted American world leadership and proclaimed support for international organization, orderly change, antiimperialism, arms reduction, and freedom of international trade. Presidents Herbert Hoover, Franklin D. Roosevelt, and Richard Nixon all identified themselves as "Wilsonians," thus testifying to the enduring importance of Wilson's ideas. Yet in his own time Wilson could not persuade the American people to join the League of Nations, and his interventionist policies in the Caribbean still stir passions. Some critics charge he sought to create an "open door empire" of American political influence and economic profit. Others accuse him of being an impractical idealist whose vision of global order nourished America's "illusion of omnipotence" and led to a dangerous overextension of American power. Both critics and admirers agree that Wilsonian policies reflected deep American desires that are still vital engines of foreign policy.

In 1910 one of Wilson's friends wrote to him that "the general principles upon which government and business must be conducted for the next generation are likely to be formulated, or at least indicated, during the next few years." Looking back more than three-quarters of a century later, this prediction has proved sound. As his friend recognized, it was Wilson's ability to ignore transient details and concentrate on underlying principles that gave him an enduring influence. His goal was not to propose radical transformations but to enunciate basic American values and to indicate ways in which those values could be reinvigorated at home and in the world. Ever since, Americans have been arguing about the correctness of his proposals, but the frequency with which they return to his definition of the issues suggests that he identified central themes of the American experience.

A biography is, or ought to be, a collaboration between writer and subject, a blend of sympathetic understanding and critical evaluation. I have found Wilson a most cooperative partner in the enterprise, and I hope the following pages do him justice. If they do not, it is certainly not the fault of my colleagues, who have been generous with help and advice. Wallace Chessman and Marcia Synnott read and made excellent suggestions about early versions of the first chapters. Herbert Johnson allowed me to read the portions of his continuing study of the development of the American air force that cast light on Wilson's military policy. With Richard Rempel I have enjoyed long discussions that clarified and enriched my understanding of major issues of reform and foreign policy in the Anglo-American world of this period. Arthur Link, David Hirst, and the other editors of *The Papers of Woodrow Wilson*, welcomed me to Princeton, advised me, and granted generous access to materials in forthcoming volumes of the papers. At Princeton's Firestone Library, Mrs. Ann Van Arsdale, in Special Collections, and Mrs. Agnes B. Sherman, in Graphic

Arts, helped to make several research trips pleasant and easy. John Cooper, the general editor of this series, and Arthur Link both read the whole manuscript and gave me the benefit of their editorial experience as well as their exceptional knowledge of Wilson and his period. I am deeply indebted to all of them. To my wife, Linda, my debt is different. Without her, I could not have done it at all.

1

YOUTH AND EDUCATION
1856-1886

It was near midnight on 28 December 1856, but in the big white house at the corner of Coalter and Frederick streets in Staunton, Virginia, everyone was too excited to look at the clock. The baby just born in the first floor bedroom was a boy, not a third girl! The baby's father, Presbyterian minister Joseph Ruggles Wilson, was ecstatic, although he pretended he had not cared whether the baby was a boy or a girl. He "used to say" that "daughters were so much sweeter than sons," reported his wife, Janet Woodrow Wilson, but that remark was never heard again after the birth of Thomas Woodrow Wilson. Jessie (as Janet was usually called) was just as proud. The baby, she wrote to her father, was "a fine healthy fellow. He is much larger than either of the others were—and just as fat as he can be. Every one tells us, he is a *beautiful* boy. What is best of all, he is just as *good* as he can be—as little trouble as it is possible for a baby to be."[1] An uncle, observing the placid baby, declared that he was "dignified enough to be Moderator of the General Assembly" of the Presbyterian church.[2] In the eyes of his adoring relatives, Tommy was plainly intended for greatness.

Tommy's older sisters, Marion (born 20 October 1851) and Annie (born 8 September 1853), immediately took second place to the much-wanted son. Eleven years later (20 July 1867) a second son, Joseph R. Wilson, Jr., was born, but little Josie was destined to be the baby of the family, expected to admire but not to equal his big brother's achievements. In later years Woodrow's relations with his sisters and brother were friendly but distant. He visited them occasionally and was generous with money for them and their families, but he rarely shared his thoughts and dreams with them.

Wilson's mother, Jessie, was born in Carlisle, England, in 1830 and came to Canada with her family in 1835 and to Ohio in 1837. Her father, Thomas Woodrow, was a notable Presbyterian minister in England but not well received in Canada and the United States. For most of his career he moved from small church to small church in the American Midwest. In the meantime, not long after the Woodrows arrived in Canada, Jessie's mother died. Thomas quickly married his dead wife's sister, but she did not welcome the children of the first marriage. Raised more by her brothers and sisters than by her stepmother, Jessie grew up convinced that family ties must be firm. When she married Joseph Ruggles Wilson in 1849, her family's needs and interests became her paramount concern.

Jessie was an intelligent, proud, but shy woman. To the members of her husband's congregation she often seemed arrogantly aloof, and apparently she did feel herself superior to many of them. She found the social and benevolent duties of a minister's wife difficult and performed them with little grace, but within the family she was a different person. There she enjoyed reading and discussing public issues and lavished affection on the children. Tommy, her special pet, later admitted that he had been a "mamma's boy."[3] He idolized his mother, and throughout his life sought from women the same sort of uncritical devotion and emotional support he had received from her.

Woodrow's father, Joseph Ruggles Wilson, was a handsome, eloquent, passionate, ambitious man, not immune to the temptations of power and the flesh. His good looks, wit, and powerful rhetoric helped him rise in the church and inspired admiration in both men and women. During the summers when he took vacations alone at fashionable resorts there were surely opportunities for flirtations, and after Jessie's death there were even rumors of a dalliance with another woman. Jessie could not have been unaware of the admiring glances other women gave her husband, and she knew that by the clerical standards of the day, his liking for a pipe, a nip of Scotch whiskey, a game of billiards, and the latest literature were rather unorthodox.

In Joseph Wilson there were elements of greatness that, unfortunately, never quite came together. Born in Ohio in 1822, he learned printing from his father, taught school briefly, and then decided on the ministry, completing his training at the Princeton Theological Seminary. In 1849 he was ordained by the Ohio Presbytery and the same year married Jessie. Six years later he was called to the important Presbyterian church of Staunton, Virginia, where his growing reputation as an attractive and powerful preacher marked him as a man to watch. In 1858 he was called to one of the most important pulpits in the southern Presbyterian church, at Augusta, Georgia. As the Civil War approached he supported the South and warmly endorsed slavery despite his Ohio birth. During the war his church often housed wounded Confederates and its grounds offered campsites for troops. Young Tommy's earliest memories were thus of the excitement—and agony—of war.

Following the war, Dr. Wilson continued his climb in the church. In 1865 he was elected Stated Clerk (chief executive officer) of the southern Presbyterian church, and in 1870 he was appointed to the faculty of the important theological seminary at Columbia, South Carolina, and was also named stated supply of the First Presbyterian Church of Columbia. Always happier teaching or preaching than ministering to the sick or comforting the afflicted, Wilson was pleased with his new position. Planning to stay in Columbia permanently, the family built a comfortable house and settled down.

Three years later the congregation of the First Church decided they wanted a regular minister, and Wilson lost his position. When he fought back by urging that students at the seminary be required to attend chapel services held at the same hour as the First Church's services, several students rebelled and appealed to church authorities. Although the General Assembly of the church upheld faculty authority, they also recommended that chapel attendance be voluntary, and Wilson, believing that the assembly had "sustained the self-will of the students," resigned and left Columbia.[4]

Just as things looked blackest, Wilson was saved by the offer of a four-thousand-dollar-a-year position as minister of the First Presbyterian Church of Wilmington, North Carolina. The timing was lucky and the pay generous, but the Wilsons disliked Wilmington, finding the seaport dull and the demands of the large, wealthy congregation burdensome. Jessie complained that the members of the church were cold and unfriendly, and apparently the dislike was mutual, for there were long periods of tension when Wilson's salary was not paid on time. Although he stayed fifteen years in Wilmington, Wilson felt that his career, once so promising, had dragged to a stop. In 1885 he resigned the Wilmington pastorate to take another teaching position (in theology) at South-western Presbyterian University in Clarksville, Tennessee.

The move to Clarksville was another half-step down. The semi-nary was not the equal of the one at Columbia, and Wilson was never happy. Three years after moving there, Jessie died, and two years later their elder daughter, Marion, also died. In 1893 Dr. Wilson retired, living for a time with his younger daughter Annie Howe and with Woodrow at Princeton, where he died, an irascible and difficult old man, on 21 January 1903. The bright hopes of his youth had never been realized, and he had a hard time coming to terms with his life.

Joseph Wilson might have been happier in a career other than the ministry. A genuinely devout man, he could never fully reconcile his Presbyterian belief in predestination with the frustrations of his career. He loved literature and politics, and it seems possible that, like his son, he would have been happier in public life than in the pulpit or the classroom. There was not, in those days, a great deal of distance be-tween those callings. Stockton Axson, Woodrow Wilson's brother-in-law, later pointed out that "in Dr. Wilson's youth a great statesman and a great divine, at least in the South, were cut on much the same pattern. . . .Both the statesman and the preacher tended to trace their dogmas back to first principles, to metaphysics."[5] Whether consciously or not, Woodrow, who was so much like his father in many ways, chose wisely when he avoided the ministry and pursued an academic and po-litical career.

From his father Tommy learned to set his goals high and never to accept second best from himself. Perhaps Dr. Wilson's dissatisfaction with his own career led him to see in his son a second chance to achieve the success that had eluded him, and he often seemed to give the impression that nothing Tommy did was quite good enough. When the boy wrote essays to please his father, they always had to be revised, no matter how carefully they were done in the first place. Ironically, in pushing the boy to live up to his full potential, Joseph Wilson seems to have aroused in him a fear that lasted for many years that he would not measure up to his father's standards. Not until he established himself as a major scholar did he outgrow that insecurity.

Certainly Joseph Wilson never wanted to make his son unhappy. Both parents doted on their boy, yet they differed sharply in how they revealed their love. An incident in 1880 illustrated this difference. That spring Woodrow, enamored of one of his cousins, cut too many classes at the University of Virginia Law School and was reprimanded

4

by the faculty. His mother took his side uncritically and blamed the faculty for being too strict. His father wrote, "You certainly acted most imprudently . . . , and it seems to me that the faculty would be deserving of censure if they should overlook so gross a breach of discipline. But, then, I will add this—that, come what will, *you possess our confidence*, because we well know your *character*."[6] Both parents expressed love, but the difference between them was carried over into Wilson's future life. From friends he demanded the same totally uncritical admiration that his mother had given him, but deep down there was an element of self-criticism that seemed to echo his father.

The kinds of goals he pursued were also determined by his father. To both Joseph and Woodrow, the only worthwhile achievements were those that went beyond merely personal satisfaction and were of benefit to society. Joseph Wilson's religion held that people were God's agents for achieving His plans on earth. That meant that people should take an active part in the struggle against evil, and that God would reward them for doing His will. Service, not personal salvation, was the center of his faith.

Woodrow was more successful than his father in achieving satisfaction in this faith. He never questioned the religious tenets laid down by his father. His simple duty was to carry out God's purposes by means of service to others, and from that would surely come God's rewards.

The sense of being God's agent on earth can easily lead to bigotry, intolerance, and rigidity. Both father and son sometimes fell into such behavior, but they were aware of the peril and tried to avoid it. No person, wrote Woodrow, could know all of God's will; one "should have a becoming sense of his own weakness and liability to err."[7]

Tommy Wilson had a happy childhood. Most of his youthful memories were of Augusta and Columbia, which coincided with the happiest years of his father's career. The Civil War, of course, disrupted life somewhat, but Augusta escaped its direct effects, and the family moved to Columbia only as the city was beginning to recover from its destruction by Sherman. Relatively affluent, the Wilsons did not suffer from the aftereffects of war as much as their neighbors did. For Tommy probably the most important effect of the war was a delay in starting school, but since recent medical research suggests that he probably suffered from dyslexia, a slow start to formal education may have been beneficial. Some of the boys with whom he played baseball in Columbia remained friends all his life.

If Tommy's formal education was delayed (he did not learn the al-

5

phabet until he was nine and did not learn to read until eleven), his father offered him plenty of informal instruction. Politics and literature were the common subjects of family conversation, and Joseph made clear his conviction that the Christian must lead in those fields.

In a democracy as in the pulpit, Joseph Wilson believed, a leader must win the support of the people. He must, therefore, cultivate spoken and written eloquence as the principal tool of leadership. "In the last sense of the word," Dr. Wilson said, "the great orator is the great *actor*."[8] He drilled the boy in precise, effective use of language, and Tommy, an apt pupil, sometimes practiced speeches in his father's empty church on quiet afternoons. "I've fallen fairly in love with speechmaking . . . ," he admitted in 1881, for an orator, "can gain a hearing when others might find difficulty in doing so, and can, by an effort, change a vote while others fail to command their hearers' sympathies."[9]

The policies to be followed by a leader were at this stage less clear in Wilson's mind than the techniques of leadership. Rhetoric in itself seemed a good thing, and he was less concerned with content than with style. When practicing for an extemporaneous speech, for example, he paid little attention to the topic and instead spent his time reading a work of literature whose style he admired—Shakespeare or Swinburne's *Tristram of Lyonesse*, for example—in order to set his "mind aglow, seeming to make it nimble and strong, with a joyous strength fit for doing at its best any work it is capable of doing at all." That, he thought, was far preferable to trying to read too much, for "the penalty for cramming one's mind with other men's thoughts is to have no thoughts of one's own."[10] One of his earliest proposals for reform of the American system was to convert the government to a parliamentary system, to maximize opportunities for debate and oratory.

Without thinking about it, Tommy absorbed the values and attitudes of his region. He later said that one of his earliest memories was of running to ask his father why people were saying that Lincoln's election meant war, and as an adult his books were sympathetic to the position of the antebellum South. Throughout his career his speeches were sprinkled with romantic images of the South. He often said it was "the only place in the country, the only place in the world, where nothing has to be explained to me."[11]

Like other whites of his generation, Wilson took a condescending and paternalistic attitude toward blacks. He defended segregation and disfranchisement as the result of sad experience during Reconstruction

6

when political power was held by Negroes, whom he saw as "ignorant and unfitted by education for the most usual and constant duties of citizenship."[12] As blacks secured education, he seemed to imply, they would be able to take a larger part in political affairs.

Yet in private Wilson seemed even less liberal, referring several times to blacks as "an ignorant and inferior race."[13] Such beliefs were bred into his very fiber, and even after living for many years outside the South he admitted that "there are certain things which I can perfectly understand in my heart and not justify in my mind."[14] As president, he and other southerners in his administration brought many of these attitudes to federal policy.

On the other hand, there were ways in which Wilson transcended his southern background. As an adult he had no noticeable accent and pruned most "southernisms" from his speech. He did not share his father's enthusiasm for the "Lost Cause" of the Confederacy, and his *Division and Reunion*, published in 1893, was one of the fairest and most impartial accounts of the Civil War and Reconstruction published by anyone, northern or southern, up to that time and for some years to come. As biographer Arthur Link has pointed out, Wilson's yearnings for the South "increased in direct ratio to the length of his absence from it."[15]

Wilson's eventual decision to leave the South was the culmination of a slow maturation process that began in 1873 when he first left home for college. Up to that time he had roamed the world in fantasies as an admiral of the Royal Navy, but he had never really been away from his family. That fall he enrolled at Davidson College in North Carolina and discovered that he was neither academically nor emotionally well prepared. The college was a small, intensely religious establishment, and although Wilson managed to survive the work, he was unhappy. A poem he copied into one of his notebooks from the *Southern Presbyterian* suggests his confused state:

> The way is dark, My Father! Cloud on
>   cloud
> Is gathering thickly o'er my head, and loud
> The thunders roar above me. See, I stand
> Like one bewildered! Father, take my
>   hand,
>   And through the gloom
>   Lead safely home
>   Thy child.[16]

7

Homesick, he kept a list of letters received from and sent to members of his family.

Yet even as he suffered the shock of separation, Wilson was beginning to move beyond his family circle and to build a life of his own. Despite recurrent illnesses, which were probably psychosomatic in part, he passed his courses and found time to participate in a debating club, for which he wrote a new constitution. He also played second base for the freshman baseball team, and by the time he went home at the end of the year, he apparently intended to return in the autumn for his sophomore year.

In the meantime Dr. Wilson accepted a pulpit in Wilmington, North Carolina, and the family moved that summer. Coming on top of his strained year at Davidson, Tommy was distressed by this decision, which meant breaking his ties with friends in Columbia. His mother assured him he would "have no lack of friends in Wilmington—of the warmest sort," but perhaps, given the bitterness surrounding Joseph's departure from Columbia, her reassurances lacked real conviction.[17] Whether out of concern for the boy, or to draw the family together in a time of stress and uncertainty, the Wilsons decided not to send Tommy back to Davidson. Instead, he studied at home during 1874–75 in preparation for a new institution, the College of New Jersey, at Princeton.

The Princeton Wilson entered in 1875 was beginning to change from "a quiet country college" to one of "the most notable institutions of the country," as Wilson put it years later.[18] Under the presidency of James McCosh, elected in 1868, it was securing a more scholarly and diverse faculty, its graduates were entering professions other than the ministry, and its undergraduate activities were becoming more varied with the addition of intercollegiate athletic competition and nonreligious organizations. Chapel services were still major events of campus life, almost all the faculty were still Presbyterian clergy, and there were regular class religious services; but a new atmosphere of secular intellectual and social activity was beginning to emerge. The first new building McCosh erected with the funds he was so successful in raising was, symbolically, a gymnasium. More than half the members of Wilson's class entered business; only 18 percent chose the ministry.

Princeton's blend of secularism and religious idealism suited Wilson perfectly, and he quickly made friends with other young men who shared his vision of a literate, service-oriented elite reforming American political life. Although few of the professors excited him, during his sophomore year he discovered for himself the pleasures of reading Macaulay's and Green's histories of the English people, the essays of Addison and Walter Bagehot, and the speeches of Burke and John Bright. From this self-education, rather than from what he heard in the classroom, Wilson formed his own political values. When he was a senior, his admiration for the British political system found expression in an article proposing that Congress and president be replaced by a parliamentary form of government. "Cabinet Government in the United States," published in the *International Review*, expressed the idea that infused Wilson's first book, *Congressional Government*.

There were also opportunities for fun. Sharp rivalries existed between classes and often found expression in athletic contests or in rough and rowdy "sprees," which amounted to licensed riots. For less active times there were the Glee Club, where Wilson's strong tenor was welcomed, and the college newspaper, the *Princetonian*, where he rose to editor. In these activities and in long walks and talks with his new friends Wilson gradually began to realize, as did some of the faculty, that he had unusual qualities of leadership and intellect.

The real reason the parliamentary system appealed so strongly to Wilson was that, as he imagined it, it fitted his own talents and training. It was a system in which he thought he could rise to the top. With a strong desire for political power, he cast about for ways of getting into politics and eventually decided to enter law school. He never had any real enthusiasm for law but recognized that it was a traditional route to political office. "The profession I chose was politics," he told his fiancée in 1883; "the profession I entered was the law. I entered the one because I thought it would lead to the other."[19]

Although a common motive for choosing law, Wilson's reason was the wrong one. Even before he entered the University of Virginia Law School (where he studied from the autumn of 1879 to December of 1880), he began to wonder if he had made a mistake, and he soon decided he had. What interested him were the philosophy and purpose of the law—the law as a reflection of the goals and values of the society—but what he had to learn were its endless details and technicalities. To a friend he wrote that he was "struggling, hopefully but not with . . . *over*-much courage, through its intricacies, and am swallowing the vast mass of its technicalities with as good a grace and as straight a face as an offended palate will allow."[20] Only ambition kept him going.

Wilson's metaphorical indigestion became, in 1880, physical as well. During the spring a chronic "cold" produced recurring bouts of "dyspepsia" that became serious enough that his family suggested he drop out of school. Instead he finished the term, and after a summer's rest returned to Charlottesville. With his studies the illness returned, however, and in December Wilson abruptly left the university without telling either his friends or the faculty of his decision. What his parents thought about that rash action we do not know, but during the next year and a half he lived at home and worked there to complete his legal education. Even in that atmosphere his digestive problems, both intellectual and physical, continued.

Nevertheless, by the summer of 1882 Wilson was ready to embark officially on his legal career. In August he went to Atlanta and joined another University of Virginia student, Edward I. Renick, in setting up a practice. The young men hoped to benefit from Atlanta's reputation as "one of the most thriving places in the South."[21] Yet despite the city's opportunities, the practice did not prosper. Atlanta was a boomtown, and its legal business required an aggressiveness and crudity neither Wilson nor Renick possessed. Wilson passed his bar examination brilliantly in October, but few clients entered the firm's offices, and he had to borrow money from his father to live. Long, empty days were spent reading history and political science while busy Atlanta rushed by outside. Georgia, Wilson concluded, was an "ignorant, uninteresting" state, and the "dreadful drudgery" of the law was not for him.[22] As the end of his first year as a lawyer approached, Wilson decided to leave the profession and the South in order to approach politics from a different direction, as a teacher and writer.

In principle, Wilson was enthusiastic about the New South of commerce and industry, which, he argued, was made possible by the destruction of the stultifying slavery system, but he was never happy in the most important city of the New South, Atlanta. He found it a cultural wasteland, totally inhospitable to the sort of literary and political career he wanted. The only reason he set up his law practice there, he told a friend, was "that in the South I would have more immediate prospects of gaining an influence over political opinion, though the North offers more abundant opportunities of large professional favor."[23] When he discovered that prospect was illusory, he lost no time in leaving the law, the city, and the region, never to return permanently.

The New South had no place for Wilson, yet he never questioned its boosters' cheerful confidence that industry would make the region as

10

prosperous as the North without changing its distinctive way of life. For Wilson, as for many others, the seductive appeal of this ideology was the faith that progress and change were entirely compatible with tradition. Made unhappy by the fact that the reality did not fit the myth, he never realized that the problem lay as much in the ideology as in his problems with law as a profession. When he left the region and the law, he took with him as a major part of his intellectual baggage, the ideological assumptions of the New South. Largely unexamined, they became the greatest legacy of Wilson's southern upbringing and the basis of his national political program.

The decision to leave Atlanta was not easily reached. He and his father agonized over it, wondering whether he had given law a sufficient trial and worrying that he might find himself always drifting from one commitment to another. It was characteristic of Dr. Wilson, however, that even as he warned Woodrow about inconstancy, he also wrote, "I will not object to any decision you may come to, and will do my utmost to secure you a position."[24]

Having reached his difficult decision, Wilson applied for a fellowship to the Johns Hopkins University in Baltimore. He did not receive the fellowship, but his father offered to support him, and so in the summer of 1883 he left Atlanta and the law for good. Despite his hatred for the practice of law, he still believed it a noble subject. "The philosophical *study* of the law—which must be a pleasure to any thoughtful man—is a very different matter from its scheming and haggling practice," he told a friend.[25]

What most bothered Wilson about leaving the law was the fear that he was shutting the door on a political career. "A professorship was the only feasible place for me," he wrote, because it was "the only place that would afford leisure for reading and for original work, the only strictly literary berth with an income attached," but he deeply regretted that it would never enable him to "participate actively in public affairs." Instead he must, he thought, "content [myself] with becoming an *outside* force in politics . . . through literary and non-partisan agencies."[26]

One of Wilson's few legal cases was an estate matter for his mother, but that had an unexpected benefit. Early in April 1883 the case took him to Rome, Georgia, where he attended church with the family of his uncle, James W. Bones. During the service his attention was distracted from the religious to the mundane when he caught sight

11

of a girl with "a bright, pretty face" and "splendid mischievous, laughing eyes!"[27] She was, Wilson quickly discovered, the daughter of the minister, Reverend Samuel Edward Axson.

Ellen Axson, then twenty-three, had "a sunny, loving heart and a quick, earnest, thoughtful mind."[28] A talented artist, she was also the homemaker of her family, tending her father, two younger brothers, Stockton, sixteen; Edward, seven; and a sister, Margaret, two. Her mother had died in childbirth two years earlier, and her father was chronically depressed. In 1884 he entered the state mental hospital where apparently he committed suicide a few months later. For all her laughing eyes, Ellen carried heavy burdens.

Ellen and Woodrow were strongly drawn to each other, but she resisted serious involvement despite his growing ardor during two more visits to Rome in the spring of 1883 and his increasingly passionate letters. Woodrow was supremely confident that no obstacle would prevent marriage. He promised that Ellen's brothers and sister would become part of their family (they did), and he swept aside even his mother's objections to the romance.

On 14 September, by a series of coincidences that the Wilsons later attributed to the workings of Providence, the couple's paths crossed in Asheville, North Carolina, where Ellen was waiting for a train to Rome and Woodrow for one to Baltimore. Neither knew the other was in town, but Woodrow, walking past the Eagle Hotel, happened to spy through a window a young lady with a familiar hair-do and rushed inside. The surprise swept away their last reserve, and out he poured a torrent of adoration. Dazed and overwhelmed, Ellen found herself agreeing to marry him before she could catch her breath. Sealing their promise with a brief kiss, they were so excited that they forgot the magic words "I love you." Woodrow, rushing away to his train, could hardly wait to begin a fiery exchange of letters that would rectify the oversight many times over. "I did not know myself how much I loved you until I found out that you love me," he wrote from Baltimore two days later. "If you could know my heart as I know it," he assured her, "you would have very few doubts and fears as to the future, my pet. No love like mine can be a mistaken love, when it is returned by love like yours."[29]

Wilson sailed into Baltimore on the floodtide of romance. He felt wonderful and was delighted to be turning away from the law and putting all his energy into the study of history and politics. "It's a strange psychological fact," he wrote Ellen, "that since my short visit to Asheville I've been able to write with much more satisfaction to myself than formerly."[30]

The doctoral program Wilson was entering, in history and political science, was the first in the United States to be modeled on German patterns, and it employed among its faculty some academic leaders, including Herbert Baxter Adams in American history, Richard T. Ely in political economy, and J. Franklin Jameson in English history. Fellow students in the "Seminary," as the group of students was called, included Albert Shaw and Davis R. Dewey, and the regular meetings of faculty and students were opportunities to discuss original research, which Wilson much preferred to the textbook recitations that had so bored him at Princeton.

At first Wilson was much impressed by faculty and students, and in the euphoria of love found delight in everything. To his college friend Bobby Bridges he wrote that "as soon as I can get into college ways and avoid kicking over the traces, I shall, I think, like the work here thoroughly well. Certainly I shall not lack for stimulating examples or for intelligent guidance."[31]

Sadly, the first impression did not last. His great, romantic passion sustained him but left him prey to sexual frustrations. And his first enthusiasm for the work of the graduate program began to wane when he found that Dr. Adams, following the German model, was more interested in "digging . . . into the dusty records of old settlements and colonial cities . . . and other rummaging work of a like dry kind" than in "the grand excursions amongst imperial policies which I had planned for myself."[32] A few months later he accused Adams of stealing his students' ideas for his own advancement while giving in return "a very meagre diet of ill-served lectures."[32]

The complaints were largely rhetorical excess brought on by finding that the program was not, after all, perfect. In fact Wilson was well treated at Hopkins, and although he never stopped complaining about the stress upon fact and detail, he was not really unhappy. In October 1883 he called on Adams and explained that his interests were in the philosophy and structure of politics rather than in the facts of history. Far from being angry, Adams welcomed his ideas and largely freed him from "institutional" studies so that he could follow his bent. Early in 1884 Ely invited him to coauthor a book on American political economists, and later that spring Adams asked him to read the first chapters of what would become *Congressional Government* to the other students, describing the work as "better than anything in that line that has been done heretofore in the Seminary."[34] The following year he was awarded the fellowship for which he had originally applied.

Outside class Wilson made friends with other students and became a leader of the Hopkins Literary Society and the glee club. In almost daily ten- and twelve-page letters he poured out his love for "the person whose love animates all his undertakings."[35] Ellen, rejoicing in his successes, assured him that his own sense of direction would carry him forward even if the faculty was disappointing.

Throughout early 1884 Wilson produced a prodigious amount of work. He kept up with the regular graduate program, including reading and attending both lectures and meetings of the seminary; he began work for the collaborative book with Ely (never published); he published an article entitled "Committee or Cabinet Government?" in the *Overland Monthly*; he wrote long daily letters to Ellen; he visited friends and took part in extracurricular activities; and he churned out chapter after chapter of *Congressional Government*. In part, his impatience with his professors may have been because he was doing more and better work than most of them.

Published in January 1885, *Congressional Government* was the first attempt by a scholar to describe the American political system not as it was supposed to function but as it actually worked. As Wilson saw it, the federal government was dominated by Congress, and Congress in turn was manipulated behind the scenes by special interests. Neither that analysis nor Wilson's recommendation for a change to a parliamentary system was entirely new, but the book had great impact because it was scholarly yet readable and understandable to a general audience. Wilson tried to be "entertaining, exact, philosophical" all at once, because he believed that "readers delight most, not in a writer who sees, but in one who enables them to see readily and pleasantly."[36] Enthusiastic reviews and brisk sales testified to his success. Short of actually holding office himself, nothing could have pleased him more.

Wilson's modest claim for the book was an understatement. It was no small achievement to have written the first serious study of how a major institution actually worked, and to have presented the findings in a style that is still enjoyable a century later. Modern political scientists still regard the book as a model, while for contemporaries it drew attention to a serious imbalance in the government.

Not suprisingly, *Congressional Government* also had some flaws. It lacked a historical perspective that might have suggested to Wilson that Congress had not always dominated the executive and that it might lose its dominance again. It ignored the importance of economic issues in shaping political battles, and it made little effort to look beneath the surface of political parties or alliances to see what held them together. It had some serious errors, such as Wilson's strange assertion that the "Senate is . . . separated from class interests."[37] But those mistakes were by no means fatal, and the book was reprinted year after year to serve as an introduction to the workings of the American political system for generations of students.

For the "mugwumps" of the day—the conservative reformers who believed that American politics had been corrupted by materialism and must be purified through structural changes—*Congressional Government*'s originality or profundity was unimportant. They embraced it because it gave literary and academic respectability to the charges they were already making. Wilson was not disappointed by that assessment; his aim, after all, was to influence contemporary political life even more than to advance scholarship.

After the publication of the book, Wilson had the usual author's doubts about what to do next and whether he could follow up his first success. His concerns lightened in the spring, however, when Ellen agreed that they be married in June, and when he accepted an offer to join the faculty of a new women's college near Philadelphia, Bryn Mawr. A year later, in June 1886, after Professor Adams had generously bent the rules to permit the submission of *Congressional Government* as Wilson's Ph.D. dissertation, he was awarded the doctorate from Johns Hopkins. Finally, at the age of almost thirty, he was ready to begin an academic career. Warmed by his first successes, he still cherished the hope that he might, after all, find a way to political power.

2

BUILDING AN ACADEMIC CAREER
1885–1902

On 7 July 1884 Ellen wrote Woodrow that she had decided to attend classes that autumn at the Art Students' League in New York. The announcement was something of a declaration of independence for her, both from the family burdens that followed her father's death in May, and even, to some extent, from her "darling Woodrow."[1] What she wanted, though she did not say so directly, was to postpone exchanging duties to her father, brothers, and sister for the obligations of marriage that Woodrow so ardently urged. In the end she was willing to give up an artistic career and devote herself to home and family, but first she wanted to know beyond doubt what she might have done.

Admitted to the school in one of the elementary classes, her abilities were quickly noticed by her teachers, and she was transferred to an advanced class, where she became one of the star students. Characteristically, her letters describing these triumphs were filled with self-deprecation and insistence that it was all a mistake, but there was no mistaking the tone of pleasure and quiet confidence that lay beneath the surface. She was extremely popular among the students as well, both with the women and some of the men. Predictably, Woodrow became a little jealous, and her reluctance to wear her engagement ring (she kept saying it was not the right size) or to cut off all contact with one especially attentive male friend, as Woodrow demanded, suggest that she enjoyed teasing him a bit. It was all part of spreading her wings.

By the spring of 1885 Ellen seems to have decided that she had learned what she wanted to know about herself. Early in January Woodrow completed negotiations with the trustees of Bryn Mawr College and accepted an associateship at fifteen hundred dollars a year. The salary was small, but Woodrow thought he and Ellen could manage on it and begged her to marry him. On 14 January she agreed to a June wedding. Never then or thereafter did she so much as hint that by so doing she had sacrificed anything she cared about. "Sweetheart, I would never give you a divided allegiance," she wrote to Woodrow when he expressed concern about whether she would try to combine a career with marriage; "I owe you my little *all* of love, of life and service, and it is all my joy to give it. Believe me, dear, it is an absolutely pure joy—there is in it *no* alloy, I have *never* felt the *slightest* pang of regret for what I must 'give-up'."[2] On 24 June 1885 they were married. After a summer's honeymoon at Arden, North Carolina, the newlyweds arrived at Bryn Mawr to begin Woodrow's teaching career in September. As he did so, his feelings about his new undertaking were decidedly mixed.

In some ways Bryn Mawr, which opened its doors to a first class of thirty-five undergraduates and seven graduate students that September, was ideally suited to a man who wanted "to gain a reputation and make his work tell as soon as possible." Particularly it was close to the "eastern centres of educational work" and to "the great libraries which alone contain adequate materials for original writing." Wilson's teaching schedule was not heavy, and the new college had a close relationship with Johns Hopkins that would enable him to keep himself "under the eyes" of the leaders of his profession.[3] Anyway, the only alternatives were not attractive, so by contrast Bryn Mawr seemed desirable.

Wilson did, however, have reservations. The salary was painfully small, and finding living quarters proved a problem. Most serious were Wilson's doubts about teaching at what Ellen referred to as "a *girls school*" and being supervised by a woman dean (Dr. Martha Carey Thomas). "It goes without saying, my darling," Wilson admitted, "that I would a *great* deal rather teach *men* anywhere, and especially in the South, than girls at Bryn Mawr or anywhere else."[4]

Wilson's attitudes toward women were conventional for the time. "A woman," he told Ellen, "is glorified and made perfect by marriage and motherhood."[5] He was made a little uncomfortable by women as college students, though he was honest enough to admit that his students were "interested and intelligent" and "the administration . . . honest, straightforward, and liberal."[6] Later, however, when professional advancement seemed slow in coming and the birth of two daughters strained his small salary, he began to find fault. "Lecturing to young women of the present generation on the history and principles of politics," he complained, was "about as appropriate" as "lecturing to stone-masons on the evolution of fashion in dress."[7] By the autumn of 1887 Wilson was actively looking for another position, and in June of 1888 he submitted his resignation to Bryn Mawr, having received an offer to become the Hedding Professor of History and Political Economy at Wesleyan University in Middletown, Connecticut.

Aside from his concerns about money and his academic career, Wilson's discontent in 1887 seems to have come from a fear that he had been sidetracked, that after the first great success of *Congressional Government* he had been "shut off from my heart's *first*—primary—ambition and purpose, which was, to take an active, if possible a leading, part in public life, and strike out for myself, if I had the ability, a statesman's career."[8] He did not care for "*book*-politicians," he told a friend, and wanted instead to meet "men who have direct touch of the world."[9] Moving to Wesleyan would not make him a statesman, but it would at least allow him to teach men.

In a sense Wilson's move in the summer of 1888 was also symbolic of a deeper break, for in April of that year his mother had died. Her death, he told his friend Heath Dabney, gave him an "oppressive sense" of having lost his youth.[10] It may also have brought home to him the difference between the uncritical devotion given him by mother and wife and the more challenging relationship with his students. "My mother, with her sweet womanliness, her purity, her intelligence, her strength, prepared me for my wife," he wrote. "I remember how I clung to her (a laughed-at 'mamma's boy') till I was a great big fellow: but love of the best womanhood came to me and entered my heart through those apron-strings."[11] It was his mother's kind of womanhood that Wilson wanted, not the feminist or scholarly variety exemplified by Dean Thomas and some of his Bryn Mawr students.

Determined to return eventually to Princeton, Wilson regarded the Wesleyan position as temporary, but he liked the college (a "university" by virtue of having five M.A. students). In many ways, Wesleyan in 1888 was about where Princeton had been when Wilson had entered in 1875. It was a small, denominational (Methodist) college successfully making the transition to a secular university. Its facilities and library were similar to what Wilson had known at Princeton, but its faculty was much better. Its trustees, mostly Methodist ministers, chose faculty with tolerance and an eye for quality. In later years Wilson remembered the Wesleyan faculty as having less "dead wood" than any other he was familiar with.[12] The professors were encouraged to pursue their own studies, to give lectures outside the university, and to experiment with teaching methods beyond the traditional textbook and recitation combination that Wilson had found so dull at Princeton.

The Hedding professorship's twenty-five-hundred-dollar salary was a substantial increase over what Wilson had been receiving at Bryn Mawr, and with additional income from lecturing and writing, it enabled the Wilsons for the first time to live in some comfort. They rented a large Greek revival house on High Street a short distance from the campus. The house had a fine view out over the Connecticut River Valley and, with two stories in front and three in back, provided enough room for their expanding family, which now included their daughters, Ellen's two brothers, various visiting relatives, and two Irish serving-girls.

The Wesleyan students loved Wilson. His teaching load was light, and he prepared his lectures with the greatest care, concentrating factual material at the beginning and filling the rest of the hour with anecdotes and illustrative descriptions that delighted the students with their humor and colorful immediacy. Above all, his students remembered the "clarity, charm, and elegance of his language."[13] Ellen's brother, Stockton Axson, who came at Wilson's urging to live with them and attend the college, recalled that he put so much energy into his lectures that he would have to lie down for half an hour to recover after each.

Wilson enjoyed Wesleyan too, playing tennis and bicycling with friends, sponsoring a college debating club and even coaching the football team. When Ellen became pregnant a third time, he hoped his good fortune would be capped by the birth of a son, but the arrival of a third daughter was only a momentary disappointment. The new baby, Nell, soon became his favorite.

In the broader world of scholarship Wilson's reputation and confidence were growing. "Since I have been here," he told Ellen in 1889, "a distinct *feeling* of maturity—or rather of maturing—has come over me. . . . I need no longer hesitate . . . to assert myself and my opinions in the presence of and against the selves and opinions of old men, 'my elders.' "[14] The obvious reason for that sense of confidence was the growing recognition Wilson was securing. In 1887 Johns Hopkins invited him to return to give a three-year series of twenty-five lectures a year in the graduate program, and the students, including a talented young man from Wisconsin, Frederick Jackson Turner, were enthusiastic about his ability. Continued until 1896, Wilson's annual lecture series broke new ground by exploring the theory and practice of government administration in the United States and Europe.

Unfortunately, Wilson never got around to turning his impressive lecture notes on administration into a book, but he did complete his second book in this period. It was *The State: Elements of Historical and Practical Politics; A Sketch of Institutional History and Administration*, published in the autumn of 1889. It was intended as a textbook for college classes in comparative government and the first step toward a broad history of the development of democratic government. Based largely on German sources through which Wilson, with his shaky German, was guided in large part by Ellen, the book described the evolution of political structures from ancient to modern times and offered detailed description of the American government as well as analysis of European governments. Because it described how governments actually worked rather than the theory behind them, it was then unique among works of political science. Together with his study of administration, *The State* established Wilson as one of the most innovative and important political scientists in America.

The State provided clues that Wilson's political opinions were developing. In it he dropped his old proposal of an American parliament and turned to specific contemporary problems. He deplored "modern industrial organization" when it "distorted competition" and enabled "the rich and strong to combine against the poor and weak." Government, he wrote, should rectify these injustices by taking over or regulating natural monopolies such as gas works, water systems, and railroads. It should restore competition, prohibit child labor, regulate working conditions for women, control hours in certain trades, and generally improve the workplace. Its goal should be to make "competition equal" and protect society against "permanent injury and deterioration." Believing that all societies evolve and change, Wilson deplored equally the revolutionary and the reactionary. "The method of political development," he concluded, "is conservative adaptation, shaping old habits into new ones, modifying old means to accomplish new ends."[15] Those who expected Wilson to be either a radical or a conservative as a political leader would have done well to ponder those words.

The public response to *The State* was friendly. Except for one critic in the *Nation*, most reviewers praised the book for its clarity, perception, and sense of a broad order in history. It was adopted as a textbook for courses at Harvard, Johns Hopkins, and the universities of Wisconsin and Indiana, among others. For almost thirty years it remained in print and for much of that period continued to sell a thousand or more copies a year, bringing its author welcome royalties.

Even before *The State* appeared, Wilson was off on another project. Albert Bushnell Hart of Harvard invited him to write a volume on the Civil War and Reconstruction for the Epochs of American History series, of which Hart was editor. Wilson was flattered as a southerner to be asked to do the volume and pleased to have a chance to try his hand at history. Published in 1893, *Division and Reunion, 1829–1889* was based on careful research and offered a balanced, judicious interpretation of a still sensitive subject. Its novel thesis that the war resulted from differences in the way the two regions had developed economically and socially was disputed by some scholars, but it has had considerable influence on subsequent scholarship. Particularly striking from a southerner was the argument that slavery was economically wasteful and that the region was better off without it. Still confident that the New South ideology would bring prosperity and happiness, he concluded that the wounds of the past were healed, and that the country would enter the new century with "a sense of preparation, a new seriousness, and a new hope."[16]

By the time *Division and Reunion* appeared (to generally favorable reviews), Wilson had achieved his goal of returning to Princeton. In February of 1890 several of his friends from the class of 1879 arranged to have President Francis L. Patton offer him a professorship of jurisprudence and political economy. He was delighted, and although he asked at first for a salary of thirty-five hundred dollars (more than anyone else was receiving), he eventually accepted an offer of three thousand and a promise that he would be required to lecture no more than four times a week and would be able to continue his Hopkins series. His Wesleyan colleagues regretted his departure but wished him well and in 1903 invited him back to be the main speaker at festivities celebrating the two hundredth anniversary of John Wesley's birth. On both sides the Wesleyan experience had been a happy one.

The Princeton to which Wilson returned in September of 1890 had not developed as rapidly or as far as President McCosh had hoped. Under the presidency of Francis L. Patton (elected in 1889) it remained small (600 students), religiously orthodox, and rather inbred. Patton was a brilliant speaker but a poor administrator, and he was unable to enforce discipline or bring himself to fire incompetent professors. The students no longer wore coats and ties as they had in Wilson's day, but fierce class rivalries and hazing were still normal. For most students intercollegiate athletics and membership in the college's eating clubs were more important than learning.

Princeton legend holds that Wilson's students tested him at his first class by bringing a drunk into the classroom. Wilson reputedly took the man by his collar and ejected him—all without turning a hair. Thereafter, he had the students in the palm of his hand.

He was more demanding than most faculty members, but his classes were enormously popular, and Princeton alumni fondly recalled his vivid lectures. He was friendly and informal with students, and many of them dropped in to see him and talk about their ideas and problems. Among the few dissenters from the universal praise he received were a few of the graduate students at Hopkins, who in later years recalled him as a fine lecturer but not very interested in scholarly research.

The impression was correct. Wilson had never been comfortable with the "scientific" method of history taught at Hopkins and, although he was willing to lecture there, consistently refused offers to join the faculty. The scientific approach, he wrote, emphasized the ugly and sordid and denigrated humans' ability to shape events and originate ideas. It infuriated him when a Hopkins English professor dismissed a book as "mere literature." "Mere literature—mere literature," Wilson allegedly declared; "I'll get even with him."[17]

He did. An article, "Mere Literature," was published in the *Atlantic Monthly* in 1893 and attacked the whole structure of formal scholarship. Literature, he wrote, had the "immortal essence of truth and seriousness and high thought," and there was "a natural antagonism . . . between the standards of scholarship and the standards of literature." Scholars' minds "are not stages, but museums; nothing is done there, but very curious and valuable collections are kept there." "I am not only not a scholar, but I don't want to be one," he averred privately to a friend."[18]

In fact, after the publication of *Division and Reunion* he largely abandoned serious historical research in favor of popular biography and broad synthetic interpretations of the meaning of the nation's history. In 1896 he rushed out a biography of George Washington; its pretentiously antique style and careless scholarship almost overwhelmed handsome illustrations by Howard Pyle but the book was justified in Wilson's eyes by the desperately needed eighteen hundred dollars it brought in to help pay for the family's new house. Of more merit and significance was the writing of a multivolume history of the United States, intended to be read more by the general public than by scholars. History, he was convinced, had important lessons for the nation if they were properly explained. America's past, he wrote, "has taught us how to become strong, and will teach us, if we heed its moral, how to become wise, also, and single-minded."[19] His concern with lessons, broad themes, American heroes, and nationalism did not make his history profound, but it certainly made it popular, and his wish had always been to influence the political life of his generation rather than to make a scholarly impact. He wrote the history of the United States, he said, "not to remember what happened, but to find which way we were going."[20]

Although there is no doubt that Wilson made intellectual contributions of lasting importance especially in political science, his main interest in both history and the analysis of politics was in reaching a wide audience and in achieving political influence. By the 1890s the popularity of his writings was giving him the national reputation he sought, though he still lamented not being himself an actor. While watching a session of Congress, he confessed to Ellen in 1898, "the old longing for public life comes on me in a flood."[21]

As his discussion of the growth of monopolies in *The State* showed, Wilson was aware of the major currents of American politics in the 1890s, but he was not comfortable with reform proposals advanced by radicals like the Populists. Their antitrust program, he declared, "smacked of the extremest purposes of experiment in the field of legislation," and when William Jennings Bryan was nominated for president by the Democrats in 1896, he deserted the party to vote for the candidates of the splinter "Gold Democrats."[22] It was incredible, he exploded, that "a good voice and a few ringing sentences" should have brought Bryan so near the White House.[23] Although he believed that the law must be "the instrument, not of justice merely, but also of social progress," and described Adam Smith as early as 1886 as "decidedly old-fashioned," there seemed to be no political home for a conservative reformer of his particular views.[24]

Wilson was equally uncomfortable with the other great political issue of the 1890s, the Spanish-American War and imperialism. He made no public comment about the war in 1898 but was quoted in 1899 by a small Connecticut newspaper as opposing the annexation of the Philippines. In the preface to a new edition of *Congressional Government* issued in 1900, however, he pointed out that the war had reduced the congressional dominance that had unbalanced the government and had begun to restore the power of the presidency. The war's most important effect, he wrote, was "the greatly increased power and opportunity for constructive statesmanship given the President, by the plunge into international politics and into the administration of distant dependencies."[25] By a means he had never anticipated, the central problem identified in *Congressional Government* was being corrected and his argument for the institution of a parliamentary form of government made irrelevant.

If Wilson had early doubts about imperialism, they faded before the end of the war. "It is not simply a question of expediency," he wrote. "It is a question also of moral obligation."[26] The "impulse of expansion is the natural and wholesome impulse which comes with a consciousness of matured strength,"[27] he decided finally. Repeating the comfortable rationalizations of the time, he argued that the United States would "moralize" and "elevate and steady" the Filipinos in preparation for an eventual grant of self-government.[28] In *The State* he had declared that "political growth refuses to be forced," and he here applied that principle in his argument that the islanders would be better off under American guidance until they learned to run their own affairs. "They must first take the discipline of law, must first love order and instinctively yield to it," he said. "We are old in this learning and must be their tutors."[29]

Even as he repeated these noble clichés, Wilson was not entirely comfortable. "I am of the class of men who are described as *imperialists*," he admitted, "and yet I have had such an intense sympathy with the men on the other side who are getting sat upon that I could almost have wished that my opinions were different that I might join their ranks."[30] The antiimperialists, he declared, were people of true courage and genuine patriotism.

One reason that Wilson's political ideas were somewhat contradictory in the late 1890s was that politics occupied only a corner of his attention. Between 1893 and 1902 he published nine books and thirty-five articles, beginning with *Division and Reunion* and ending with the five-volume *History of the American People*. The quality and scholarly validity of these works fell rapidly after 1893, but their sheer volume was testimony to prodigious work and self-discipline. All of this was accomplished, moreover, despite conscientious devotion to his teaching, increasing involvement in university affairs, a growing family, a heavy outside speaking schedule, and the first ominous signs of a health problem.

When Wilson came back to Princeton in 1890, his appointment as professor of jurisprudence and political economy was supposed to be a first step toward the establishment of a law school. He hoped that the school would teach the law through the case method introduced at Harvard, but that it would go beyond that to emphasize the philosophy and purpose of the law as well. Thus students would be prepared to be administrators, statesmen, and jurists as well as attorneys. Neither in Europe, where law students concentrated on the philosophy of the law, nor in the United States, where law schools stressed practical training, did there exist such a school as Wilson envisioned.

He spent his first three years at Princeton developing an undergraduate curriculum to prepare students for the law school and campaigning for its establishment, but unfortunately President Patton neither raised money for the new program nor mentioned it to the trustees. Frustrated and angry, Wilson tried to throw his energies into his writing and speaking obligations, but he suffered from episodes of depression and recurrences of his old intestinal troubles. Early in 1895 he was further upset to discover that the new house he and Ellen had planned would, because of an error in his calculations, be much more expensive than he had expected. It was largely because of this discovery that he agreed to write *George Washington*, driving himself to finish the work in time for an early deadline.

By the late spring of 1896, after finishing *Washington*, Wilson was nearing exhaustion, and he finally agreed to take his first trip to England that summer. Shortly before he was to leave, however, he suffered a severe attack, perhaps a cerebral stroke, which left him with weakness, numbness, and some pain in his right hand and arm. His physician urged him to go on his trip anyway, and he did. Largely ambidextrous, he easily learned to write with his left hand and let nothing stand in the way of his enjoyment of England, much of it seen from a bicycle. In fact, instead of complaining about his illness, Wilson seemed to deny its existence—behavior in striking contrast to his earlier loving attention to every symptom of his internal problems. When he returned to Princeton that fall, his family and friends were surprised at his energy and purposefulness, although the weakness of his right arm lingered for months. The episode, Stockton Axson thought, seemed to have "freshened his sense of mission in the world."[31]

Mission and service were the themes of the address on "Princeton in the Nation's Service" that became his main work after his return. Princeton was about to celebrate its sesquicentennial, and Wilson was to be the principal speaker. He took as his theme praise of the broad liberal education offered at Princeton and a warning that science could not solve all the world's problems. Science, he declared, "has not freed us from ourselves."[32] Princeton's particular function, he argued, was to blend liberal training with religious instruction so that the college's graduates would be inspired to serve the nation through responsible political and social leadership. The college should be, he said, "a school of duty" where young men would learn to be "concerned with righteousness in this world, as well as with salvation in the next."[33]

Wilson's speech was a triumphant success and identified him as the leader of the faculty and the logical successor to President Patton. In that role his only real rival was the organizer of the gala three-day sesquicentennial celebration, classics professor Andrew Fleming West. Over the next decade West and Wilson frequently clashed over the future of the college, and, although neither would admit it, over personal ambitions.

"Andy" West was, like Wilson, the son of a Presbyterian minister and himself a strong churchman, but there the similarity ended. If Wilson cared little for scholarly research, his work nevertheless revealed a distinguished and original intelligence; West was neither a great scholar nor a profound intellect. Rather he was a rotund, gregarious, affable man with great charm and a backslapping style whose administrative talents and interests outweighed his concern with scholarship. Unlike Wilson, who hated asking anyone for money, West was a natural fundraiser, and it was largely because of his talents in that line and his social contacts with wealthy alumni that Princeton's trustees in 1900 appointed him dean of the new graduate school.

For all West's friendships and polish, however, he did not become President Patton's successor in 1902. In the late nineties the abler members of the faculty became more and more distressed at Patton's lax standards and failure to implement promised reforms. West unwisely allowed himself to become identified as the leader of this group of malcontents, and when Patton was forced to resign in 1902, he blamed

26

West for his troubles and blocked his succession to the presidency. Instead, Patton recommended Wilson, who had kept in the background of earlier struggles. On 9 June 1902 the trustees unanimously elected Wilson the thirteenth president of Princeton.

When elected, Wilson had a national reputation both as a scholar and as a popular intellectual leader. At Princeton he was identified with the transformation of the college into a modern university, which President McCosh had begun and Patton delayed, and in that commitment he enjoyed strong backing from both faculty and trustees. Although he had dueled with West, his election as president seemingly sealed his triumph and promised an administration characterized by rapid academic reform. It became apparent that Wilson's growing reputation might, in the future, lead to even greater opportunities for service. As he prepared to take up his new duties in the summer of 1902, he spent a restful vacation in New England and from there wrote to Ellen that after so many years of frustration, the way ahead again seemed bright. "The right to *plan* is so novel," he said, "the element of vexation, the sense of helplessness we had for so long, is so entirely removed, that it is a pleasure to think out the work that is to be done."[34] Both physically (the lingering effects of the 1896 illness were now gone) and in terms of his career, Wilson felt that delay and impairment were behind, and a new opportunity for achievement and service was ahead.

3

PRESIDENT
OF PRINCETON
1902–1910

When Wilson became president of Princeton, the college was still cast largely in the mold of the nineteenth century, in which Greek, Latin, and mathematics dominated the curriculum, and the inculcation of religious piety was a major goal. Presidents McCosh and Patton had realized that this program was growing old-fashioned, but they had done little to accommodate to change beyond admitting some newer subjects, which were segregated into a School of Science.

Other colleges had grappled with the explosion of knowledge and the proliferation of subject areas much earlier than Princeton. Led by reformers like Harvard's Charles W. Eliot and Cornell's Andrew D. White, such universities decided that all disciplines were intellectually equal and should be admitted to the curriculum. The result, in the case of Harvard, was to eliminate nearly all required courses and to make everything elective, and at Cornell, to place a great stress on applied or practical courses that would prepare students for citizenship and careers.

A third academic trend at the turn of the century was exemplified by Wilson's graduate school, Johns Hopkins, which had been one of the first American universities to adopt the German model of emphasizing original research, conducted for its own sake. Deliberately attempting to minimize concern with practical results and to eliminate moral training, the research universities were mainly graduate institutions.

Wilson was uncomfortable with all three of these patterns in higher education. The traditional curriculum, he thought, was hopelessly outdated; it would, in fact, have excluded his own subjects if rigidly applied. The idea of making all courses elective, however, also appalled him, since he definitely did not believe all subjects were equal. Even less was he attracted to the idea of professional, utilitarian training. And his own experience at Johns Hopkins had convinced him that the Germanic universities tended toward pedantic trivia.

Wilson believed that a university's mission was not to produce only ministers, businessmen, or scientists, but to train citizens whose value to the community would lie in their ability to understand and solve the general issues confronting the nation. Regardless of what professions Princeton's graduates chose to follow, they would be part of "a great invisible brotherhood that binds a man by uncommon standards of honor and of service."[1]

That purpose sounds vague and somewhat mystical, and to some extend it was. Wilson hoped to create a community of men who, regardless of their special interests or professions, would share a commitment to serving others and would have the ability to see through specific issues to great underlying principles. "Our duty," he said in 1911, "is to take men and reintroduce them to the country as it is; to make them forget the interests of their fathers and to see how the interests of all the people are linked together. We must resaturate each generation in the general views of life."[2]

Wilson's concern with "the general views of life" was so great that one historian has said, with a good deal of truth, that he "may well have been more concerned with where the students ate, conversed, and slept than with the formal details of their curriculum."[3] The broad interests and ideals of service he sought to teach could, he believed, only be absorbed in a close-knit community. "The spirit of learning can be conveyed only by contagion," he said, "and contagion occurs only by personal contact."[4] His hope was to create a community of scholarship, where faculty, undergraduates, and graduate students would work and live in intimacy, stimulating in each other the development of broad ideas and noble ideals.

In his inaugural address, "Princeton for the Nation's Service," in October 1902, Wilson set out this aim. The university "should seek to make the men whom it receives something more than excellent servants of a trade or skilled practitioners of a profession. It should give them elasticity of faculty and breadth of vision, so that they shall have

a surplus of mind to expend, not upon their profession only, for its lib-
eralization and enlargement, but also upon the broader interests which
lie about them, in the sphere in which they are to be, not breadwinners
merely, but citizens as well, and in their own hearts, where they are to
grow to the stature of real nobility."[5]

Among other things, Wilson intended to maintain the communal
atmosphere of a small liberal arts college within the structure of a modern university. He had no intention of giving up Princeton's school of
electrical engineering, despite its professional orientation, and he
hoped to establish a graduate college and a school of law that would
embody ideals of research. What was more, although his inaugural address emphasized training for public service as Princeton's mission, he
also believed that the sciences deserved a central place in the curriculum. One of his first actions as president, in fact, was to appoint Henry
B. Fine, a mathematician, dean of the faculty. Out of all these seeming
inconsistencies and diversities Wilson planned somehow to weld a co-
hesive, coherent university.

Several years before becoming president, Wilson told his brother-
in-law Stockton Axson that if he were "autocrat of the college" he
would reform the curriculum, change the teaching methods, and restructure the college's residential arrangements.[6] Had he been given the
kind of autocratic power he imagined, there is no doubt he would have
done exactly what he told Axson. As it was, power had to be shared
with faculty, trustees, and alumni; nevertheless, Wilson came impres-
sively close to doing all he wanted.

The moment was ripe for change. Almost everyone connected
with the university recognized that its facilities needed to be developed
and its curriculum reformed. Recent growth in the faculty had added
younger scholars like Wilson who were eager to raise the college's academic quality, and a substantial turnover in the board of trustees had
brought in new members, several of them Wilson's friends and class-
mates, who would support a dynamic president. Wilson could hardly
have asked for a better opportunity to implement his ideas.

For Wilson's family, the elevation to the presidency was not without strain. A close-knit and intensely private family, the Wilsons found
the public life and incessant social obligations of the presidency difficult. Ellen redecorated the president's house, "Prospect," in charming
style, redesigned the gardens, and managed the social schedule brilliantly, but she sometimes regretted the change that had come to them.
Woodrow, more prominent than ever, was often away on speaking en-

gagements, leaving Ellen to cope with the house, its staff, and their extended family, which included Wilson's nephew, George Howe, Jr., Ellen's brother Eddie, her sister Madge, and Wilson's father.

Joseph Wilson, a complete invalid by 1902, became Ellen's heaviest burden before his death on 21 January 1903. "He seems to suffer constantly," Ellen wrote her cousin in December, "and when coming out from his stupors moans and cries—even screams,—for hours. . . . It is simply harrowing." Although they hired a full-time attendant for the old man, Ellen was near breaking. "I thought I had nerves that could be depended on," she confessed, "but I regret to say I have developed a habit of lying in bed awake half the night and holding myself!"[7]

Dr. Wilson's death a month short of his eightieth birthday brought only momentary release for Ellen. Soon after the funeral her brother Stockton, a popular professor of English at Princeton, had a serious mental breakdown. Suffering from frightful depression, he demanded Ellen's constant attendance until finally, later in the spring, he had to be hospitalized. For Ellen and Woodrow the situation was doubly horrible. Not only did they pity Stockton, but they could not fail to note the repetition of the pattern of depression and insanity that had ended with Samuel Axson's suicide twenty years before.

Wilson began to unveil his plans for the university at the trustees' meeting in October 1902. There he recommended strengthening and reorganizing the faculty, raising salaries, and encouraging research, but he also suggested some major innovations. One was the creation of a British-style tutorial system under which lectures and recitations would be replaced or supplemented by small group meetings of students and especially hired tutors whose duty it would be to stimulate and direct the students' self-education by recommending reading and discussing ideas in relaxed, informal settings. To make such a program work, Wilson said, it would be necessary to build enough new dormitories to house all students on campus. The dormitories would, in effect, become home to students and tutors. There, he believed, "the very best effects of university life are wrought between six and nine o'clock in the evenings, when the professor has gone home, and minds meet minds, and a generating process takes place."[8] Equally important, he argued, was the creation of a graduate college and its location "at the very heart" of the college community, where it would pump its intellectual stimulation into all the arteries of the institution.[9]

Wilson's ideas stunned even trustees accustomed to handling great corporate affairs. At a time when the college was running an annual deficit of six to ten thousand dollars, he was proposing innovations that he estimated would cost not less than twelve and a half *million* dollars. Equally staggering was the idea that the college would set out in directions essentially different from those being taken by any other major institution. Yet such was the power of his personality and his faith that all objections faded for the moment, and the trustees accepted his vision, commencing a major fundraising program that did indeed bring in millions of dollars (although never as much as Wilson could spend).

Having secured the trustees' support, Wilson reorganized the faculty and set up a committee to review the curriculum, of which he was chairman. In April 1904 the committee's report, largely written by Wilson, was unanimously endorsed by the faculty. Based upon Wilson's conviction that "the object of undergraduate study is general training rather than specialized skill, a familiarity with principles rather than the acquisition, imperfect at best, of a mass of miscellaneous information," students were allowed to choose their general degree programs—philosophy, art and archaeology, language and literature, or mathematics and science—but within those programs all students were required to take the same broad courses.[10] For the ablest seniors, a taste of graduate school's more specialized training was to be available in honors seminars ("pro-seminaries").[11] To Harvard's President Eliot the new curriculum seemed a "little archaic," but it was a modernization of Princeton's existing course of study that preserved the qualities of the old system that Wilson thought vital.

With the curriculum reformed, Wilson immediately proposed the inauguration of a British-style tutorial (or as he preferred to say, "preceptorial") system. Whereas traditional education at Princeton had been by lecture and recitation, Wilson proposed to make students active participants in their own education by shifting the responsibility for learning to them. He intended to create, he said, "the reading man, the man who gets the subject up for himself and in the end is put through his paces by the board of examiners."[12] Recognizing that most students could not manage that task by themselves, he sought to hire a group of young preceptors who would live and work closely with the students, helping them to select and understand their reading, and serving as examples. So important was the exemplary function of the preceptors that Wilson decided "whenever necessary to prefer a gentleman of somewhat inferior attainments in scholarship to a fully equipped scholar who was not a gentleman," but by offering generous salaries, attractive conditions, and an exciting challenge, he was able to secure preceptors who were both "gentlemen" and "scholars."[13] By no means the least of the attractions was Wilson himself. "I had never before talked face to face with so compelling a person," one former preceptor recalled many years later.[14]

The new system was inaugurated with forty-seven preceptors in the autumn of 1905. It was terribly expensive, swallowing up so much of the hard-raised funds of the university that there was some opposition at the outset, but it aroused such enthusiastic support among students and faculty that over the next few years it was gradually expanded. Stockton Axson, a somewhat biased judge, declared that curriculum reform and the preceptorial system had created "nothing less than an intellectual awakening" at Princeton, and the trustees' curriculum committee reported in 1906 that "expectations" of the program had been "more than fulfilled."[15]

Anyone familiar with the endless debates that delay even minor reforms in most academic settings will recognize that the radical changes Wilson proposed and secured so quickly were extraordinary. Independent, strong-minded men on the faculty and the board of trustees did his bidding without question. Seemingly mesmerized, they behaved as if they had no wills or ideas of their own. It was a situation that could not possibly last, yet Wilson, far from moderating his demands and seeking others' opinions, demanded greater and greater changes and seemed ever less willing to listen to the ideas and opinions of others. The result was an inevitable collision of mighty forces.

Why he behaved in this self-defeating fashion remains a subject for debate among historians. Seemingly missing from his mental makeup was the politician's instinctive understanding of when it is time to stop and let people digest changes before proceeding to others. Having made himself temporarily the "autocrat of the college," his vision of the future blinded him to the necessity of dealing with others. No success satisfied him. Instead each spurred him on to greater efforts, greater dreams, greater demands. "I am so constituted that, for some reason or other, I never have a sense of triumph," he admitted a few years later.[16] Each peak climbed opened vistas of new ranges to be conquered.

Ironically, Wilson's public triumphs were accompanied by a series of private problems. His father's death, Stockton's recurrent breakdowns, and two serious illnesses in his daughter Jessie, were followed by a partial paralysis in his right hand in June 1904. He dismissed it as "writer's cramp," but it persisted for months. That autumn he developed an intestinal hernia that had to be corrected surgically, and after the operation he suffered from phlebitis in his leg and had to be off the job until February 1905. A few months later Nell had to be operated on for tubercular neck glands, and in the midst of that crisis came the tragic news that Ellen's youngest brother, Eddie, had drowned along with his wife and baby. Raised from childhood by Ellen and Woodrow, Eddie seemed almost a son to both of them, and his death was shattering, especially to Ellen, who hardly spoke for weeks and went about her duties "in a daze."[17] Alarmed about her, Wilson arranged for her to spend the summer of 1905 at an artists' colony at Lyme, Connecticut, where she resumed painting and recovered some of her balance, but the bright spirits that had originally captivated Wilson were dimmed forever.

Whatever Wilson may have felt and thought about these disasters, he showed nothing externally. Preparing for the next series of reforms at the college, he threw himself into work harder than ever. Between 6 January and 19 May 1906 he gave twenty-one speeches to alumni and public groups who sought him out for discussion of topics of the day. It was a foolishly grueling schedule, but insatiable ambition allowed him no rest. Then, on the morning of 28 May, he awoke blind in one eye.

The event, obviously serious, threw everyone in the household into panic. Woodrow underwent what Ellen called "a dreadful week" of medical tests during which he was tense and irritable—"*very* nervous— annoyed by the things he usually enjoys,—as for instance the lively chatter of the young people."[18] Later in the week he moved to a neighbor's to escape the confusion inevitable in the president's house in the period just before commencement.

The first reports from the doctor—or at least what Woodrow told Ellen—were encouraging. The blindness was caused by a burst vessel in the eye, a symptom of "a general condition of overstrain."[19] If he stopped all work for an extended rest, everything, including the eye, would probably be all right. When the trustees met on 11 June, they immediately passed a resolution calling upon Wilson to take a prolonged vacation.

Meanwhile, either the doctors made another diagnosis, or Woodrow was franker with Ellen. By 27 June, as the Wilsons prepared to leave for the Lake Country of England, Ellen understood the basic problem to be hardening of the arteries and high blood pressure, "a dying by inches, and incurable."[20] Fortunately, she said, because of the eye problem the disease had been discovered in its early stages, and at least one of the specialists Wilson consulted believed it could be arrested.

Ellen's contradictory reports probably reflected the reactions of the whole family—fear that the disease would kill yet hope it could be halted if not cured. In that spirit the Wilsons sailed for England, where Woodrow obediently put himself in the hands of the best specialists they could find. Resolutely putting aside all university work, he made recovery of his health his only concern, recognizing wisely that until he was well, he could do nothing else. The family rented a cottage at Rydal, near where Wordsworth had lived, and there Wilson relaxed and took walks through a countryside that quickly became one of his favorites.

Although the doctors had originally been pessimistic about Wilson's recovery and predicted a very long convalescence, he astonished them all with his powers of recuperation. By the end of August the Edinburgh specialists he consulted pronounced his eye "perfectly healed" (an exaggeration; his vision was permanently impaired) and told him "it would probably be better for a man of [his] temperament to go back to work than to lead an aimless and perhaps anxious year."[21] That was not advice that needed to be repeated to Woodrow Wilson.

The rather vague and somewhat inconsistent accounts of Wilson's 1906 illness make a conclusive diagnosis improbable at this late date. Possibly it was a more serious episode in a series of strokes Wilson had been having for some time, or it may in fact have been just what the doctors said—the rupture of a vessel in the eye. The important point is that the event had a significant impact on Wilson's behavior, giving the achievement of his academic and personal goals a new urgency and making him impatient of all opposition or delay.

In a sense, Wilson's personality enabled him to adjust to the threat to his health better than most people. Although intense and driving, he had a remarkable ability to compartmentalize his life, so that when he was working, his concentration was total, and when he was relaxing, that also was complete. His closest family and friends understood that on social occasions he never wanted to talk business. That was one reason many of his best friends were seemingly frivolous women; few men were able to keep the necessary barrier between business and social matters for long. After his return from England in the autumn of 1906 Wilson set aside more time for recreation and improved the efficiency of his working time. He agreed to take a winter as well as a summer vacation, and he began to play golf regularly, although his weak eye created some problems. The result of these changes, ironically, was that he became more rather than less productive while at the same time apparently reducing stress. In November 1907 he suffered one more health incident, but thereafter he entered the healthiest and most successful decade of his life.

The adjustments were fortunate, for by 1906 Wilson was beginning to emerge as a national figure. From all over the country came invitations to speak to various audiences on topics religious, educational, and political. From his youth he had been training himself as an orator, and now he was eager to seize the opportunity. Each invitation seemed to lead to others, and each broadened his reputation as a speaker and a possible political candidate.

Wilson's speaking style is not easy to analyze. Although like Theodore Roosevelt he could coin a pungent phrase, the power of his speeches often seemed to come from something other than their memorable lines; indeed it is often difficult to draw a sentence or two from them that captures their essential points. A keen sense of how his words sounded and the use of such techniques as the repetition of phrases showed his debt to southern preachers, as did the lively sense of humor and fund of anecdotes he inherited from his father and constantly added to. He was a master at constructing an argument, so that his talk seemed to build logically and inevitably toward the point he wanted to make, even though he almost always spoke from sketchy notes rather than a prepared text. As stenographic reports of his speeches reveal, each sentence was polished and grammatical, and the sentences fitted together into coherent, logical paragraphs, which in turn mounted to a unified argument. The result was a speech that was fresh and spontaneous, yet as impressive when read as when heard.

Especially crucial to Wilson's success as a speaker was his ability to put arguments in such a way that his audience felt that he was merely saying well what they had always felt. Often he felt that indeed he *was* only articulating the people's feelings, but he realized that part of his effect was also art. A "novel idea," he said, must be "worked over so thoroughly with old ideas and in old phrases that it wont [sic] look new. Then it will look as if it had been handled; and it will be put in old words which [an audience] have heard time out of mind, and they will get the impression that there is nothing new about [it] at all. The art of persuasion is to mingle the old with the new, and thus do away with the prejudice against new things."[22]

Wilson was hardly just an average citizen, even if professing to articulate Everyman's desires was his stock in trade. It took much more than normal insight to be able to identify and state what was in the public's subconscious, and even more to suggest appropriate action. One of Wilson's greatest strengths as a scholar, speaker, and leader was his ability to penetrate an issue to its basics, ignoring all but essential details. Generally undogmatic and eager for results, he was also able to alter and add to previously held opinions if conditions changed or he discovered new facts. The ability to analyze a situation rationally, and to make use of that knowledge in solving it, is a rarer ability among humans than most of us care to admit. Having it in unusual degree coupled with persuasive talent made Wilson a natural leader.

Wilson's remarkable leadership talents, however, were sometimes blocked by his greatest defect. Sometimes after a period of success he seemed to overreach himself, to develop excessive ambitions and to lose altogether the ability to analyze problems rationally and to shape his behavior accordingly. His last years at Princeton were marked, unfortunately, by just such a collapse of judgment and behavior.

Wilson was well aware in 1906 that his plans for Princeton were incomplete and in danger. Although his reforms had raised the quality and intellectual tone of the college considerably, it still lacked the graduate school that he envisioned as its intellectual center and saw as essential for holding the distinguished faculty he had recruited. What was more, just as the college's intellectual life was developing, there were competing forces turning the students' interests toward social rather than intellectual pursuits.

Princeton's social system had been evolving along with the college. There were no fraternities, but even while Wilson was a student, there began to develop a number of eating clubs that served a similar function. At first merely a pleasant alternative to the bad food offered in local boarding houses, by the early 1900s the eating clubs had proliferated and become the social centers of college life. Some of the mansions erected by wealthy alumni for the clubs along Prospect Avenue were reliably reported to have cost more than a hundred thousand dollars and their furnishings were comparably luxurious. Club membership was restricted to juniors and seniors and was highly competitive. A quarter to a third of each class was not taken into any club, and those excluded sometimes believed their college years ruined. The spring of sophomore year during which selections for membership were made became a period of obsessive tension when studies were completely forgotten; extralegal organizations sprang up among freshmen, sophomores, and even prep school students headed for Princeton, to channel the favored ones into one club or another. Just as the town of Princeton was changing from country village to luxurious suburb of New York, so it seemed that the college was changing from denominational school to rich man's playground, not into the great university Wilson envisaged. Increasingly, Wilson regarded the clubs as a fundamental threat to all the other reforms he was trying to achieve.

The heart of the issue was Wilson's drive to create a community based not on social ties but on common involvement in intellectual activity. "We must *reintegrate*," he insisted, "and create a *college* comradeship based on *letters*. We have tutor and pupil. Now we must have pupil and pupil in a comradeship of studies."[23]

Wilson first expressed his concern about the clubs at the trustees' meeting in October 1902, but other matters prevented him from addressing the problem seriously until 1906. That summer, while recovering from his illness in England, he inked in on a map of the campus a series of colleges or quadrangles, as he preferred to call them. Each would have dormitories, an eating hall, classrooms, and living facilities for some faculty. In these colleges within the university students from all classes would live together and form, he hoped, a small intellectual unit. At the December 1906 meeting of the trustees he announced his proposal, and the board, taken by surprise, agreed to appoint a committee, with Wilson as chairman, to study and report on the idea.

In June 1907 Wilson wrote and delivered the committee report on his plan to the trustees. Not surprisingly, it stressed the importance of making Princeton "an organic whole" and urged the "absorption" of the clubs into quadrangles that would avoid the "rivalries and cliques" characteristic of the club system. The quadrangles would provide instead a setting "where members of all four of the classes [would] be associated in a sort of family life, not merely as neighbors in the dormitories but also as comrades at meals and in many daily activities,—the upper classes ruling and forming the lower, and all in constant association with members of the Faculty fitted to act in sympathetic cooperation with them in the management of their common life."[24]

Few of the trustees grasped the essential point that Wilson objected less to the social snobbery of the clubs than to their competition with the university's intellectual goals, and the president's forceful presentation of his position swept away their vague objections. After brief discussion, the board voted to accept the committee's recommendations. Only one trustee voted no, not because he objected to the plan, but because he thought it needed fuller consideration.

Swept up by the power of Wilson's leadership, the trustees had followed him blindly. Several of them soon began to wonder if they had made a mistake, and an outburst of alumni and faculty opposition to the proposal convinced them they had. Failing to anticipate the growing opposition, Wilson had not, as he had done so well with curriculum reform, the preceptorial system, and fundraising, prepared the way for his proposals by a careful program of speeches and written statements that might have developed alumni and faculty support. Whether he was overconfident as a result of previous successes, or whether his health affected his judgment, he had blundered badly.

Despite heartening support from friends who understood what Wilson wanted to do and some touching letters from former students who felt their lives at Princeton had been blighted when they were excluded from the club system, most alumni reaction, especially from the well-organized groups of the East and Midwest, was hostile to the plan. Younger alumni in particular remembered the clubs as the heart of their Princeton experience (thus proving the validity of Wilson's judgment) and were determined that nothing be done to change the situation. The inability of many faculty members to grasp the plan's intellectual significance, and their petty complaints that they had not been consulted in its formulation were disillusioning to Wilson, and the defection of some close faculty friends, like Jack Hibben, was a bitter personal blow. More politically serious was Grover Cleveland's rejection of the plan. The former president, now Princeton's most famous resident, was an influential if not always well-informed member of the board of trustees. Cleveland made no secret of his belief that quadrangles would be a waste of money. In so thinking Cleveland was probably influenced by his friend Dean Andrew West of the graduate school, who feared that the quadrangle proposal would postpone indefinitely the construction of the graduate college. Wilson and West soon joined battle over that issue.

During the summer of 1907 Wilson took refuge in the Adirondacks, but he did not escape the "quadrangling," as Ellen referred to the controversy.[25] A friend remarked that he seemed "nervous and excitable," weakened physically and mentally by the strain.[26] Stockton Axson reported ominously that he had never seen the president "more stiffly bent and insistent on a project" and warned that if forced to major concessions, he might resign.[27] Discouraged, Wilson told Axson that there was little hope the opposition would fade with time "be-cause," he said, "these people are not fighting me out of reason; they are fighting on the basis of their privilege, and privilege never yields."[28] It was hard to understand why, if he really believed that, he had pre-pared so poorly for the struggle.

By mid-summer Wilson was convinced that the only hope for his proposal lay in securing a multimillion dollar contribution from some wealthy donor to "lubricate the evolution," as he wrote to his friend Cleveland H. Dodge.[29] Efforts to secure such a gift from Mrs. Russell Sage, John D. Rockefeller, or Andrew Carnegie produced nothing, however, and by September his friends on the board were becoming afraid that he faced a humiliating rebuff. A reversal of position by the chairman of the board, Moses Taylor Pyne, and an alarming drop-off in contributions to the endowment drive underlined the seriousness of the situation, and during September and October the president's friends sought a face-saving compromise. Wilson proved stubborn. Unwilling to retreat, he would agree only that the trustees be given more time to study the issue.

The board meeting on 17 October 1907 was a disaster for Wilson. The majority rejected his proposal for more study of the plan and voted to rescind the approval granted in June. The most Wilson's friends could get was a nebulous resolution stating that the board respected Wilson's personal convictions in the matter and would not hinder him in trying to persuade others. Furious, Wilson started to draft a letter of resignation but did not submit it because he convinced himself, at least temporarily, that the board's position had left him free to push the quadrangle plan. No sooner did he start to speak out, however, than Chairman Pyne told him bluntly that the board's rejection was "final and could not be changed." The only reason the plan "was not turned down harder," wrote Pyne to another trustee, "was to save the feelings of the President."[30]

The most unfortunate aspect of the quadrangle controversy was that both Wilson and his opponents were right. As Wilson said, the clubs did compete with the educational objectives of the university, yet at the same time Wilson's proposal was, in Pyne's words, "absolutely Utopian."[31] The money was simply not available to finance it, and it was madness to antagonize the alumni just when the university was most in need of their support for other projects.

Ironically, although Wilson lost the quadrangle battle, his struggle gave him a reputation as a crusader for democracy. He of course consistently argued that he had no objection to the exclusivity of the clubs. His objection was entirely on educational grounds. But in the national political atmosphere created by the progressive movement, his struggle was readily interpreted as democracy against privilege. Although it was not obvious to him at the time, this public misunderstanding was creating a political opportunity that would replace his dimming prospects at Princeton.

Wilson planned to reintroduce the quadrangle plan at the January 1908 trustees' meeting, but by that time a new controversy over the graduate college forced him to set it aside. From time to time he returned to the subject in public and private, stating and restating his belief that "the reforms which I have most at heart are those which would lie toward obtaining the attention of the undergraduates for the more serious tasks of the University. So long as they are left to organize and conduct an elaborate social life of their own, their interest and energy will of course be absorbed in that, no matter how pure and unobjectionable that life may be, or free from snobbish qualities even. It will be their chief and most absorbing interest."[32] But in reality he knew the battle was lost, or more accurately, he believed that its principle was subsumed in another struggle, over the establishment of a graduate college at the center of the university where it was to create the sort of intellectual atmosphere he had hoped the quadrangles would provide.

Princeton had begun to call itself a university at its sesquicentennial in 1896, but its graduate program was so limited when Wilson took over as president six years later that the title was hardly deserved. From the outset, Wilson frequently talked about strengthening graduate programs by erecting an actual set of buildings, a graduate college, in which graduate students could live, eat, and exchange ideas, both among themselves and with faculty members. In a talk to the Princeton Graduate Club in November 1902, he described the purposes of graduate training as the provision of a more exact knowledge of a field than was afforded undergraduates and the creation of independent scholars, but he also came to believe that the graduate college would have an important role as an example of scholarship for the undergraduates. He authorized the dean of the graduate school, Andrew West, to travel through Europe during the autumn of 1902, studying graduate programs. West's mission was "to keep an eye open for anything of use to Princeton from vines, trees, and flowers, to methods of teaching—and the secrets of professorial greatness."[33]

Upon his return, West wrote a pamphlet summarizing his findings.

He strongly advocated the erection of a self-contained graduate college, where students and faculty could stimulate each other in a comfortable setting. The visible presence within the university of "such a body of men devoted to high and serious work," he wrote, "should quicken all good purposes" of "every graduate who lives within its quadrangle" and of "every undergraduate who passes it in his daily walks."[34] It appeared he was in complete harmony with Wilson's desire to stimulate an intellectual environment on the campus by means of example. Enthusiastically, Wilson wrote in a brief preface to West's pamphlet that the graduate college would "stimulate and set the pace for the whole University."[35]

Despite Wilson's interest in the graduate college, he kept putting other projects, such as the recruitment of new faculty and the inauguration of the preceptorial system, ahead of it when the time came to decide how to allocate scarce money. After a few years of this, Dean West understandably began to doubt the president's commitment. A start was made in 1905 when an estate known as Merwick, on Bayard Lane near the campus, was purchased by M. Taylor Pyne and made available for the temporary use of the graduate college, but the facilities were at best only a stopgap. Something permanent was needed, and that possibility emerged only in October 1906 when Mrs. Josephine Ward Thomson Swann died, leaving her estate of almost three hundred thousand dollars to the university for the construction of a "John R. Thomson Graduate College" in honor of her husband, who had been United States senator from New Jersey from 1853 to 1862.

By 1906, when the Swann bequest was announced, West's ideas about the graduate college were no longer in harmony with Wilson's. As dean at Merwick, West envisioned the college as a place of refined culture, separated from the hubbub of the campus, while Wilson believed ever more deeply that it must avoid the pedantry of German universities but be a center of serious scholarship, open to talent, and an inspiration for the undergraduates. West, presiding at Merwick over formal candlelit dinners where students and masters wore academic robes and grace was intoned in Latin, seemed more concerned with the appearance and style of a European university than with intellectual pursuits. Because the two had powerful followers and were unadmitted rivals for control over the university, their struggle over the graduate college had far-reaching implications.

Ironically, just at the moment that the Wilson-West conflict began to appear serious, a solution appeared. Massachusetts Institute of

Technology asked West to become its new president. For Wilson the offer was a way out of a difficult situation, but instead of urging the dean to accept, he drafted for the board of trustees a resolution imploring "one of the chief ornaments and one of the most indispensable counsellors of the place" to stay.[36] His strange action may have reflected some pressure from trustees who particularly liked West, but it also lends support to the theory that Wilson's June illness had somewhat damaged his judgment.

Strengthened by a vote of confidence, West pushed forward with his plans based on the Swann bequest. In May 1907 he presented his proposal for construction of the college on the grounds of Merwick, "near the campus and yet sufficiently retired to ensure the residential separation of the graduate from the undergraduate students. Without this much separation—but no more," he argued, "the proper life of the Graduate College cannot be successfully developed."[37] From Wilson's point of view, which had strengthened with the evolution of his educational philosophy since 1903, West's proposal presented a major challenge, particularly since it was accompanied by other differences over the purpose and structure of the proposed college. "My hopes and my chief administrative plans for the University would be injured and deranged at their very heart were the Graduate College to be put at any remove whatever from . . . a central site," Wilson informed the trustees.[38] The lines of battle were drawn.

Under intense strain, Wilson suffered in November 1907 what he described as "an attack of Neuritis" which left his right arm partially paralyzed.[39] Thus reminded of his mortality, he readily accepted his doctors' advice to take a winter vacation, and late in January 1908 he went to Bermuda. At the end of a holiday there the previous year he had been introduced to a charming woman in her mid-forties, Mary Allen Hulbert Peck, and he now quickly renewed the acquaintance. Mrs. Peck, literate, witty, and well traveled, was just the sort of woman Wilson liked, and the fact that she was separated from her husband did not pose any embarrassing difficulty in Bermuda's relaxed atmosphere. In his first letter to Ellen he wrote that he had already seen Mrs. Peck twice, "and really she is very fine. You must know her . . . ," he declared, "for I know that you would like her."[40]

Apparently Ellen, replying in a letter now lost, expressed something less than enthusiasm for Woodrow's new friend, for he wrote to her on 4 February that although he was "seeing a great deal of Mrs. Peck," he was "remembering your injunction" and was never alone with her. The situation, he insisted, was "thoroughly wholesome."[41] And perhaps it was, but a scribbled shorthand salutation to "My precious one, my beloved Mary," on the back of another paper may make us doubt his feelings if not his actions.[42]

Upon Wilson's return to Princeton at the end of February, Mrs. Peck seems to have been the subject of a sharp disagreement. The next summer, when Wilson departed alone for another holiday, this time in England, his letters betray far less than his usual confidence in Ellen's love. "Darling," he asked, "will you be very generous to me and make love to me in your letters this summer—if you feel like it?" "Do you love me and want me?" he asked in another. "I know I do not give you satisfactory proof [of my love]," he admitted, "but it is there as the greatest deepest force of my life. Try to believe it and realize it and accept it with a *little* joy!" "By whatever compass of thought I steer," he insisted, "I find the needle in me swinging around to you." "But you are *mine*, are you not," he asked in some lingering uncertainty despite her letters which, although now lost, apparently brought forgiveness.[43]

Not until near the end of July was Wilson confident enough to mention directly what had happened:

> You have only to believe in and trust me, darling, and *all* will come right,—what you do not understand included. I know my heart now, if I ever did, *and it belongs to you*. God give you the gracious strength to be patient with me! "Emotional love,"—ah, dearest, that was a cutting and cruel judgment and utterly false; but as natural as false; but I never blamed you for it or wondered at it. I only understood—only saw the thing as you see it and as it is *not*,—and suffered,—am suffering still, ah, how deeply!—but with access of love, constant access of love. My darling! I have never been worthy of you,—but I love you with all my poor, mixed, inexplicable nature,—with everything fine and tender in me. Suffering and thinking over here by myself, *I know it!*[44]

Sincere as was Wilson's penitence, and deep though his love for Ellen, he did not give up the relationship with Mary Peck after 1908. Fragmentary surviving correspondence gives us only a glimpse, but it is enough—she advising him not to leave his spoon in his teacup while he drinks, he deceiving Ellen about his time of arrival from a trip to make room for a visit with Mary. Whether that visit took place or not we do not know, but their correspondence continued and reflected continuing closeness. In the 1912 campaign rumors of an "affair" circulated, heightened by Mrs. Peck's divorce that July. Yet although they remained friends, Wilson had apparently crossed some personal Rubicon. Even after Ellen's death on 6 August 1914, he made no hint of a closer relationship with Mary. A marriage to a divorced woman would of course have been politically devastating in that period, but the evidence suggests that Wilson by that time regarded her as no more than "a dear companion and chum."[45] She, for her part, still cherished dreams. When he told her of his engagement to Edith Bolling Galt in October 1915, she replied sadly, "I have kissed the cross. . . . The cold peace of utter renunciation is about me, and the shell that is M.A.H. still functions. . . . I shall not write you again this intimately but must this once. . . . Write me sometime, the brotherly letters that will make my pathway a bit brighter."[46]

Between Woodrow and Mary there was at some point a romance if not an affair. It was incredibly indiscreet for so public a man, particularly because of his deep love for Ellen and happy life with her. He risked not only his public standing but his private happiness as well. For a man of his background, such behavior must have carried a heavy burden of guilt, yet Wilson could no more live without the adoring support of a woman or women than without oxygen. Approaching his twenty-fifth wedding anniversary and with what he must have realized was a serious health problem, Wilson needed reassurance that he was still a virile, attractive man, particularly because of the strains of his professional life and Ellen's somewhat withdrawn emotional state. In Bermuda's romantic atmosphere, Woodrow and Mary were drawn together by mutual need as well as by shared interests and tastes. Above all, Mary offered in abundance the uncritical admiration that Woodrow always craved.

Ellen's handling of the romance was wise and delicate. She reminded Woodrow of his duty and of their love but did not withdraw from him. Nor did she shun Mary or make a scene in meeting her, although she did not deny herself the pleasure of poking a little subtle fun at Mary's vanities. Despite Mary's attractions, Ellen was confident that Woodrow really loved her, and she knew that she had the advantage of position. Perhaps, had she not felt that in her depression she was failing her husband, she would not have let the matter go even as far as it did.

While all this was going on, the trustees were trying to find a way out of the Wilson-West dispute. Reluctant to take sides, they twice postponed the issue but eventually rejected the Merwick site on the basis of the technicality that the Swann will required the graduate college to be located on the "grounds" of the university. Delighted, Wilson promptly moved to cut West's power over the graduate college also, securing from the trustees in April 1909 a new regulation that confined West's power merely to administration of the buildings of the graduate college while control over graduate course work would be transferred to a faculty committee. Yet since Wilson wanted the graduate college to be the heart of the graduate school, this was a clumsy division of power that infuriated West without eliminating him. Secretly, the dean was planning a counterattack that he hoped would win the war.

In May 1909 West struck, announcing an offer from William Cooper Procter, head of the Procter and Gamble soap company and a Princeton graduate, to contribute five hundred thousand dollars toward the construction of a graduate college on the lines envisioned by West. A month later he seemingly clinched his victory by producing a letter from Procter that named as his preferred site none of those previously discussed, but a recently donated golf course a half mile or more from the existing campus. It now appeared that West's triumph was total; he would have the sort of college he wanted at a distant site where he could thumb his nose at Wilson.

Wilson tried hard to change Procter's mind, but West's hold on him was too strong. As time passed and all possible compromises were rejected by one side or the other, a sharp division appeared in the board of trustees and in the faculty between West's and Wilson's supporters. To Wilson's sorrow and bitterness, Pyne, who had been the dominant figure on the board throughout Wilson's presidency, and Jack Hibben, his closest friend on the faculty until the quadrangle controversy, sided with West. Whatever the outcome of the site battle, so much bad feeling had been created that Wilson's position as president was becoming untenable.

At the October 1909 meeting of the board of trustees matters came to a head. Pyne offered a resolution accepting the Procter gift, and one of Wilson's allies proposed an amendment declining it unless Procter agreed to a more central site. When the amendment failed and the main resolution passed, Wilson was furious. "They have refused to follow my leadership," he told Mary, "because money talked louder than I did," though he still hoped the situation could be saved, perhaps by eliminating West.[47] Increasingly, the struggle was becoming a contest between the two men in which issues were secondary to personal hostility. Where the graduate college would be located was of course

46

important, but it was also true, as Pyne pointed out, that if the university started turning down half-million-dollar gifts, fund raising was going to become awfully difficult.

At this eleventh hour Wilson made one last effort to find a compromise by suggesting a half-baked scheme that proposed the construction of two graduate colleges—one on the campus with the Swann bequest, and the other on the golf course with the Procter gift. Pyne rightly regarded this "very astounding proposition" as "ridiculous" and feared that if Wilson pressed it, it would mean the withdrawal of Procter's offer.[48] Procter, however, refused to back down, and Wilson thus concluded that he had "come to the end," as he told Pyne in a hastily written note on 22 December.[49] "I cannot accede to the acceptance of gifts upon terms which take the educational policy of the University out of the hands of the Trustees and Faculty and permit it to be determined by those who give money," he explained in a letter written on Christmas day.[50] To his friend Cleveland Dodge, however, Wilson put the matter somewhat differently. "What I have said to Pyne in the letter means . . . ," he wrote, "that West must be absolutely eliminated, administratively."[51] As Pyne recognized, Wilson's compromise proposal was not workable, nor did it address the real issue.

Faced with what amounted to an ultimatum from Wilson and support for the president's position from most of the ablest members of the faculty, the trustees naturally concentrated upon the issue at their meeting on 13 January 1910. A few days before the meeting Pyne and Procter got together, and Procter drafted a letter withdrawing his offer. Pyne dropped this bombshell on an unsuspecting Wilson just a few moments before the trustees' meeting was to begin, and Wilson fell straight into the trap. Completely disconcerted, he told the meeting that the real issue was West's "ideals," and that the faculty could make a success of the graduate college no matter where it was located.[52] That was foolish, since he had previously denied that personalities played any part in the issue and insisted that location was the crucial consideration. The revelation of his hostility to West gave his enemies a chance to argue that his position was based on personality rather than principle.

During the next few weeks Wilson attempted to regain lost ground by explaining the issue repeatedly to alumni groups without mentioning West's name, and by counterattacking with a ghostwritten editorial in the *New York Times* where the issue was explained as a battle between privilege and democracy. The editorial proved to be a second tactical error. Although it was true that West had an elitist conception of the graduate college, he denied any such thing in public, and Wilson's enemies accused the president of trying to haul in the quadrangle plan indirectly by means of the graduate college issue. What was more, the editorial infuriated Pyne, who now became determined that Wilson must go. At the April trustees' meeting Wilson spurned a last compromise proposal engineered by his friends and a few days later publicly attacked the Pyne faction as enemies of democracy. Roused totally, Wilson was now determined to win outright or lose all.

The impasse could not last. Behind the scenes Pyne, West, and Procter schemed to renew Procter's offer in such a guise that the university could not reject it, while at the same time Wilson's attacks upon wealth and privilege, which made the Princeton situation worse, also made him a more popular national political figure. For months leaders of the Democratic party of New Jersey had been considering him as a possible gubernatorial candidate, and he now emerged as a frontrunner. Defeat at Princeton, wrote Ellen, would leave him "free again . . . to accept the nomination for governor and go into politics," and to do so, she pointed out shrewdly, on the basis of a defeat that would actually be seen in political terms as an asset, a principled fight for democracy against privilege.[53] Wilson, no fool, also saw the advantage of sticking to the high ground of principle. "He that observeth the wind will not sow and he that regardeth clouds will not reap," he preached to a student audience.[54]

On 22 May 1910 the issue was at last resolved. That day Wilson learned that West had been made an executor of the estate of Isaac Wyman, an aged Princeton alumnus who at his death left an estimated two million dollars for the construction and endowment of a graduate college. Ironically, Wilson had called on Wyman eight years earlier in an effort to secure a gift for the university, but it was now West who would control the money. It turned out several years later that the Wyman estate actually amounted to less than three-quarters of a million dollars, but the bequest and West's control of it meant defeat for Wilson. Frankly admitting the situation, he said immediately that West must stay and that the college must be built where West wanted it, which of course also cleared the way for a renewal of the Procter gift. Pyne and his allies were delighted and could not refrain from rubbing Wilson's nose in his defeat. By mid-June, when the New Jersey gubernatorial nomination was offered to him, Wilson was ready to accept it and to turn his back on Princeton.

Before he left, however, Wilson fought one last battle with Pyne over the election of a new trustee, and this time he had the satisfaction of winning. The victory somewhat restored his perspective, and he was able to look back with satisfaction on his eight years as president of the university. Although unable to fulfill all his dreams and defeated on the issues of the graduate college and the quadrangles, he succeeded in turning Princeton from a mediocre college into a leader among American universities. He had recruited a superior faculty, reformed the curriculum, and reshaped teaching methods in a way that kept the advantages of a small college in the setting of a university. Even in losing he became a national spokesman for educational reform and for a kind of liberal arts education that produced both scholars and men committed to public and private service. In his last baccalaureate sermon on 12 June 1910, he reminded the students that all the members of the university community were merely temporary residents and that the university's influence would outlast them. "Here men come and go," he said, "the men of her Faculty and Trustees as well as the men of her classes, but her force is not abated. She fails not of the impression she makes. Her men are formed from generation to generation as if by a spirit that survives all persons and all circumstances."[55] Whatever his own fortunes, he could feel justly that he had had a large part in shaping that spirit.

As he turned from Princeton to politics, Wilson was fulfilling a lifelong dream, which of course eased the sting of defeat. Alone among the major participants in the controversies that marred his last years as president, Wilson had a coherent, overall vision of what he wanted the university to become. Others, like West, tended to see it from a much narrower perspective, or, like Pyne and many other trustees, to see it in social or utilitarian terms that were to a considerable extent in conflict with Wilson's ideas. That these differences among strong-willed men led to battle should be no surprise. What is surprising is that Wilson, whose whole academic career had been devoted to study of politics and leadership, should have neglected his own lessons.

4

GOVERNOR
OF NEW JERSEY
1910–1913

"We have beaten the living, but we cannot fight the dead," Woodrow told Ellen when the Wyman bequest was announced.[1] With the graduate college battle lost, there was no longer any reason to stay at Princeton. The moment might have been profoundly discouraging, except that defeat was submerged in a new opportunity. New Jersey's Democrats needed a gubernatorial candidate for the 1910 election, and some of the most influential of them were talking about Woodrow Wilson as just the man they wanted.

Wilson's hope of being a statesman had been the mainspring of his interest in the law, and he had set aside his political ambitions reluctantly when he entered academic life because he thought he would never have enough money to run for office. His speaking and writing since then, however, had been devoted to influencing people and events from the sidelines even if he could not be on the field himself. He was not interested in theories or abstractions, he often said, but in practical matters. Principles, he said, "must hold water, real wet water, or they must be mended so they will," and leaders must concern themselves with the "*practicable* formulation of action, and the *successful arousal* and *guidance of motive in social development.*"[2]

During his early years at Princeton Wilson thought of himself as a conservative Democrat as opposed to the semipopulist reformers led by

William Jennings Bryan. "Since 1896," he told the Virginia Society of New York in 1904, "the Democratic party has permitted its name to be used by men who ought never to have been admitted to its counsels, men who held principles and professed purposes which it had always hitherto repudiated." Such men, he charged, were mere "radical theorists, contemptuous alike of principle and experience."[3] Only the passivity of conservatives, he told a South Carolina editor, had allowed such men to "play fast and loose" with the Democratic party.[4] "Would that we could do something, at once dignified and effective, to knock Mr. Bryan once for all into a cocked hat," he wrote in a 1907 letter to railroad executive Adrian Joline.[5]

The Joline letter came back to haunt Wilson when it was published by his enemies during the 1912 campaign, but he was less conservative than he sometimes sounded. Although he was no admirer of Bryan and spoke out against some reforms espoused by the national progressive movement, such as the direct election of senators and woman suffrage, he was not a reactionary oblivious to problems or opposed to all change. "The country . . . needs and will tolerate no party of discontent or radical experiment," he said in 1904, "but it does need a party of conservative reform, acting in the spirit of law and of ancient institutions."[6]

Wilson's "conservative reform" was essentially the religious belief that people must be moral in their private and public lives. "We all know what is right, and when we do wrong we know it," he told Princetonians during a fight to oust from the board of trustees two men involved in a life insurance scandal.[7] It was precisely that concern with individual morality in the corporate world that became his central theme in a series of speeches about controlling big business, a major concern of the progressives.

Wilson's approach to the problem of big business was at once sophisticated and simplistic. He recognized the advantages of efficiency and scale achieved by large corporations and acknowledged that they had "come to stay." Attempting to restore a vanished era of free competition by breaking big companies into smaller competing units ("trust-busting," in the jargon of the day) he dismissed as "the statesmanship of destruction" because it flew in the face of economic reality. Likewise, he believed that government regulation of big business, as advocated by some reformers, tended toward "socialism" and "centralized and corruptible control," which was "a danger of the very sort we seek to escape."[8] Wilson's view made a good deal of sense.

51

His understanding of the economic forces that had produced big business as well as his criticism of some of the proposals for controlling it were realistic, but his own reform program was naive. The remedy for corporate misbehavior, he suggested, was to make the officers of corporations legally and morally responsible for the acts of their companies. "The whole trouble now is," he said, "not that [men] unite in corporate undertakings, but that they sink their consciences in the corporations of which they form a part and act as instruments rather than as men. . . . The defect of our legal system is that it allows individuals thus to lose and hide themselves."[9] Appealing though that idea was on the surface, it betrayed Wilson's ignorance of the complexity of corporate organization, the diffusion of authority within companies, and the moral ambiguity inherent in many economic decisions.

By 1906 Wilson, while still thinking of himself as a conservative, was outlining a series of proposals that, six years later, would be defined as "progressive." In October 1906, for example, he gave a speech in Chattanooga in which he proposed tariff reduction, control of corporate misbehavior by making executives responsible for company acts, the banning of such business practices as overcapitalization, and currency reform to make the monetary system more elastic. There, in broad outline, were the main measures of Wilson's "New Freedom" program of 1912. The transition from "conservative" to "progressive" that Wilson supposedly made between 1906 and 1910 was, in fact, not a great deal more than relabeling of positions he had long held.

One shrewd observer of the political scene, George B. M. Harvey, editor of *Harper's Weekly*, sensed that Wilson's conservative tone and progressive ideas might make him politically effective. Casually acquainted with Wilson since 1901, Harvey began in 1906 to publicize him as a possible political leader. A time would soon come, he predicted in introducing Wilson to the members of New York's Lotos Club, when the country would turn eagerly to "a man who combines the activities of the present with the sober influences of the past." The idea of voting for Wilson for president, he said, gave him "a sense almost of rapture."[10] The powerful and conservative members of the Lotos Club were somewhat skeptical of the editor's enthusiasm, but Harvey was sure he had a winner. To underline his seriousness, he published Wilson's portrait on the cover and repeated his own remarks in the 10 March 1906 issue of *Harper's*.

Wilson was equally enraptured by Harvey's idea. Before going to

52

bed after the Lotos dinner, he sent a warm note of thanks to the editor, and the next day he rushed home to tell his family all about it. Ellen threw a little cold water on the excitement when she asked, "Was he joking?" but Woodrow's ambition continued to burn. "He did not seem to be," he replied.[11] From then on Wilson stepped up his schedule of speeches on overtly political topics while Harvey, relishing his role as kingmaker, sought opportunities to introduce his protegé to powerful friends and to stoke the potential candidate's ambition by relaying their favorable comments back to him.

During 1907 and 1908 Princeton's battles continued to absorb most of Wilson's attention, but he seized every opportunity he could to talk about his conservative reform program around the country. By 1909, as the national progressive movement gained strength in both parties, and as the situation at Princeton became tenser, Wilson's speeches were taking on a more radical tone, even if their substance did not change much. Frustrated and angered by the entrenched power of wealth over the college, Wilson found welcome relief in joining the national chorus of praise for the common man and attacks on big money. Abraham Lincoln, he declared in Chicago, was "a man of the people," who went beyond the ordinary to understand and articulate goals most people only dimly sensed. Lincoln was great, Wilson declared, using the present tense, "not because he speaks from their ranks, but because he speaks for them and for their interests."[12] Between Lincoln, the self-educated voice of the masses, and the "restless, rich, empty-headed people" who bedeviled his life at Princeton, there was so great a contrast that it led him to wonder if education was doing anything useful.[13] The colleges, he often said, needed basic reforms if they were to produce educated people as good as the supposedly uneducated Washington and Lincoln. That, he feared, was exactly what wealthy men like William C. Procter were trying to prevent. "We should cry out against the few who have raised themselves to dangerous power, who have thrust their cruel hands into the very heartstrings of the many, on whose blood and energy they are subsisting," he proclaimed in a moment of despair as his failure at the college became obvious early in 1910.[14]

Wilson's distress at his personal situation paralleled, to a great degree, the feelings of many Americans in the early 1900s about the national situation. Just as it seemed to him that wealth was resisting reform at the college, so it seemed to many Americans that wealth was preventing state and national reform. Once again, as had been true when Wilson became president of Princeton, he was ready to lead just as there was a general demand for change.

In November 1909 Henry Eckert Alexander, publisher of the Trenton *True American* and a leading New Jersey reformer, wrote to Wilson suggesting they meet to talk about new leadership for the state. Alexander was right that the people of New Jersey were becoming impatient with their state's reputation as one of the last islands of bossism and corruption amid a rising flood of national reform, and he was correct also in sensing that Wilson might be recruited to lead local reform efforts. For a time it had appeared that the "New Idea" movement in the Republican party might bring reform to the state, but as the 1910 elections approached, it seemed that Republican reformers had failed in their bid to wrest control of the party from the bosses. Alexander hoped the Democrats could move into the breach.

The Democratic bosses who still controlled the party recognized the growth of reform sentiment and sought a way to use it to their advantage. Early in 1910 one of the shrewdest, James Smith, Jr., met with George Harvey, and Harvey recommended Wilson as a conservative reformer. Skeptical at first, Smith eventually decided that whatever Wilson's political views, he looked respectable and was so politically naive that the bosses would be able to manipulate him after the election. His opinion was confirmed when Harvey asked Wilson whether he would accept a nomination, and Wilson replied that if the nomination came to him "on a silver platter . . . , without any requirement or suggestion of any pledge whatsoever," he would give it serious consideration.[15] Wilson's concern with preelection promises marked him in Smith's mind as an amateur; what interested the bosses was the postelection distribution of jobs and favors. Smith thus agreed to throw the machines' support behind Wilson.

Late in June 1910, after the graduate college affair ended in humiliation for Wilson, he came to a decision. "I am sure I can be elected Governor of New Jersey," he told Stockton Axson. "The convention meets in September, and I believe that I had better listen to the people who have been wanting to present my name to it."[16] Characteristically, he explained his decision to friends not as a matter of ambition but of duty. "I have all my life been preaching the duty of educated men to undertake just such service as this," he wrote to one, "and I did not see how I could avoid it."[17] To another friend he admitted that duty might lead on beyond Trenton. The governorship, he wrote, was "the mere preliminary of a plan to nominate me in 1912 for the presidency."[18]

On 12 July Wilson met with a group of New Jersey political leaders at the Lawyers' Club in New York. Once again he emphasized that the nomination must come to him "without any obligations, stipulated or implied," but on the crucial issue of patronage, what he had to say was music to the ears of his listeners.[19] "I have always been a believer in party organizations," he declared. "If I were elected Governor I should be very glad to consult with the leaders of the Democratic Organization. I should refuse to listen to no man, but I should be especially glad to hear and duly consider the suggestions of my party."[20] Content, the bosses did not listen as closely as they should have to Wilson's precise words. They had yet to learn, as his Princeton opponents had, that his words were sometimes carefully chosen to convey an impression to listeners that pleased them but still left him free to do as he wished.

Three days later, on 15 July, after clearing his decision with the trustees at Princeton and assuring Ellen that he would try not to let political attacks wound him as the Princeton struggles had, Wilson announced his willingness to serve. He would do nothing to seek the nomination, but if it were offered freely to him by a "decided majority" of the Democrats of New Jersey, he would accept it.[21]

Within a few days it became obvious that while a "decided majority" of the bosses supported Wilson, reformers definitely did not. Many reformers had never heard of Wilson, and those who knew of him had little faith in his sincerity or ability. Scenting victory after long years of struggle, most reformers thought the reward should go to known leaders. The state's labor leaders, who unearthed antiunion quotations from some of Wilson's earlier speeches, agreed.

On the advice of Harvey, Wilson made no attempt to reassure the reformers and spent most of the summer with his family at Lyme, Connecticut, avoiding reporters and saying nothing about state politics. Since the bosses were busily lining up support for the convention, it was more important to avoid alarming the machine politicians than to win the support of the progressives who were well-meaning but poorly organized. A few days before the convention was to meet on 15 September Harvey reported, "We have no question of the result. . . . All reports are good. There will be only one ballot."[22]

When the Democratic delegates began to pour into Trenton for the convention on 14 September, they were treated to torchlight parades with brass bands, but the public show was meaningless. Behind closed doors Harvey, Smith, and the bosses worked to solidify votes for Wilson and to transcribe the platform, already outlined by Wilson and Harvey in August. As long as they controlled the nomination and the candidate, the party regulars had little interest in the platform. They believed it meaningless and were quite willing to let Wilson fill it with progressive promises of tax reform, worker compensation laws, regulation of public utilities, and elimination of election corruption. On 15 September convention delegates, ignorant both of Wilson's role in drafting the platform and the bosses' contempt for it, adopted it unanimously, and the next day the machines demonstrated their power by ramming through Wilson's nomination on the first ballot. Frustrated progressives were convinced that once more victory had been snatched from their hands at the last moment.

Earlier in the day Harvey had instructed two of his lieutenants to bring Wilson inconspicuously to Trenton in the afternoon. The two drove to Princeton and up the drive to Prospect where Wilson, who had been playing golf in the morning, met them at the door wearing a plain gray suit over his golfing sweater. "Gentlemen," he said, "I am ready," and they departed for Trenton. Wilson slipped in a side door of the Trenton House hotel and up to Harvey's room to wait. He seemed entirely relaxed, although the others in the room were visibly nervous. At 5:10 P.M. came a knock on the door. The nomination had been made unanimous. "I am ready," Wilson repeated.[23]

As the candidate entered the Taylor Opera House to deliver his acceptance speech, the machine delegates cheered as instructed, though few of them recognized their candidate. The progressives waited in sullen silence, expecting nothing. One man, obviously seeing Wilson for the first time, burst out, "Gawd, look at his jaw!"[24] It was a brief moment of levity in a strained and artificial situation as the delegates settled down to listen to Wilson's acceptance.

Expecting platitudes, reformers were delighted when Wilson declared that he had given "absolutely no pledge of any kind to prevent me from serving the people of the State with singleness of purpose."[25] The bosses, who now heard in public what had only been said in private before, were a little concerned, but the progressives were pleasantly surprised. As he then went on to enumerate each of the platform's promised reforms and to pledge his allegiance to each, their interest continued to grow. Could it be that the machine candidate might be a reformer in disguise?

Following his acceptance speech, Wilson did not campaign for two

weeks while he attended to college business. He even avoided reporters, merely announcing that he would speak in each county of the
state before the election. In the meantime, the Republicans nominated
as their candidate Vivian M. Lewis of Patterson, a moderate progressive
with long political experience. Wilson seemed to believe he would win
an easy victory, telling friends that he would pay his small campaign
expenses from his own pocket, but Lewis's nomination promised a vigorous campaign and possibly a close election.

Colonel Harvey, who understood the situation much better than
Wilson, quickly took him in hand, persuading him to expand his campaign plans and to begin raising money (eventually about $119,000).
On his own, Wilson undertook to study the issues, and by 28 September when he opened his formal campaign in Jersey City, he was ready.
Although his first speech was fumbling, he soon recovered, and drawing
upon his years of experience, emerged as an effective and attractive
campaigner. He also demonstrated a shrewd political instinct. When
his opponent promised that he would be a "constitutional governor,"
meaning that he would not interfere improperly with the legislature,
Wilson quickly announced that he intended to be an "unconstitutional
governor," meaning that he would make every effort to influence the
legislature—in the interests of the people. The attack was hardly fair to
Lewis, but it was effective. It allowed Wilson to emphasize what he intended to be his main campaign theme, his determination to subject
state government to relentless publicity and to keep himself "in constant touch with the general body of opinion" to make sure it did what
the people wanted.[26] He drummed on that and on the related argument
that the Republicans, having been in office so long, had become responsible only to the special interests, not to the public. The Democrats, having been out of office, were free to adopt reforms, he argued,
conveniently ignoring the boss system that had arranged his own
nomination.

During October Wilson gradually moved from generalizations to
specifics. On 30 September he went beyond the platform to suggest
stricter laws governing corporate charters and a constitutional amendment providing for the direct election of senators. Then, in his series
of speeches in each county, he dealt in detail with each of the main
platform planks. These speeches went beyond generalizations to analyze
complex issues and to explain what he thought should be done to regulate the corporations, prevent election fraud, control public utilities,
conserve water resources, and protect workers injured on the job. In

them he was so specific and so effective that although the Republican platform had been vague on most of the issues, Lewis was forced to keep saying that he, too, would do the same things.

Wilson's willingness to confront the issues and describe what he wanted to do won him many friends, but leaders of the progressive movement were still doubtful. Whatever Wilson said, they could not ignore his support from the machines. Of these progressives, the most important was George Lawrence Record. So great was Record's standing among progressives of both parties that if Wilson could win him over, victory would be nearly assured.

Never elected to office, Record had been the intellectual force behind every progressive movement and piece of legislation adopted in New Jersey since the 1890s. A Democrat until the turn of the century, he had become a Republican when that party showed reformist stirrings, but his passion was reform, not party. Wilson intrigued him, though he was reluctant to commit himself without knowing more.

On 5 October Record wrote Wilson suggesting they meet in public debate on the issues. Wilson wisely declined this invitation to debate a private citizen, but against the judgment of his advisers he offered to reply in writing to any questions Record wanted to ask. On 17 October Record sent a long letter with nineteen specific questions, to which he challenged Wilson to reply with a simple "yes or no."[27]

A week later Wilson answered. To most of Record's questions—if Wilson favored a public utilities commission with power to fix rates; if a primary law should control party nominations; if United States senators should be elected by popular vote; if a strong corrupt practices law should be passed; and if the boss system should be broken—Wilson replied simply, "yes." In a few cases he went beyond what Record had suggested, and at one dramatic point he dealt with a question Record had not asked, but which Wilson surmised, correctly, was implied. That was about his relations with the Democratic bosses. "If elected," he promised, "I shall not, either in the matter of appointments to office or assent to legislation, or in shaping any part of the policy of my administration, submit to the dictation of any person or persons, special interest or organization. . . . I should deem myself forever disgraced should I in even the slightest degree cooperate in any such system or any such transactions as you describe in your characterization of the 'boss' system."[28]

Nothing in Wilson's letter to Record was new, but its forceful restatement in reply to questions put by a Republican had a powerful effect. "Damn Record," said Republican leaders privately, "the campaign's over." Record himself supposedly said, "That letter will elect Wilson governor," though he was not as unhappy about the situation as other Republicans.[29] Wilson's friends, who had opposed his determination to answer Record, were now jubilant. Harvey declared the letter "the most effective political document" he had ever read, while Jersey City Democrats Joseph Patrick Tumulty and Mark A. Sullivan prophesied that the letter "makes certain your triumphant election," a prediction echoed by Wilson's rival for the nomination, Otto Wittpenn.[30] The only questions left unanswered seemed to be the size of the Democratic vote and whether Wilson would be able to carry with him a Democratic majority to the legislature.

With the hope of getting out the vote for the Democrats, Wilson stepped up his campaigning in the last two weeks, delivering seventeen powerful speeches before closing his campaign on 5 November. "It's an astonishing thing," he told Hackensack voters, "that the only thing that stands between us and good government are the people who do the governing," and he stressed that progressivism was no monopoly of either party as he urged Republicans to cross over to support him and the Democrats.[31] The real issue, in his opinion, was the quality of leadership. "You cannot put it on the government of New Jersey that it has not yielded the things you want," he told a Passaic audience; "you have to put it on the men who have conducted the government of New Jersey."[32] Although issues were important, the essence of Wilson's campaign was a promise of leadership responsive to public opinion, and in the end that was what he asked the voters to endorse.

New Jerseyans apparently liked what they saw, heard, or sensed. On 8 November they gave Wilson 233,682 votes, Lewis 184,626. It was a landslide, with Wilson getting 54 percent of the vote and carrying fifteen of the state's twenty-one counties. In addition, Democrats won four of seven contested state senate seats and swept forty-two of the sixty seats in the assembly. In the recent past only one other gubernatorial candidate, a Republican, had done that well in a normally Republican state. From all over the country congratulations poured in from friends old and new, all of whom suddenly realized that Wilson had emerged as a possible Democratic presidential candidate for 1912.

Behind him now were the battles at Princeton, though they would haunt his nightmares for years to come. That autumn his enemies on the board of trustees had delivered a final blow by rushing through acceptance of his resignation from Princeton's presidency even before the election, but he could laugh about that now, even if the laughter was a little hollow. At last he had achieved a lifelong dream. "You are bringing Princeton into the nation's service," Frederick Jackson Turner telegraphed, and no compliment could have sounded sweeter in Wilson's ears.[33]

In the days after the election the Wilsons labored to pack up twenty years of academic life and to prepare for a new career even as the politicians came and went at Prospect. Since New Jersey had no governor's residence, the family decided not to move the approximately fifteen miles to Trenton but to take an apartment in the familiar surroundings of Princeton. Freed of the duties of university entertaining, and with their daughters now largely independent, Ellen welcomed the opportunity to return to painting. Woodrow, looking forward eagerly to his new job and delighted to be out of the old one, was in fine fettle. Only Stockton saw dark clouds on the horizon, predicting gloomily that Wilson's new duties would "kill him quickly."[34]

Somewhat to her own surprise Ellen discovered an aptitude for politics. Joseph Patrick Tumulty, Wilson's newly appointed private secretary, declared that she was a better politician than her husband, and even allowing for some Irish blarney, there was truth in the compliment. Where Woodrow might be brusque and righteous, she was warm and humane, complementing his intellectual approach to politics with a sensitivity to people and their needs. She drew Wilson's attention to the need for reform in the treatment of the mentally retarded and the insane and alerted him to other social issues, "especially where they relate to women and children," as she modestly defined her role.[35] In March 1911 she did her husband an enormous service by arranging a quiet family dinner at the Princeton Inn with William Jennings Bryan. Soothed by her grace and charm, the two men discovered to their mutual surprise that they got along well, and the political antagonism between them that had been so great an obstacle to Wilson's presidential ambitions began to disappear.

Between Wilson and 1912, however, lay two years of the New Jersey governorship, and its tough realities made themselves evident at once. The first fight, upon which the success of his whole term might hinge, came in January when the state legislature chose a new United States senator. If the bosses won that, the hopes of the progressives would be shattered and Wilson's chances of success blighted.

Even before the election progressives had warned Wilson that Boss Smith, who had served one term in the United States Senate from

1893 to 1899, would ask to be returned to Washington in payment for his support of Wilson. Progressives favored James E. Martine, a likable but shallow Bryan Democrat, but Wilson was not enthusiastic about either candidate. Embarrassed, he told George Harvey that while he had "a very high opinion of Senator Smith . . . , his election would be intolerable to the very people who elected me and gave us a majority in the legislature."[36]

If Smith had been counting on Wilson's political inexperience, he soon found he had made a mistake. Smith had hardly announced his plan to run when Wilson went to call on Bob Davis, boss of Hudson County, in the hope of dividing the machines. Davis, bedridden and dying of cancer, said that he had already promised Smith his support but offered Wilson a deal. If Wilson would stay out of the senatorial battle, "we'll support your whole legislative program." The offer must have been tempting, but Wilson did not hesitate. "If you beat me in this first fight," he answered, "how do I know you won't be able to beat me in everything?"[37] There, in a nutshell, was the real situation, and Wilson's understanding of it won Davis's respect. He would not break his promise to Smith, but he would not enforce discipline on his followers either. Over the next weeks many of Davis's men came over to Wilson.

Wilson followed up his talk with Davis by meeting with nearly every member of the incoming legislature. By early December he believed Smith would be defeated and Martine elected, but Smith refused to withdraw. On 8 December, after a personal visit failed to persuade the boss to pull out, Wilson issued a statement endorsing Martine. Smith accused the governor-elect of "a gratuitous attack on one who has befriended him," and the issue was out in the open, to the delight of people all across the country who viewed it as a test of Wilson's leadership ability.[38] "I feel pretty confident . . . ," Wilson wrote to Mary Peck, "but a nasty enough fight is ahead, and I shall . . . have to go out on the stump again and conduct something like a systematic campaign against the whole gang: for Smith is only one of a gang that has had its grip upon the throat of the State for a generation."[39]

During December and January Wilson traveled around the state as if he were campaigning, denouncing Smith and urging support for Martine. It was an unprecedented appeal to the public in a senatorial campaign, and it was effective in keeping pressure on the legislators. When the Democrats met in caucus on 23 January 1911 thirty-three were pledged to Martine, and despite last minute efforts by those Wilson de-

nounced as Smith's "agents and partisans," the first ballot in the legislature the next day produced forty votes for Martine, just one short of
the number needed for election.[40] Smith received only ten votes, and
later that day he released his supporters. "I feel that I should no longer
stay the consummation of the Executive's purpose," he declared drily.[41]

Wilson declined the honor and ascribed his triumph to the people,
as if events would have taken their course without his being on the
scene. "Why congratulate me?" he asked. "It is the people who are to
be congratulated. All you have to do is to tell them what is going on
and they will respond."[42]

As Wilson had seen from the outset, defeating Smith weakened
the machines and strengthened his influence with the legislature. On
17 January 1911 he took advantage of this situation to lay his reform
proposals before the legislators. Methodically, he took up each plank of
the Democratic platform and explained that although making basic
changes in state law would be complex, he was determined to proceed.
"Our business," he declared, "is to adjust right to right, interest to interest, and to systematize right and convenience, individual rights and
corporate privileges, upon the single basis of the general good." To assure action he would "take the liberty from time to time to make
detailed recommendations . . . , sometimes in the form of bills if necessary." Although he did not say so explicitly, the "recommendations"
would also be to ensure that his proposals were acted upon. "I look forward with genuine pleasure," he concluded half in promise and half in
threat, "to the prospect of being your comrade" upon "the journey of
duty."[43] Just how close a comrade he would be most legislators probably
did not then suspect.

The details of Wilson's legislative program began to be hammered
out at an unusual bipartisan meeting he convoked at the Hotel Marti-
nique in New York City on 16 January. The governor-elect presided
over the meeting, but its main direction came from Republican progressive George L. Record, who arrived at the meeting loaded with documents and proposals. At Wilson's urging the meeting agreed that
Record, although not a legislator nor even an appointee of the new administration, should draft the crucial legislation. He was asked to write
a bill providing that candidates for office be nominated by public primaries rather than by party conventions, and another bill regulating
campaign contributions and banning such corrupt election practices as
ballot box stuffing. Overjoyed at this opportunity to fulfill his long-
standing commitment to reform, Record had the requested drafts on

Wilson's desk within ten days, along with a proposal to make employers responsible for injuries to employees. Wilson had his own ideas about the employers' liability bill and did not use Record's, but the other two bills, unchanged from Record's drafts, became his first two major legislative proposals.

Wilson's willingness to depend upon a Republican nonlegislator to draft major legislation was certainly unorthodox, and it created an atmosphere of excitement around the new administration. Shrewd observers noted that Wilson's willingness to consult Record would certainly help him get his measures through the state senate, still controlled by Republicans. Everyone agreed that Wilson was making good on his promise to be an "unconstitutional governor" and watched with interest to see what he would do next.

They did not have long to wait. Less than a month after the New York meeting, Wilson's first measure, an election reform bill, was introduced into the legislature by Assemblyman Elmer H. Geran, a former student of Wilson's. By providing that candidates for office be selected through public primary elections rather than by party caucuses, the bill fulfilled Wilson's promise that the people would have a dominant voice in government.

Machine politicians were appalled by the Geran bill and fought it vigorously. Wilson leaped into the battle immediately, announcing on 15 February that the roll of those opposing the bill would "make an excellent list, easily accessible, of those who either fear to establish the direct rule of the people or who have some private and selfish purpose to serve in seeing that the more concealed and secret methods of politics are not taken away from them and made impossible."[44] Yet at the same time he also professed his willingness to consider reasonable amendments to the bill. "I am not standing here to ask that I may have my way," he said in one speech, "but I am challenging every man who wants another way to convince the people of New Jersey that that is the right way. . . . But," he added, "we are done in this day, gentlemen, with private arrangements, and every man who wants to make out his case has got to make it out in public."[45] The essential issue, he insisted, was to write "as good a bill as can be got" and not "to talk it to death." Everyone must "waive all minor objections," to pass an effective bill. On the principle of reform he would allow no compromise, however flexible he might be on details. "I am going to stand for this thing through thick and thin," he declared.[46]

Early in March when the bill seemed to be losing momentum,

Wilson took another of those unprecedented steps that were coming to be the hallmarks of his administration. On 6 March he attended the Democratic caucus of the assembly—something no governor had ever done before—and for more than two hours spoke to the members, answering questions, debating points, and urging Democrats to support the Geran bill and other reform proposals. Afterward he told reporters hungry for all the details of this remarkable event that a number of ideas for amending the Geran bill had been advanced, and that he "took it that all of those who advanced such suggestion[s] would vote for the bill whether or not their ideas were accepted."[47] Of course the legislators had made no such promise and no party discipline existed to enforce such a commitment, but Wilson's statement stepped up the pressure on Democrats to do as he wanted. A week later, on 13 March, he again met with the caucus for three more hours of earnest persuasion.

It was now obvious to the bosses that the naive schoolteacher they had made governor was a tough and resourceful politician well on his way to putting them out of business. They panicked and began making mistakes. On 10 March Hudson County bosses summoned members of their delegation to a conference, only to discover to their horror that eight of the eleven were going to support Wilson and the "popular cause." To the bosses this was incredible heresy, and the "two Jims," James Smith and James Nugent, issued a plaintive statement declaring that Wilson had made the Geran bill "a personal partisan measure" that he was determined to pass "regardless of any consequences to the Democratic party."[48]

Newark boss James Nugent, who was also chairman of the state Democratic party, had been accustomed to appearing on the floor of the legislature and roaming the halls of the capitol giving orders to Democrats, even though he was not a member of the legislature. On 20 March Governor Wilson invited Nugent into his office to suggest that he take a less obtrusive part in the legislature's affairs and to ask his support for the Geran bill. The boss must have been dumbfounded at such effrontery. He shot back that he expected to beat the bill and accused Wilson of using patronage to line up support for the measure. Wilson, eyes blazing in icy rage, leaped to his feet and gestured to the door. "Good afternoon, Mr. Nugent," he said. Nugent, unaccustomed to being thrown out of anyone's office, was slow to understand. He tried to carry on the debate, but Wilson advanced on him repeating, "Good afternoon, Mr. Nugent." Now in full retreat, Nugent paused only long enough to suggest that Wilson was no gentleman. Wilson's voice got quieter and harder: "Good afternoon, Mr. Nugent," and the boss went flying out of the office.[49]

Of course the story was all over Trenton, the state, and the country within hours. Wilson claimed that he felt "debased" by the incident, but it dramatized the reform case as nothing else could have done.[50] The next day the assembly passed the Geran bill by thirty-four to twenty-five and sent it to the Republican-controlled senate. Wilson had been afraid the Republicans would fight it, but his collaboration with George Record paid off. With Record's strong support for the bill (which of course he had written), Republican senators confined themselves to correcting a few mistakes and inconsistencies in the assembly's bill. On 13 April the senate passed the bill unanimously, and six days later the assembly accepted the senate version.

As with Boss Smith's defeat, Wilson refused to take personal credit for the passage of the Geran measure. The bill, he told reporters, "is the result of a popular uprising in which the voices of the people made their demands so clear that there was no escape."[51] Despite Wilson's modesty, however, the campaign for the bill had made Woodrow Wilson front-page news all across the country. Suddenly he was beginning to be seriously discussed as a possible presidential candidate for 1912.

Wilson was not displeased by the talk, but he realized that for the moment the best thing he could do was to concentrate on reform in New Jersey. With the Geran bill in hand, three other measures now became priority concerns. One was a corrupt practices act, which would limit and regulate campaign contributions. A second proposal was for strict regulation of public utilities, and the third was to set up a system of worker compensation for job-related injuries. Together with the Geran bill, these three measures covered the main planks of the 1910 Democratic platform, and Wilson believed that if he could get the legislature to enact all four of them, it was all he could reasonably hope to achieve in his first year. As it turned out, when the fight over the Geran bill was won, the heart went out of the opposition, and passage of the other three measures became easier.

Leadership on a corrupt practices act again came from George Record. While Wilson was concentrating on the Geran bill, Record worked with Republican senators to hammer out a bill setting strict disclosure standards for private campaign contributions, banning all corporate contributions, and outlawing such obviously crooked practices as false registration and ballot box stuffing. Candidates were even forbidden to solicit contributions during campaigns for their churches or clubs, or to make unusual contributions to such organizations themselves. On 19 April Wilson signed the Geran bill into law, and the next day the senate passed Record's corrupt practices act unanimously. The same day the assembly, anxious to adjourn, also passed the bill not only unanimously but without debate. Half of Wilson's major goals were thus accomplished.

His third reform priority was public utility regulation. A state with many commuters, New Jersey had responded warmly to Wilson's campaign promises to control the rates charged by railroads, trolley lines, and other public utilities. Early in the legislative session Senator Harry Osborne, Democratic minority leader, conferred with the ubiquitous George Record and drafted a bill based on a 1906 New York statute known as the Hughes law. Introduced in the senate on 23 January by Osborne and in the assembly on 6 February by Charles M. Egan, the bill received Wilson's warm backing. It created a public utilities commission with power to set rates and standards of service for all railroad, trolley, power, telephone, sewer, gas, and other public utility companies in the state. The assembly passed the Egan bill on 13 March, the senate adopted the Osborne bill on 5 April. On 21 April, the last day of the session, both houses passed a conference bill that reconciled the two measures. Three-quarters of Wilson's program was now complete.

The last of his major goals was the workers' compensation measure. Such a law was an urgent concern of organized labor too, despite the existence of a weak employers' liability law dating from 1909, because the courts continued to rule that anyone taking a job tacitly agreed to accept any risks. Since workers could almost never win damage suits against employers, there was no incentive for companies to make working conditions safer. Thus even before 1910 there was widespread agreement that reform was needed, and Wilson's Republican predecessor had appointed a special commission headed by Senator Walter E. Edge to investigate the situation. When Wilson was elected, he talked to Edge and learned that the commission, although mainly Republican, would cooperate in the preparation of a new law.

The day Wilson was inaugurated, 16 January, worker compensation bills were introduced in both the upper and lower houses. The senate bill, sponsored by Edge, was slightly amended and passed by that house on 15 March. In the assembly, however, it was opposed by Cornelius Ford, chairman of the Committee on Labor and Industries and president of the New Jersey State Federation of Labor. Ford thought the

Edge bill provided too little compensation for injured workers. Wilson and other state labor leaders argued that the bill was the best that could be passed at the moment, and that establishing the principle of employer liability was a vital gain. On 3 April Ford gave in and the assembly unanimously approved the Edge bill. It set aside the legal assumption that accidents were the fault of the worker and established a scale of payments for injury or death of a worker, unless the employer could show that the employee had been willfully negligent. Wilson signed the bill into law on 4 April.

The passage of the four major bills Wilson had requested completed his program for the legislature but not its accomplishments. Also passed in the same session were wages and hours legislation for women and children, a factory inspection law, laws regulating food storage and inspection, public school reforms, and a law permitting cities to adopt the commission form of government and the initiative, referendum, and recall (all popular reforms intended to make government more efficient and more responsive to the people). Wilson received credit across the country for all of these, but in reality he took an active part in the passage of only the municipal reform act, and even on that he joined the battle in its late stages.

In fact it can be argued that Wilson joined the whole reform movement in New Jersey in its late stages and rode it to prominence. The charge is true in the sense that he was associated with no statewide reform group or program before 1910, and it is likewise true that others, especially George Record, were authors of his reform bills. Yet without Wilson there might have been no reform in New Jersey in 1911. His role was not to originate reform ideas or to draft specific legislation but to bring together reformers from both parties, to break or at least bend the power of the machines, and to provide the dramatic leadership that stirred and prodded the legislature into action. Nor should it be ignored that the measures he supported passed without crippling amendments. To say that he was an opportunist in the sense that he benefited from the work of many others is true but misleading. Without his ability to strengthen and exploit the prevailing progressive mood of the state, reformism might have dribbled away to nothing as it had so often before.

Only one real failure marred Wilson's record in this 1911 session of the legislature. He was unable to persuade the Republican-controlled senate that it should approve the proposed Sixteenth Amendment to the U.S. Constitution. Although the amendment, which authorized a federal income tax, had been recommended by a Republican Congress and president, Wilson could not win the support of New Jersey Republicans. When the amendment became part of the Constitution, it was without New Jersey's assent.

Wilson's harmony with the 1911 legislature was evident in the nearly unanimous votes with which most of his appointees were approved, and the very small number of bills he vetoed. His appointments, which excluded machine Democrats and put in office some New Idea Republicans, including George Record, were warmly praised by progressives from both parties. The appointments, together with the legislative record, transformed New Jersey's reputation from corrupt backwardness to leadership in the mainstream of the national progressive movement.

Wilson's successes in New Jersey stimulated speculation about his chances for the Democratic presidential nomination in 1912 and encouraged some friends to begin quietly organizing. In the spring of 1911 some of them opened a New York office, collected a little money, and began distributing copies of his speeches and of articles about him. Later that spring they arranged a speaking trip through the West that put the governor before a national audience and introduced him to reform leaders across the country. "With the successful conclusion" of that trip, declared the *Springfield Republican*, "Governor Wilson . . . may be said to be a candidate in the fullest sense."[52]

After the state legislature adjourned in April 1911, Wilson could give his full attention to campaigning without sacrificing anything but his family, who saw little of him that summer. But by autumn he was feeling the pressure familiar to all local officials running for higher office to be in two places at the same time. Although he campaigned actively for progressive candidates running for nomination in the first primary to be held under the new Geran law on 27 September, he had less time for state affairs than in the past.

Nevertheless, it was obvious that if progressivism were defeated in the New Jersey fall elections, Wilson's presidential aspirations would be dealt a serious blow. The bosses hoped to do just that. Their bitterness was revealed when, on 27 July, James Nugent, after an evening "indulging in champagne," offered a toast in a public restaurant to "the Governor of New Jersey . . . , an ingrate and a liar."[53] Not only did Nugent refuse to apologize for this insult, but on 10 August he brought a gang of thugs to a Democratic state committee meeting and prevented a quorum from gathering. Although such behavior so outraged other Democrats that Nugent was voted out of the state chairmanship as soon as he and his men left the room, his actions only reflected in a crude and public way the feelings of many machine Democrats.

Even after progressives won most nominations in the September primary, Wilson found the struggle with the machines was not over. As the November election approached, he learned that the Smith-Nugent machine in the state's most populous county, Essex, intended to sit out the election in the hope that the Republicans would thereby win control of the legislature and Wilson would be embarrassed. During October, therefore, Wilson redoubled his campaigning. Since the bosses had in effect made the issue a challenge to him personally, Wilson said little about other issues. In a speech on 9 October, for example, Wilson said vaguely that "most all" the things the Democrats had promised in 1910 they had already accomplished, "and those that we did not have time to do we have put upon our program for the next session."[54] What he was really asking for was a vote of confidence, a personal endorsement of his leadership.

That he did not get. On 7 November New Jerseyans restored Republican control of the legislature, with a thirty-seven to twenty-three majority in the assembly and an eleven to ten majority in the senate. By simply telling its people not to vote, the Smith-Nugent machine in Essex had cut the Democratic vote in that county by about 44 percent and permitted the Republicans to sweep the county. Wilson commented bitterly that the bosses' action was likely to "cause a very serious reaction even among machine politicians . . . because it is obviously a bad game to deprive your own party of power in order to accomplish a personal revenge," but there was no denying that he had been dealt a sharp blow.[55] A *New York Times* reporter summed up the situation precisely when he wrote, "Whether Gov. Wilson's name will go before the Democratic National Convention for the Presidential nomination will depend in a measure on what progress he makes with the Republican Legislature during the next four months."[56]

On 9 January 1912 Wilson made a good start by sending a deliberately low-key message to the legislature. Opening with a call for cooperation between the parties, he used most of the message to stress an important if unglamorous theme of reform, the reorganization of state government to provide "efficient, responsible and economical" services to the people. Far too many of the functions of state government, he argued, were conducted wastefully by an "utterly confusing" welter of boards and commissions that overlapped and duplicated one another, obstructed business, made the assessment and collection of taxes unfair, and left the state charitable and correctional institutions uncoordinated. He urged the reform of the legal system to make it as accessible to the "poor and unschooled" as to the wealthy, and he recommended reexamination of the "basis and principle" of the tax system to make it fair to all. He closed the address by urging the passage of legislation to abolish railroad grade crossings, a proposal that already had bipartisan support.[57]

Sometimes criticized by historians as the half-hearted effort of a man focused on the presidential campaign, Wilson's message was a realistic attempt to propose important but unexciting reforms upon which there might be hope of bipartisan agreement. The weakness of his proposals was that they did not arouse public enthusiasm, so there was little hope of getting Republicans to cooperate when they had a chance to block his presidential aspirations. It soon became clear, in fact, that Republican leaders intended to go in the opposite direction, dismantling as much as possible of the 1911 reforms.

To have made progress on his recommendations, Wilson would have had to set aside his campaign and concentrate fully on state affairs. Of course he did not do that. Leaving the legislature to its own devices, he made no specific recommendations to it, lobbied very little for reform bills, and never met with the Democratic caucus. By contrast with his tremendous activity of the previous year, his seeming lack of interest in legislative matters in 1912 was especially striking. Only when the legislature passed measures with which he disagreed did he go on the attack, returning fifty-seven of the bills passed (about 10 percent) with vetoes. The Republicans, he charged, were a "petty partisan band" whose main goal was to embarrass him and defeat the will of the people.[58] That there was truth in the charge did not reduce the impression of conflict that so many vetoes inevitably created, nor did it absolve the governor for his own lack of constructive leadership.

To some extent at least Republican charges that Wilson failed to offer direction to the legislature and that his veto messages revealed "a deplorable lack of study of many of the measures" were justified.[59] During the legislative session he campaigned in at least twelve states and made about forty speeches in various parts of the country. He later claimed correctly that he had been out of New Jersey only two days while the legislature was actually meeting, but his busy schedule and concentration on the national race prevented his giving more than cursory study to most of the nearly six hundred bills passed by the legislature. Given the Republican majority, there would have been conflict between governor and legislators even if Wilson had not been running for president, but the campaign certainly prevented him from exercising the dynamic leadership that might have reduced the problem. As a result, the state slid backward toward the old order. It was remarkable, however, how little damage that slide seemed to have on Wilson's national standing.

During the 1912 election the split between Theodore Roosevelt and William Howard Taft that crippled the national Republican party was reflected in New Jersey politics as well, and the Democrats recaptured control of the legislature. On 13 January 1913 Wilson, now president-elect of the United States, returned to New Jersey to deliver his third and last annual message. Reminding his listeners of the "remarkable" achievements of the 1911 session, he passed silently over the 1912 session and called for the enactment in 1913 of reforms left over from 1911.[60] Particularly, he recommended tax and constitutional revision, reform of the jury system and of the state's incorporation laws, further municipal reform, and more power for the Public Utility Commission.

Freed of the burden of campaigning by 1913, Wilson was now absorbed by cabinet making and planning the policies of his new national administration. He was able to find little more time for state affairs than in 1912. When he resigned as governor on 1 March to assume the presidency, the only major part of his program that had passed was reform of the state's antitrust laws. On 19 February Wilson signed seven bills, commonly called the "Seven Sisters," that attempted to prevent the formation of monopolies and to ban incorporation of holding companies in New Jersey. "These laws mark a new era in our business life," he told the press optimistically on 20 February, but in fact the bills were failures and were later repealed.[61] The rest of Wilson's reform proposals remained in political limbo when he resigned.

Even if Wilson did not revolutionize the government and society of New Jersey while governor, he did accomplish most of what he set out to do in 1910. As he had at Princeton, he laid out a program, and with a dazzling display of leadership overwhelmed opposition and secured almost all he asked for. There, however, parallels end. If Wilson failed as governor, it was but a partial failure and was not for the same reasons or in the same ways as at Princeton. Those who suggest a recurrent pattern of self-destructive behavior leading to failure are in error.

The crucial year for any assessment of Wilson's alleged failure is 1912, during which he warred with the Republican-controlled legislature and secured no significant reform measures. Unlike the situation at Princeton, the problems of this year were not the result of resistance to Wilson's overbearing demands, but of a lack of direction from him coupled with a clearly partisan opposition, which differed philosophically from him and was determined to embarrass him. In the circumstances Wilson's behavior seems rational and appropriate, free of the self-destructiveness that intensified his failure in the last years at Princeton. Moreover, the 1912 struggle with the legislature was marked by no personal battle comparable to that with Dean West at Princeton. To the contrary, his most personal struggle while he was governor was against Boss Smith at the outset of his most successful period rather than part of failure. Inasmuch as Bosses Smith and Nugent also waged highly personal fights against Wilson, there was nothing irrational about Wilson's seeing these conflicts in personal terms.

In a significant way Wilson's alleged failure of 1912 revealed not a personal weakness but a defect in the progressives' assumptions. The reformers placed much faith in structural reforms like the primary, the direct election of senators, and reform of election procedures, all of which were intended, as Wilson put it, to "establish the direct rule of the people."[62] The assumption was that if the power of corrupt or special interests could once be broken, government would thereafter respond automatically to the people's interests. Wilson's year of absentee leadership, however, revealed the falsity of that assumption. What gave reform its vigor in New Jersey was not structural change but vigorous, ingenious leadership. When the cat was away, the mice returned to play.

Under Wilson's direction New Jersey shed its reputation as one of the most corrupt and boss-ridden states and moved to a place among the leaders of reform. If the reforms adopted failed to cope with all the evils of industrialization and urbanization, as they undoubtedly did, the fault was no more Wilson's than it was of progressives in general, who assumed that relatively limited and modest reforms would rectify all problems in the political and economic system. Wilson and most other progressives were as concerned about the dangers of big government or socialism as they were about big business and political corruption. Willing to go much farther in the direction of constant government intervention in society and regulation of the economy than most Americans of the nineteenth century had been, they were far less comfortable with an activist government than most Americans have been since the New Deal.

Within the rather narrow goals set out by progressivism, Wilson was a marked success as governor of New Jersey. He and other progressives demonstrated that state government could be revitalized to deal with modern society. The irony of his success, however, was that triumph at the state level made him a national figure and a potential candidate for the presidency. The best leaders were thus plucked from the states and thrust upon the national stage, where to be successful they had to argue that the very problems they had been dealing with effectively at the state level could only be attacked from Washington. The success of state reform movements seemed to doom them and to focus attention on the national government. Wilson, for one, certainly made no attempt to resist the siren's song.

5

PRESIDENTIAL CANDIDATE
1912

Wilson's national political popularity reached a peak in the spring of 1911 a few months after his astonishing victory in the New Jersey gubernatorial race catapulted him onto the national stage. When, building on that first popularity, he defeated Boss James Smith for the senatorial nomination, seized control of the Democratic party from the bosses, and shoved a reform program through the legislature, Democrats all over the country were enchanted. Successful as a reformer, Wilson still spoke in terms palatable to conservatives and thus seemed the brightest light in the Democratic sky. In that optimistic moment, Wilson's friends launched a drive to create a national campaign organization.

It was well they did. A year later the first bloom of popularity was fading fast. After hard campaigning across the country, Wilson won the endorsement of many prominent Democrats, but as he became better known, it was apparent that he offered no magical panaceas for the nation's problems. He himself had been the novelty; his ideas were familiar. His lackluster second year as governor of New Jersey and the entrance of two other serious candidates, Champ Clark and Oscar W. Underwood, into the presidential field also diminished his lead. By the spring of 1912 he was no longer the frontrunner for the nomination, and it was quite possible he would lose out altogether.

Early in 1912 Wilson broke with George Harvey, whose conservative reputation was harming his campaign, and turned over organizing to former student William McCombs and businessman William Gibbs McAdoo, whose full-time commitment gave Wilson's candidacy new energy and impetus. Although McCombs was somewhat unstable and McAdoo hungrily ambitious, both were dedicated to Wilson, and they made an effective combination. A third insider, the soft-spoken Texan, Edward M. House, had no official position in the campaign organization but knew most Democratic leaders across the country and quickly became Wilson's closest friend and confidant.

Changes in the campaign's organization threatened to be too late. Champ Clark, drawing on political assets piled up during a long career in the House of Representatives, quickly won victories in early primaries. Clark's folksy style and Bryanite political record stood him in good stead in the Midwest, particularly since Bryan himself remained scrupulously neutral among the candidates. The only area where Clark made little progress was the South, but there Wilson's hopes were blocked by Oscar Underwood of Alabama, who was popular as a tariff reformer but conservative on other issues. Even in Ellen's and McAdoo's home state of Georgia the Wilson forces failed, and several other southern states also endorsed Underwood. As the weeks went by, it began to look as if Wilson, having flashed across the political sky in 1910 and 1911 with Halley's comet, would disappear into the outer darkness also.

Discouraging though the situation was, it was not hopeless. Clark could not secure enough delegates to assure nomination on the first ballot, and Wilson won some victories. Pennsylvania gave him seventy-six delegates, the Carolinas blocked an Underwood sweep of the South, Oregon and Delaware brought few votes but some encouragement, and there were scattered delegates from states generally committed to Clark or Underwood. Many Underwood delegates, in fact, said that Wilson was their second choice, and although Nebraska went for Clark, Bryan remained neutral.

But as the convention neared, such small successes were not enough to maintain progress. By late May the Wilson campaign seemed nearly dead. The New York office was as empty as McComb's accounts, and even the manager himself was discouraged. In Texas, Colonel House, ever anxious to be a kingmaker, quietly offered his support to Bryan if the Commoner should decide to run again. When Wilson fell ill, rumors circulated that he had suffered a breakdown.

Wilson laughed at the rumors as "absurd" and declared in the face of mounting evidence that "politically, things are in fairly satisfactory shape." Underwood's and Clark's support, he insisted, was only "perfunctory" and would crumble.[1]

Although even Wilson's most dedicated supporters did not share his optimism in early May, by the end of the month the situation began to improve. On 28 May Wilson defeated the New Jersey bosses once again, winning twenty-four of the state's twenty-eight convention delegates despite the machines' effort to secure an uncommitted delegation. The same day Texas chose forty Wilson delegates, and shortly thereafter he won support in North Dakota, North Carolina, Utah, and Minnesota as well. As the last states chose their delegates, only West Virginia supported Clark, and Wilson's forces went to the convention with 248 votes, far fewer than they would have liked, but enough to keep Clark, with 436 pledged delegates, from a first-ballot victory.

Nevertheless, prospects were not bright. "Just between you and me," Wilson confessed to Mary Peck, "I have not the least idea of being nominated." In addition to Clark's strong support, he feared that the convention would be controlled by "the professional, case-hardened politicians who serve only their own interests," and with whom he suspected Clark would be willing to strike a bargain.[2] On the eve of the convention his gloomy prediction seemed to be borne out when the Democratic National Committee nominated the conservative Alton Parker, 1904 presidential nominee, as temporary chairman of the convention.

The Parker nomination proved to be a serious error by conservatives, however, for it outraged progressives, especially William Jennings Bryan. Denouncing Parker as a "reactionary" whose choice would be "criminal folly," the Commoner fired off telegrams to Wilson, Clark, and other candidates asking them to join him in a fight against Parker.[3]

Wilson's advisers, believing that his only chance lay in making deals with some of the machines, urged him to ignore Bryan's appeal, but Wilson refused to equivocate. "You are quite right," he telegraphed Bryan. "The Baltimore convention is to be a convention of progressives,—of men who are progressive in principle and by conviction. It must . . . express its convictions in its organization and in its choice of the men who are to speak for it."[4]

McCombs was distraught. "All my work has gone for nothing," he said to McAdoo, but he could hardly have been more wrong.[5] Where Wilson was direct, Clark waffled, with the result that Wilson emerged in the eyes of Bryan and the progressives as the one candidate committed to reform. Adding to the effect was the fact that Clark's managers admitted that they were supporting Parker as part of a deal with Tammany Hall bosses who would, in return for the honor accorded Parker and New York, deliver New York's ninety votes (and a convention majority) to Clark. Despite his liberal voting record, Clark was now tarred with the brush of reaction, while Wilson looked ever more progressive.

The maneuverings of the Clark forces succeeded in winning Parker the temporary chairmanship, but they left many delegates feeling uncomfortable and restless. Taking shrewd advantage of this situation, Wilson's men secured the seating of friendly delegations from several states where disputes arose over delegation credentials. Although in some cases the delegates thus seated were progressives, Wilson's managers did not overlook the opportunity for political bargaining. The delegation seated from Illinois, for example, was controlled by a notorious machine, but its bosses promised to support Wilson at the right moment. By such tactics Wilson's strength was quietly increased, yet because the bargaining was done in secret, his reputation for progressive virtue remained unsullied.

After the bargaining over delegates was finished, nominations were to begin on the evening of 27 June, but before the roll call of the states could start, Bryan was on his feet asking consent to introduce a resolution. It was a bombshell. Bryan wanted the party to denounce the convention influence of members of "the privilege-hunting and favor-seeking class," and specifically to expel from the convention such notorious members of these groups as Thomas Fortune Ryan (Virginia) and August Belmont (New York).[6] Such an attack on individual delegates was unprecedented, and it set off a near riot in the convention. Members of the New York and Virginia delegations leaped to their feet and competed with each other in screaming insults at Bryan, and even progressives moaned that the resolution would shatter the party. Bryan, at first adamant, eventually listened to the pleas of his friends, and after several hours of hysterical debate agreed to withdraw the section of the resolution naming Ryan and Belmont. The rest, essentially innocuous, passed by a vote of 883 to 201½. For Wilson's managers the uproar provided a heaven-sent opportunity during which they worked frantically to solidify his support and to block a Clark stampede.

It was near midnight when nominations finally began. Alabama led off by placing in nomination its favorite son, Oscar W. Underwood. A thirty-minute demonstration dominated by the strains of "Dixie" followed, and then Arkansas yielded to Missouri. Senator James A. Reed rose to nominate Champ Clark. Another uproarious demonstration ensued, this one lasting an hour and five minutes. After the nomination of a Connecticut favorite son, it was nearly 2:15 A.M. when Delaware yielded to New Jersey, and Judge John W. Wescott stood to nominate Woodrow Wilson. Even before he could open his mouth a wild demonstration began, with the Texas and Pennsylvania delegations leading the way. By the time Wescott launched into his rip-roaring speech, it was almost 3:30 in the morning. Then followed nominations of Governors Thomas R. Marshall of Indiana and Judson Harmon of Ohio, so it was full daylight and nearly 7:00 A.M. before the bleary delegates began to vote. Their first vote showed Clark with 440½, Wilson with 324, Harmon with 148, and Underwood with 117½, with four others trailing. The exhausted convention then adjourned until afternoon.

Through the next eight ballots that afternoon there were only minor shifts until New York, as expected, swung its ninety votes from Harmon to Clark on the tenth ballot. Wilson, remembering that since 1844 no candidate with a majority had been stopped, "sat down and wrote to Col. W. F. McCombs, releasing all his delegates."[7] The next morning, as the Wilsons were having breakfast at home in New Jersey, the mail was delivered, including a catalog from a coffin company. "This coffin company is certainly prompt in its service," Wilson quipped. "They've got their catalogue here by the first mail."[8]

By that time Wilson could afford to joke. His message had never been given to the convention, and he was still in the race. When his telegram reached Baltimore, McAdoo snatched it away from McCombs, who was ready to give up, and telephoned Wilson, persuading him not to concede. Given the progressive mood of the delegates, McAdoo argued, New York's support might do Clark more harm than good.

McAdoo turned out to be right, although it took thirty-five more ballots to prove it. Bryan endorsed Wilson on the fourteenth ballot, but not until Indiana switched to support him on the thirtieth ballot did he secure a lead over Clark, and not until Illinois gave him its fifty-eight votes on the forty-third ballot did it become clear he would really win. Even then, three more ballots were necessary before Underwood could be persuaded to drop out, finally clearing the way for a Wilson nomination.

Popular accounts often credited Bryan with Wilson's victory, but the Commoner never made that claim himself, and historians have usually agreed that Bryan played a role in arousing the progressive sentiments of the convention upon which Wilson capitalized, but that the Nebraskan influenced few delegates' votes. The convention's outcome resulted from a combination of Clark's mistake in allowing himself to be associated openly with conservatives and machine politicians, and the skill of Wilson's managers in making secret bargains while publicly maintaining the candidate's progressive virtue. Particularly crucial in preventing Clark from consolidating his near victory was the success of McCombs, McAdoo, A. Mitchell Palmer, Albert S. Burleson, and other Wilson men in persuading the Underwood forces to stay in the race by means of a promise that if Wilson decided to withdraw, he would throw his support to Underwood.

Wilson was grateful to Underwood for his help and wanted to reward him with the vice-presidential nomination, but the Alabamian declined the honor. Thereupon Burleson suggested Indiana governor Thomas R. Marshall, to whom Wilson was extremely cool. "He is a very small calibre man," said Wilson.[9] Burleson agreed but pointed out that Marshall would balance the ticket sectionally and might help to carry his doubtful state. Reluctantly, Wilson assented, which must have relieved McCombs considerably, for he had gained Indiana's support by promising the nomination to Marshall. Ignored by Wilson and the rest of his administration even during the president's incapacitating illness in 1919 and 1920, Marshall is known to history only as a man who liked a good cigar. In his memoirs he summarized his role plaintively: "I soon ascertained that I was of no importance to the administration beyond the duty of being loyal to it."[10]

By the time the convention reconvened on the evening of 2 July to adopt a platform and nominate the vice-presidential candidate, the delegates were exhausted. "A listless convention, yawning and looking at time-tables," dozed as a "hoarse reading clerk gabbled swiftly through the planks of the platform," adopted it without discussion, nominated Marshall, and adjourned.[11] When the news reached Wilson at the governor's summer home, Sea Girt, he met with reporters on the lawn and issued a statement that he felt "the responsibility" of the nomination "even more . . . than the honor."[12] Not until two hours later, when a brass band marched up and began playing "Old Nassau" did the solemn spell break. On the lawn a thousand spectators cheered themselves hoarse and then seized partners and danced in celebration.

From the house the family watched with mixed feelings. "Maybe," Ellen mused, "these husbands ought not always to be encouraged to get the things to which their ambitions lead them, but how can wives who love them do anything except help them?" It was Margaret, however, who voiced the mingled sense of apprehension and elation that everyone felt. "Can you imagine father failing in anything?" she asked. No one answered.[13]

Wilson himself had been optimistic about his chances of election earlier in the spring, but the long, hard preconvention and convention fights sapped some of his confidence. Even more distressing was the news that the Republican party had split so that instead of the placid incumbent, William Howard Taft, he would also have to face the much more formidable challenge of Theodore Roosevelt. To the American people, Wilson admitted, Roosevelt was "a real, vivid person, whom they have seen and shouted themselves hoarse over and voted for, millions strong," while he was "a vague, conjectural personality, more made up of opinions and academic prepossessions than of human traits and red corpuscles." "I am by no means confident," he admitted, and other reformers were also skeptical about him.[14] Contrasting Wilson's tone of cool moderation with Roosevelt's fiery rhetoric, Toledo's reform mayor, Brand Whitlock, speculated that "Wilson seems to be . . . trying to conciliate the reactionaries in his party." His acceptance speech on 7 August, said social worker Lillian D. Wald, was "an essay of lofty sentiments . . . , but might be construed as a political hedge and an evasion of the sturdy things Bryan practised in Baltimore."[15]

The main reason reformers were doubtful about Wilson was that they had little idea of where he stood on most issues. Unlike Roosevelt, who had been a major political figure for years and who had been advancing a clear reform program since 1910, Wilson was a newcomer to politics whose whole energy had been focused at the state level. He had paid little attention to national issues and had few specific ideas to offer. One of the few topics upon which he had a definite opinion was the tariff, and he thus devoted a large part of his acceptance speech to promising that the tariff would be revised downward, "unhesitatingly and steadily downward," but that hardly excited anyone.[16] Most Democrats agreed with him, at least in principle, and reformers seldom thought the tariff a burning issue. In private, even Theodore Roosevelt favored tariff reduction, although he dared not say so in public because of differences within the Republican party. If Wilson were to be successful, he had to develop positions on more urgent issues such as trust regulation and currency and banking reform.

On those issues Wilson's acceptance speech was a disappointment. Big business, he declared, was the result of "a world-wide economic tendency" and not inherently "dangerous to the liberties, even the economic liberties, of a great people like our own," provided its size was not "an unwholesome inflation created by privileges and exemptions which it ought not to enjoy." He was sure, he added, that businessmen would join in "common counsel" to seek ways of regulating improper practices.[17] Likewise, he suggested that all interested parties get together to draw up a plan for banking and currency reform, but he gave no clue as to what such a plan might be.

On 6 August Theodore Roosevelt had laid out his program to the Progressive party convention. Like Wilson he stressed balance and moderation, but there were important differences between the two speeches. Where Wilson called for tariff reduction and evaded the trust issue, Roosevelt recommended continued protectionism and proposed the creation of a federal business regulatory commission modeled on the Interstate Commerce Commission. Attacking Wilson for an archaic approach to government that sought state solutions to national problems, Roosevelt set a fighting tone that inspired wild cheers and sent the convention delegates home happy. Even though the Progressives suffered from serious organizational weaknesses, Roosevelt's speech presented a challenge that had to be met if Wilson were to have a chance of winning.

In fact, at the time of his acceptance speech Wilson was beginning to rethink the trust issue, but his ideas were still muddy and vague. From his old friend David Benton Jones in Chicago, who was reorganizing the International Harvester Corporation, he received a letter in mid-July arguing that Roosevelt's plan for regulation of business by the government would fail and that only restoration of real competition could control business practices and restrain prices. The government, wrote Jones, "must establish and maintain *competitive conditions* in the industrial field. It cannot compel competition, but it can prevent a corporation from monopolizing the raw materials of production and it can and must prevent agreements and practices which limit or restrain trade in the distribution of its products. If it does this it is certain that in time competition or the danger of competition will be a powerful regulator of prices."[18]

Jones's letter is worth noting because not only did it propose an approach to the trust issue like the one Wilson eventually advocated, but it was the same idea that many professional economists were recommending. In the jargon of the economists, Jones was describing the doctrine of "potential competition," which meant that when a company's profits became excessive, competitors would be attracted into the field, underselling the trust and exercising a natural check on the company's misdeeds.[19] As Jones pointed out, however, the ability of trusts to monopolize raw materials or to conspire with competitors to restrain trade could prevent potential competition from having its beneficial effect. Government's role was to ban unfair practices in order to release natural economic forces. Continuous government oversight and regulation such as Roosevelt suggested would be unnecessary, Wilson concluded, because making unfair practices illegal would "so restrict the wrong use of competition that the right use of competition will destroy monopoly."[20]

On 28 August Wilson discussed the same subject over a three-hour luncheon with the Boston reform lawyer Louis D. Brandeis. Brandeis apparently gave the candidate the same advice as Jones, and Wilson emerged from their conversation to explain to reporters that "monopoly is created by unregulated competition . . . , and the only way to enjoy industrial freedom is to destroy that condition."[21] After the Brandeis conversation Wilson made the "potential competition" idea the centerpiece of his antimonopoly proposals. In so doing he took a very different approach from Roosevelt and set up the sharpest difference on issues between the two men during the 1912 campaign.

Wilson launched his attack on Roosevelt and the Progressives in a Labor Day speech at Buffalo on 2 September. The Buffalo speech was the real kick-off of the campaign, and it established that the main conflict would be between Roosevelt and Wilson, with the unfortunate Taft largely ignored by both. It also revealed for the first time the results of Wilson's previous month's thought about the monopoly issue.

Challenging Roosevelt's proposals for government regulation of business, Wilson charged that "when once the government regulates the monopoly, then monopoly will have to see to it that it regulates the government." "Do you," he asked his audience, "want to be taken care of by a combination of the government and the monopolies?"[22]

Essentially, Wilson was suggesting that Roosevelt's promises of reform would lead to a corrupt paternalism that would worsen existing problems. Not only were Roosevelt's recommendations in regard to business wrong, so was his whole philosophy of government. An administration set up as Roosevelt wanted, Wilson declared, would be "an organization of government which makes [reform] impossible."[23]

"What I fear . . . ," Wilson went on to say, "is a government of experts." Roosevelt of course pounced on that remark to imply that Wilson favored government by fools, but that was a distortion of an important and basic part of Wilson's ideas. What he was challenging was not so much expertise but elitism, the idea that the functions of government had become so complex that ordinary citizens could not understand and direct them. That notion alarmed him. "God forbid that in a democratic country we should resign the task and give the government over to experts," he said. If democracy were to survive, the people must make the effort to understand the issues, and leaders must trust the people, "because if we don't understand the job, then we are not a free people."[24]

Wilson insisted that the people did understand the issues. "I have never heard more penetrating debate of public questions than I have sometimes been privileged to hear in clubs of workingmen," he asserted, "because the man who is down against the daily problem of life doesn't talk about it in rhetoric, he talks about it in facts. And the only thing I am interested in is facts, and I do not know anything else that is solid to stand on."[25] Even discounting that statement for its flattery of the audience, it fitted closely with Wilson's often repeated assertion that the task of the leader was not to originate proposals but to sense and articulate the desires of the people, translating their wishes into practical policies to solve practical problems. Leaders must have expertise, but they must use it to do what the people wanted, not impose alien concepts on the nation from the top. As Wilson saw the issue, the question before the electorate was whether to trust the people or to move toward an aristocracy of experts.

Roosevelt was not one to run from a fight. In a speech at San Francisco on 14 September he attacked a remark Wilson had made five days earlier: "The history of liberty is a history of the limitation of governmental power, not the increase of it."[26] The comment was intended, once again, to underline what Wilson thought were the dangers of government by experts not responsible to the people, but Roosevelt chose to take it as a restatement of Wilson's former limited government, state rights philosophy. "Mr. Wilson's proposal," Roosevelt jeered, "is really to limit the power of the people and thereby to leave unchecked the colossal embodied privileges of the present day."[27]

Roosevelt's attack forced Wilson to make explicit his rejection of the concept of limited government toward which he had indeed inclined in the past. "I am not afraid of the utmost exercise of the powers of the government . . . ," he declared, "provided they are exercised with patriotism and intelligence and really in the interest of the people who are living under them."[28]

During a speech at Indianapolis on 3 October Wilson for the first time used the phrase that became his campaign slogan; he asked his listeners to join him in organizing "the forces of liberty in our time in order to make conquest of a new freedom for America."[29] The New Freedom for which he called was the freedom of the government from domination by special interests, but it also meant freedom of opportunity for all Americans. The tariff must be reduced "in the interest of those who work and spend and plan and struggle" so that artificial advantages for trusts would be removed and foreign markets opened to American goods. A trust policy must be established that would "destroy monopoly and . . . leave business intact," that would "give to those who conduct enterprise no advantage except that which comes by efficiency, energy and sagacity." "Currency and banking questions must be discussed and settled in the interest of those who use credit, produce the crops, manufacture the goods, and quicken the commerce of the nation, rather than in the interest of the banker and the promoter and the captain of finance."[30]

The beneficiary of the new freedom, it became clear as the campaign went on, was to be "the great middle class from which the energies of America has [sic] sprung." The middle class, said Wilson, was the "originative part of America" that "saves, that plans, that organizes, that presently spreads its enterprises until they have a national scope and character." From that class came the best of leadership, and it was into that class that "the ambitious and gifted workingman makes his way up." America's prosperity, he asserted, depended "upon the invention of unknown men, upon the origination of unknown men, upon the ambition of unknown men."[31]

Wilson's concept of class was economic rather than social, and he denied there were impassable barriers between classes. "There are no social classes in America," he asserted. "There isn't a class in America so high that men haven't climbed into it from the bottom, if there is any bottom." He explained that his aim was "to show that every man born of every class [has] the right and the privilege to make the most of himself."[32]

Wilson's faith in economic and social mobility was one reason he, like Roosevelt, believed the country's problems could be solved by modest reforms. "America is not a country of revolutions," he said, but

84

he thought the system was in need of reform to make it work correctly. Failure to make such reforms might, he warned, lead the people to "do extreme things four years from now if [we] cannot do moderate and sensible things now."[33]

Dramatic as that statement sounded, it meant only that Wilson thought the problem serious, not catastrophic. Reform was urgent because "the laws of this country have not kept up with the change of economic circumstances."[34] The situation, he sometimes told audiences, was like that of Alice in *Through the Looking Glass*, who discovers while running with the Red Queen that she must run and run just to stay in the same place. America, Wilson thought, had not been running fast enough to keep available the same economic and social opportunities that had been so beneficial in the past.

It is arguable of course that both Wilson's and Roosevelt's reform programs were too limited to cope with the economic transformation that had overtaken America—that neither could make Alice run fast enough to stay in one place. Neither sought to replace or even to alter radically the capitalist system, only to assure that its opportunities were available to everyone. To their left, the Socialist candidate Eugene Debs insisted that was not enough, and when the votes were counted, nearly a million Americans seemed to agree with him. For the great majority of Americans, however, Wilson's and Roosevelt's reform proposals, rather than Debs's socialism or Taft's conservatism, were what the country needed. Americans were not in a mood for radicalism.

Indeed what Wilson (and Roosevelt) offered was more an approach to reform than a specific program. As Wilson himself gradually realized, the concept of "potential competition" was weak in explaining how new, small firms were supposed to compete with giant, well-established trusts. At the end of September Wilson asked Brandeis to "set forth as explicitly as possible the actual measures by which competition can be effectively regulated."[35] The lawyer quickly obliged with detailed recommendations, but Wilson apparently realized that such technicalities were poor campaign material. Instead of using Brandeis's suggestions, he simply assured audiences that the Democrats would "take care of the little businessman and see that any unfair interference with the growth of his business shall be a criminal offense."[36] For all his criticisms of Roosevelt's paternalism, Wilson found himself tending in the same direction.

Instead of making specific proposals Wilson preferred to carry his audiences with him to the uplands of high principle and to spread out before them the promised land into which they could descend. "We must shape our course of action by the maxims of justice and liberality and good will, think of the progress of mankind rather than of the progress of this or that investment," he argued. If Americans would create "a land where there is no special privilege, then they will come into a new era of American greatness and American liberty."[37] The will to reform was, it seemed, more important than the specifics.

The effect of Wilson's exhortations on his audiences was magical. By assuming that they would join him in noble self-sacrifice without spelling out what they would be asked to give up, he allowed them to feel idealistic at no cost. Because the desire to feel noble without having to act nobly is a strong human emotion, Wilson's audiences commonly went home feeling delighted with themselves and with him. A few hours later they might have trouble remembering exactly what he had said, but the glow lingered.

The New Freedom's central theme was economic and social mobility, but somewhat inconsistently, Wilson also proposed some measures that might be called "class legislation": the legalization of unions; regulation of working conditions; and protection for workers' health and safety. Wilson tried to argue that labor legislation would benefit everyone because "the United States consists of working men," but that was an obvious evasion of his own inconsistency.[38] His understanding of the problem and of the need for action was honest and sensible. He was less successful at fitting his recommendations into his philosophy of government than Roosevelt, whose paternalism accommodated social-welfare plans much more readily than Wilson's libertarianism.

Wilson also had trouble with the immigration issue during the campaign, but for a different reason. In his *History of the American People* he had voiced the prejudice of middle-class Americans of Anglo-Saxon descent against the new immigrants from southern and eastern Europe whose numbers had increased greatly in the late nineteenth century. His lament that the "sturdy stocks of the north of Europe" had been replaced by those who had "neither skill nor energy nor any initiative of quick intelligence" was unworthy of him even in 1902, and by 1912 it was political dynamite.[39] Republicans and representatives of immigrant groups denounced him with vigor, and Wilson found himself backpedaling throughout the campaign.

Instead of trying to explain away his earlier prejudices, Wilson would have been better advised to admit frankly that he had changed his mind about immigration. In 1906, well before he entered politics, he had joined a group opposed to immigration restriction, and by 1912 he was genuinely opposed to "any niggardly immigration policy" that excluded anyone of "sound morals, sound mind, and sound body who comes in good faith to spend his or her energies in our life."[40] Had ethnic voters had a crystal ball with which to look forward a few years to his vetoes of immigration bills, they would have realized his conversion was sincere.

Black voters had less reason for optimism. Wilson's racial views were shaped in the paternalistic mold characteristic of upper-class white southerners during his youth. Never a rabid racist, he believed blacks should have a definite but inferior place in society. That place did not include Princeton, from which he discouraged black applicants while president. When he received the Democratic nomination, however, he saw no inconsistency in seeking black support. Black leaders were suspicious and pressed him to disavow rumors that he would institute segregation in the federal government bureaucracy. Wilson replied evasively. He promised to "seek to be President of the whole Nation" and to "know no differences of race or creed or section," but he would not promise to veto segregationist legislation, nor would he guarantee patronage to blacks except to say he would avoid "unfair discrimination."[41] Unsatisfactory though that was to blacks, most of them ended up voting for him because he was a lesser evil than the "lily white" Progressives of the South.

It never occurred to Wilson to try to speak for or to ethnic or racial minorities. He was convinced that there was a single "American" set of ideas and aspirations that it was his duty to try to articulate, and he believed it was his ability to express those ideas and values that led to his successes. "I would rather know the common impulse of America than to originate," he said.[42] His deepest conviction was that "the American people accepted him as a spokesman" because "he could put into language what was but dimly in the minds of others."[43] He flattered and inspired his audiences by assuming that of course they would act only on the basis of the noblest and most unselfish principles. It was this ability to move and inspire an audience that Wilson sometimes mistook for instinctive understanding of their wishes. Certainly there was a flow between leader and followers, but it was by no means clear that the original ideas came from the people to be articulated by him, as Wilson claimed. His power over an audience and seeming rapport with its members could, upon occasion, give him the illusion that he was expressing unspoken popular wishes when in fact no such wishes existed.

Sometimes Wilson's success in inspiring crowds carried over to his relations with individuals; it did so frequently in his dealings with the preceptors he hired at Princeton, for example. But practical politicians, accustomed to a more convivial approach, were sometimes chilled by what they took to be arrogance or baffled by an intellectual idealism that they assumed must conceal other motives. Unable to play the role of superficial intimacy that politics often demands, Wilson led by calling on the best and most unselfish instincts of both masses and individuals, but while an audience could go home after listening to a speech, it was harder for an individual to whom he appealed to escape. Those who shared his values and ideals found him a profoundly inspiring leader. Others, whose values were different, thought him cold and remote. Depending on circumstances, his leadership style might produce triumph or catastrophe.

In mid-October Wilson had just returned from a triumphant trip to the West when he received word that Roosevelt had been shot by a lunatic as he left his hotel for a speech in Milwaukee. With characteristic bravado the Rough Rider had insisted upon going on with the speech even with the bullet lodged in his chest, but as soon as he finished, he was rushed to the hospital. There doctors determined that the wound was not critical and ruled that Roosevelt must rest for a time. Wilson promptly announced that except for previously scheduled engagements, he would also suspend campaigning while Roosevelt was laid up. The gesture was politically shrewd, and it also enabled him to rest a voice severely strained during his western trip.

Wilson declared that assassination risks were an inevitable part of campaigning and said he would take no additional precautions to protect himself, but his wife and Colonel House decided that was foolish. House telegraphed an old friend, Captain Bill McDonald, a former Texas Ranger, to come to New Jersey, and the Wilson family acquired a new member. Wherever the candidate went, there too was the tall, lanky McDonald, six-shooter on his hip. In the evenings he delighted the Wilson ladies with modest but blood-curdling accounts of his encounters with desperadoes, all told in a voice so soft it could hardly be heard across the table. They never tired of hearing how many men he had shot, "always," as Ellen pointed out, "on the side of the law."[44]

At the time Roosevelt was shot, he too was losing his voice, but more importantly his campaign had lost its momentum. In a speech at Chicago he seemed almost to concede to Wilson's position on the trust issue, saying "I'm not for monopoly when we can help it. We intend to restore competition; we intend to do away with the conditions that make for monopoly."[45] When he returned to make a final major speech at New York on 30 October, he said nothing about trusts. Instead his speech stressed his familiar theme that the government must take responsibility for the welfare of the poor and oppressed. It was not an idea that fitted neatly into Wilson's libertarian concepts; the Democratic candidate had said little about it, but in his remarks on labor Wilson had expressed similar concern about the underprivileged, so on this point there was little difference between the two men. The clear disagreements that had seemed to emerge early in the campaign were blurring by its end.

The election results on 5 November pretty well confirmed what everyone expected. Wilson carried forty states to win handily in the Electoral College, but his 6,293,019 votes amounted to only 43 percent of the total and were actually 100,000 less than Bryan won in 1908. Roosevelt did surprisingly well, winning only six states but earning an impressive 4,119,507 votes. Taft ran third, carrying two states and gathering 3,484,956 popular votes. United, the Republicans would have defeated Wilson easily. Socialist Eugene Debs, with an unprecedented 901,873 votes, was fourth. Despite the colorful campaign, the 1912 voter turnout was only about 150,000 higher than in 1908: apparently the voters, like the professionals, had sensed that the issue was never really in doubt.

Wilson genuinely believed that his election portended a fundamental shift in American politics. It was not only that the Democrats had at last won after sixteen years of opposition, nor even that the specific reforms he had proposed would bring radical change. Rather he envisioned his victory as the beginning of a basic power shift within the American system from the special interests to the people. That change, he told his Princeton neighbors on election night, must be undertaken "by slow process of common counsel," and it might require "a generation or two" to "work out the result to be achieved." The mistaken policies of past years, he declared, had not been adopted "malevolently" but from a failure to evoke and adhere to the highest ideals of unselfish service. "I summon you for the rest of your lives," he told Princeton students, "to support the men who like myself want to carry the nation forward to its highest destiny and greatness."[46]

6

ORGANIZING THE
ADMINISTRATION
1913

After a month's postelection family vacation in Bermuda, Wilson got down to the difficult business of choosing cabinet members for his new administration. Always a hard job for a new president, cabinet selections were especially difficult for Wilson because he knew so few Democratic leaders across the country and because the party had been out of power for sixteen years, which meant that there were not many prominent figures to choose among.

One inevitable choice was William Jennings Bryan. Three times a presidential candidate and the party's reform conscience since 1896, Bryan was described by Wilson as a necessary appointment as early as May 1911. It was essential, he told House, to have Bryan "in Washington and in harmony with the administration rather than outside and possibly in a critical attitude."[1] Yet the prospect had little appeal. Wilson liked the Commoner, but he was afraid that Bryan would try to seize control of the administration. Before finally offering Bryan the position of secretary of state on 21 December, Wilson tried hard to convince himself that the Nebraskan might be palmed off with an ambassadorial appointment to England or Russia, but House and Ellen both insisted that would not do.

Bryan tried to ease the situation. A teetotaler, he asked Wilson if he could refrain from serving alcohol at official functions and whether he would be free to promote an international peace program dear to his heart; the president-elect readily agreed to both requests. As it turned out, on more sensitive matters, such as policy and appointments, Bryan kept his mouth shut unless asked. Wilson was greatly relieved, and his liking for Bryan grew rapidly. The secretary of state, he told House in April 1913, had turned out to be "altogether different from what he had anticipated."[2]

Wilson was unwilling to appoint to office men whose only qualification was their loyalty. William F. McCombs, an early supporter and key campaign organizer, was shunted aside because Wilson thought he was mentally unstable. Joseph P. Tumulty, Wilson's press secretary in New Jersey, was nearly left behind because the president-elect thought he might not be sophisticated enough to deal with the Washington press, despite his "dog-like devotion."[3] Only House's intercession allowed Tumulty to stay on as Wilson's secretary.

On the other hand, Wilson was eager to reward supporters who were qualified for federal posts. Walter Hines Page, an old friend and early supporter, became ambassador to Great Britain; Albert S. Burleson, an active worker at the convention and a former congressman from the key state of Texas, was appointed postmaster general. William Gibbs McAdoo, ambitious, sophisticated, and an excellent administrator, became secretary of the treasury. Louis D. Brandeis, who had done much to shape Wilson's thinking about the trust issue, was his first choice for attorney general, but intense opposition to Brandeis in his home state of Massachusetts made the appointment impossible. Another early and important supporter, Newton D. Baker, would have become secretary of the interior except that Baker preferred to finish out his term as reform mayor of Cleveland. In all these cases Wilson was easily able to satisfy his desire to reward loyalty while seeking able appointees.

Of all Wilson's friends and advisers, none was closer to him than Edward M. House, and Wilson was eager to have House in the cabinet. On 8 January he offered the Texan his choice of cabinet offices, with the exception of the State Department, already promised to Bryan. House was too shrewd to be tempted. Confined to a single office he might be prevented from influencing the president on issues outside his official responsibilities. "I very much prefer being a free lance," he wrote in his diary, "and to advise with him regarding matters in general, and to have a roving commission to serve wherever and whenever possible."[4] The essence of his power, House well understood, lay in his personal influence over Wilson, and by rejecting office he actually increased that influence because he convinced Wilson that he was without political ambition. Seeming to spurn power, House really confirmed his grip upon it.

House's mark on the new administration is obvious. When the Brandeis appointment fell through, it was he who suggested a New York lawyer with antitrust experience in the Roosevelt administration, James C. McReynolds, to be attorney general. He also urged upon Wilson the appointment of Burleson because of the Texan's influence with Congress. He recommended an old friend, David F. Houston, chancellor of Washington University, for the Agriculture Department, and Houston became the only candidate for that office. And when Baker declined the Interior Department, it was House who came up with the name of Californian Franklin K. Lane, then a member of the Interstate Commerce Commission.

Other cabinet members were discussed by Wilson and House but chosen primarily by Wilson. These included the Raleigh, North Carolina, newspaper editor, Josephus Daniels, as secretary of the navy, and William C. Redfield, a New York congressman whose tariff opinions had impressed Wilson, as secretary of commerce. Wilson also wanted to appoint A. Mitchell Palmer, a Pennsylvania congressman, as secretary of war, but Palmer, a Quaker, declined. Virtually on the eve of the inauguration Tumulty suggested Lindley M. Garrison, a distinguished New Jersey judge, and Wilson hastily made the offer. Dumbfounded, Garrison accepted. William B. Wilson, a former congressman and leader of the United Mine Workers, was an obvious choice for the new post of secretary of labor, created in 1912 when Congress split the Department of Commerce and Labor.

Names of cabinet members were announced on 4 March 1913, and were generally approved as respectable if not distinguished by both progressives and conservatives. It was obvious that some of the members might have been chosen for political reasons, but it was equally apparent that none was there because of any bargain or deal. For better or worse, the choices were Wilson's.

That fact was more significant than most people realized at the time, for it turned out that Wilson gave unprecedented administrative liberty to his cabinet. He did not delegate authority; he simply ignored departments for weeks and months at a time. He often took personal charge of matters that interested him, but to other affairs he paid no attention at all. Some cabinet members complained that he offered not even general direction.

The truth was that the president's energies were limited and his attention narrowly focused. He often said that he had a one-track mind, and those who knew him well agreed heartily. His health, good at this period, was nevertheless delicate, and he deliberately curtailed his work to conserve his strength. Even during the war years, when pressures were heavy, he rarely spent more than three or four hours a day in the office, leaving in the afternoons to go for long automobile rides or to play golf. Saturday nights he often went to light theatrical productions. Sundays were for church and rest. Meals were always punctual, and when there were guests, which was less often than with many presidents, they were usually friends who knew enough to talk about light, pleasant things, not affairs of state. Those who broke the unspoken rule seldom returned. Although Wilson's incredible powers of concentration and exceptional efficiency enabled him to do more in his short days than most could in a full working day, he necessarily had to delegate a good deal of responsibility.

Nevertheless, in that spring of 1913 Wilson had no lack of faith in his ability to make a lasting improvement in the national government. On election day Walter Hines Page had written to him suggesting that he call an extra session of Congress to deal with tariff reform and other pressing issues and had recommended that he return to the practice, abandoned since the days of John Adams, of delivering his messages to Congress in person rather than having them read by a clerk. Page's suggestions struck a spark. They would dramatize Wilson's reform program, just as similar innovations had played up his ideas in Trenton, and they would permit him to make the most effective use of his greatest asset, his oratorical skills. Wilson himself would become the lens through which the power of public opinion would be brought to hot focus upon Congress. On 15 November he announced that he would call a special session of Congress in the spring of 1913 to deal with tariff reform and to redeem other party promises.

To prepare the ground for the session, Wilson delivered a series of speeches, almost as if he were still campaigning. In New York on the day after his return from Bermuda he warned businessmen that if they deliberately created a panic to block reform, he would see to it that they were hung on "a figurative gibbet" "as high as Haman."[5] "Prosperity," he argued, "is not a thing which can be consumed privately or by a small number of persons, and the amount of wealth in a nation is very much less important than the accessibility of wealth in a nation. The more people you make it accessible to, the more energy you call forth, until presently, if you carry the process for enough, you get almost the zest of a creative act."[6] What Wilson was calling for was a truly national effort, cutting across class lines and submerging personal selfishness in the general welfare, to lift the whole nation to new levels of prosperity and happiness.

A month later, in Chicago, he spelled out a four-point plan to achieve this broad ideal. His first recommendation was for an intelligent conservation program, worked out in cooperation between government and prudent businessmen, "both to husband and to administer, as if for others as well as for their own profit, the natural resources of this country." Second, he called for all "raw materials obtainable in this country" to be available to "everybody in the United States upon the same terms." The same principle of equal access must also apply, he urged in his third recommendation, to credit. And finally, he urged that the nation be "set absolutely free of every feature of monopoly."[7] If these measures were taken, he promised, there would "come a season of prosperity in this country which it has never known or dreamed of" because competition would revive. "The only thing that makes society various and rich is that men who we never heard of can come in at any time and put us on our mettle to beat them."[8]

Such language inspired some people but alarmed many businessmen, who feared that the reforms Wilson promised meant disruption of the existing corporate structure. In his inaugural address on 4 March 1913 Wilson reiterated his reform agenda but then went on to try to reassure the anxious business community. He would, he promised, respect property and individual rights; he would act only after having the facts; he would "restore, not destroy"; he would act "in the spirit of those who question their own wisdom and seek counsel and knowledge"; and he would make "justice, and only justice" his guiding principle. Yet despite his sober tone and reassuring words, there were many on Wall Street who observed the advent of the new administration with apprehension. To those people, Wilson's calls for a national crusade to "lift everything that concerns our life as a nation to the light that shines from the hearthfire of every man's conscience and vision of the right" seemed to fit ill with his promises of prudence and consultation.[9]

In fact, behind the scenes Wilson was actively engaged in the consultation he promised. On Christmas Eve he had a long, pleasant talk with House Speaker Champ Clark, and two days later, although in bed with a bad cold, he talked about banking reform for two hours with Congressman Carter Glass of Virginia, Chairman of the House Banking Committee, and Professor H. Parker Willis, the committee's main consultant on the subject. Four days later, despite the persistent cold, he had a long talk with Oscar Underwood about tariff revision and plans for the special session. On 26 February he sent House to talk to financial leaders in New York and to assure them privately that "there would be no measure enacted into law, over his signature, which was in the least degree demagogic."[10]

With Underwood, whom Wilson referred to as "a whole-souled, frank gentleman," the president-elect came to quick agreement.[11] Underwood's committee was already hard at work drafting a new tariff bill, and the congressman was only concerned that Wilson not call the special session of Congress before he had it ready. They quickly agreed that the session would be called for early April, and Wilson willingly left details of the legislation to Underwood.

The currency question was more difficult. Wilson did not want to confuse Congress and the country by asking for currency and banking reform at the same time as tariff revision, but he also wanted to have a bill ready to go if the tariff issue were settled quickly. He was not sure, however, what he wanted in the bill. His preelection statements on the matter had been vague, and his long conference with Glass and Willis left them pretty much in the dark about what he thought. Willis had drafted a bill creating a series of privately controlled regional reserve banks, which Wilson seemed to approve in general, but he told them that the system needed some sort of "general central mechanism" to exercise "control" or "oversight" over the whole system. As Willis pointed out, there was considerable difference between "control" and "oversight."[12]

Further complicating the matter for Wilson were pressures from various directions. Bryan was adamantly opposed to the creation of any sort of banker-dominated "central bank" and seemed not to understand that central control over the system did not necessarily mean a central bank. Many influential bankers, on the other hand, remained committed to the idea of the proposed Aldrich Act, which would have created just such a privately owned central bank as Bryan feared. Both Bryan and the bankers were open to persuasion on the matter, but until Wilson sorted out his own ideas, drafting a bill and securing support for it would be impossible. Even with the full power of the administration behind a proposal, warned Glass, it would be difficult to pass, and divided leadership would ensure defeat. It was sensible advice, and Wilson heeded it, setting the matter aside to be worked out after the inauguration.

Believing that recent inaugural ceremonies had become too ostentatious, Wilson had asked the committee organizing his to make "the ceremonies as simple as may be consistent with dignity and order."[13] The committee obeyed the request by eliminating the inaugural ball, but nothing could reduce the determination of Democrats to celebrate after sixteen years. On 4 March the clouds parted above the Capitol as Wilson stepped forward to read his brief inaugural address. Spread out before him, fifty thousand people cheered lustily, and that afternoon three hundred thousand, many in uniforms or costumes, passed jubilantly before the reviewing stand where the new president watched with his family. That evening there were fireworks over the Washington Monument.

Then the celebrating was over, and the Wilsons went home to the White House. *Home.* The word must have seemed strange to them. Leaving Princeton had been painful, and neither Woodrow nor Ellen had ever been in the White House before the evening of 3 March, when they had paid a call on the Tafts. The outgoing first family had been kind and helpful about the transition, but the new burdens were heavy, and Washington did not seem homelike. "I am turning away from this place in body but not in spirit," Wilson told students and neighbors who gathered to say goodbye in Princeton on 1 March, "and I am doing it with genuine sadness."[14] To Mary Hulbert he lamented, "We leave familiar scenes, which we may possibly never know again, and go out to new adventures, amongst strangers. New adjustments must be made all along the line,—a new life must be worked out,—a life full of strain and anxiety."[15] A friend of Ellen's wrote, "She really dreads Washington, I think."[16]

As it turned out, the transition was less difficult than the Wilsons feared. The White House was run by a large, well-trained staff of servants, whose wages were paid by Congress, as were the costs of entertainment and travel. Congress also willingly appropriated money to finish five bedrooms and three baths on the previously uncompleted third floor of the mansion, and to redecorate the living quarters in the light, bright colors Ellen preferred to the Victorian gloom that had pervaded the place. From the president's salary of seventy-five thousand dollars and traveling allowance of twenty-five thousand the Wilsons had only to pay whatever personal servants they wanted, feed themselves and the servants, and buy their clothes. With her experience in running a large house and entertaining extensively at Princeton, Ellen quickly had domestic affairs running smoothly.

Uninterested in fashion or social life beyond that required by duty, Ellen soon began to discover that the wife of the president can have a considerable influence on policy. Blazing a trail that would be greatly broadened by Eleanor Roosevelt and other First Ladies, Ellen talked to Woodrow about and offered advice on many matters of state, but she also struck out for herself. On 22 March 1913 she received a call from Charlotte Hopkins, chair of the District of Columbia section of the women's department of the National Civic Federation. From Mrs. Hopkins Ellen heard of the disgraceful living conditions of Washington's black population, crowded into shacks in alleys around the Capitol itself. After touring some of the worst slums and seeing model low-cost houses built by the "Sanitary Housing Company," Ellen became a stockholder in the company, a member of the National Civic Federation, and a quietly tireless organizer of reform efforts. At other times she toured government office buildings and urged the improvement of lighting, ventilation, and restroom facilities, which were often primitive, especially for women workers. In public hospitals she examined conditions and talked to the patients, urging the adoption of measures to provide better care. All of this work, as well as volunteer social work done by Margaret Wilson, helped to focus public attention upon some of the social problems of the national capital. Disappointingly little came of it, however, partly because of Ellen's illness and death in 1914, and partly because of a system of segregation in Washington that prevented any real housing reform. Ellen's efforts had called attention to a problem that would nag at the nation's conscience but prove insoluble so long as racial injustice prevailed.

There was no commitment on the part of the new administration to solving racial problems. As a recent historian of the subject has written, "Race relations was something they handled with the little finger of the left hand—and they preferred to do it quickly, almost summarily."[17] Coming into office with some sense of obligation to black voters but with no specific promises on record, Wilson's policy was shaped by his and his colleagues' background and by political pressures on him.

Whatever commitment to racial justice he may have felt, he always saw other matters as more important—first the passage of reforms, and then the war.

Racial discrimination and even segregation had existed in the federal government ever since the Civil War but had increased sharply under Roosevelt and Taft. The Wilson administration, with Southerners for president, five of ten cabinet members, and many lesser officials, was unlikely to change direction. Nevertheless, administration leaders attempted to follow a separate but equal policy, which most of them really thought was fair to both races. The policy was the brainchild of Secretary of the Treasury McAdoo, and it called for the segregation of black employees into specific sections and divisions. In this way, McAdoo hoped, contact and friction between the races would be minimized, yet blacks would have jobs and opportunities to achieve status and authority. The arrangement, Wilson asserted, was "to the advantage of the colored people themselves."[18]

McAdoo tried to implement his idea in the office of the register of the treasury, which was already about 40 percent black. As its chief Wilson nominated a black Oklahoman, Adam E. Patterson, and sent his name to the Senate for confirmation. Unwittingly, he had stumbled into a hornets' nest. Southern racists were furious that the administration had not undertaken a purge of all blacks from federal jobs, and led by Senator James K. Vardaman of Mississippi and "Pitchfork Ben" Tillman of South Carolina, they made the Patterson appointment the focus of their attack. "This appointment, if confirmed," declared Vardaman, "will create in every negro in the country a hope that he may some day stand on social and political equality with the white man."[19] With Vardaman, Tillman, and other southerners threatening to obstruct the tariff and currency bills, Wilson gave in and withdrew the Patterson nomination in August.

In the meantime other Southerners in the lower echelons of the federal bureaucracy seized upon the administration's willingness to separate the races as license for acts of vicious cruelty. Especially in McAdoo's Treasury and in the Post Office Department, where Texan Burleson presided, black employees were segregated from whites, separate toilet facilities were decreed, and civil service rules were bent to permit the demotion or transfer of black employees. In a particularly barbarous example, six of the seven black minor executives among the thousand employees in the Post Office's Washington headquarters were first exiled to the dead letter office and then, along with all black clerks, transferred to the city post office in Washington. By the end of the summer of 1913, only one black man remained among the thousand white employees in the federal headquarters building, and he worked at a desk surrounded by screens intended to prevent his fellow workers from visual contamination.

Horrifying as such tales are, they are not fully representative of Wilson administration racial policy. Treasury and the Post Office were the worst examples; in other departments and offices segregation made less progress and was sometimes successfully resisted by both blacks and whites. Wilson and McAdoo at first paid little attention to how the secretary's ideas were being implemented, but as black opposition to the policy, led by the National Association for the Advancement of Colored People, built up, and as the passage of reform legislation lessened the administration's dependence on Southerners in Congress, the president began to curb racial extremists.

Soon after Wilson signed the Federal Reserve Act on 23 December 1913, he reappointed Robert H. Terrell, a black graduate of Harvard Law School, to the municipal court bench in Washington. Vardaman exploded, but Wilson not only stuck by Terrell but rubbed salt into the wound by appointing another black man as recorder of deeds for the District of Columbia. Both were confirmed; in addition it became clear during 1914 that the implementation of new segregation policies in the lower levels of the administration had virtually come to a halt. In Congress nearly sixty bills were introduced to require segregation throughout the federal bureaucracy, but none received administration support, and none passed.

On the other hand, Wilson refused to be pressured by blacks into changing the McAdoo policy of separate but equal. On 12 November 1914 William Monroe Trotter, a Bostonian, Harvard graduate, and racial militant, led a group of blacks to an interview with the president. The shorthand transcript of the meeting is less dramatic than some published accounts, but it makes clear that while Wilson admitted the reality of racial prejudice and of some individual injustices, he defended his policy as "not intended to do an injustice" and in fact "for the benefit of both" races.[20] Prejudice, Wilson argued, would disappear only when blacks freed themselves of dependence on whites and proved their ability independently. When Trotter challenged his assertion that segregation was really for the good of blacks, Wilson lost his temper and ordered the delegation out of his office. By so doing, he later admitted ruefully to Josephus Daniels, he had "raised that incident into an issue that will be hard to down."[21]

The Trotter interview caused some momentary embarrassment but did not alter administration policy. Neither was the premiere of the D. W. Griffith film *The Birth of a Nation* at the White House in February 1915 proof of rampant racism, as is often claimed. The film was based on a 1905 novel and play, *The Clansman,* by Thomas Dixon, one of Wilson's students at Johns Hopkins in the 1890s. Knowing nothing of the movie's content, Wilson allowed it to be shown at the White House because Dixon told him that film was the new medium of universal communication. According to the only person present at the showing who was ever asked directly what happened, the president seemed lost in thought during the film and left afterward without saying anything.[22] Publicity for the movie made no allusion to Wilson, and Dixon's unpublished memoirs do not quote him on the subject. Not until 1937 did an article in *Scribner's Magazine* assert, without citing any source, that Wilson had described the film as "like writing history with lightning," a remark so irresistibly colorful that its dubious authenticity has not kept it out of even careful accounts of Wilsonian racial policies.[23]

In the latter part of the Wilson administration, racial matters were again of less concern than other issues. A growing crisis with Mexico, a renewal of reform efforts before the election of 1916, and of course the war in Europe crowded racial issues out of the picture. After the United States entered the war in April 1917 racial policies were unaltered because it seemed easier and less disruptive to carry peacetime patterns over into war. War production led to a vast internal migration of blacks out of the South, which made racial tensions and segregation national as well as regional problems. Neither in civilian war production nor in the military was there any real challenge to segregation, however, and black troops were usually confined to service and support functions under white officers. If the administration felt any discomfort about fighting to make the world safe for democracy while maintaining segregation, little sign of it appeared.

The administration's record on racial matters was not as bad as sometimes depicted, but it was certainly not good. Overall, blacks made up about 10 percent of the total population and held about 6 percent of civil service jobs in 1910. By 1918 the percentage of black civil servants was down to about 5, but even more important was the deep discouragement of blacks, who had found themselves excluded from the party of Lincoln by Roosevelt and Taft, and who now found their hope in Wilson betrayed as well. A bloody tide of lynchings and race riots in 1917, 1918, and 1919 seemed to confirm that the administration's attitude had licensed hatred and bigotry. Not until July 1918 did the president belatedly respond to this challenge with a proclamation describing racist mobs as the enemies of democracy. Wilson undoubtedly wished blacks well, but in a period of growing black militancy, a pervasive reform atmosphere, and the disruption of world war, his conservative paternalism was an inadequate response to the need.

From his youth Wilson had believed and argued that the "form of government [could] be changed by personal leadership."[24] The collapse of the reform movement after he left New Jersey suggests that the impact of his leadership did not outlast him. The racial policies of his administration demonstrated that even good leaders have blind spots and that integrity and benevolence do not always assure adequate or effective actions. Although he was right in believing that strong leadership can effect political change, Wilson overestimated the durability of the forces he aroused and underestimated the limitations of his own vision.

7

DOMESTIC REFORM
1913–1916

Soon after his inauguration Wilson granted a long interview to the journalist John Reed. The interview was never published, perhaps because Wilson decided he had been too frank about sensitive issues, but it offers a valuable insight into Wilson's approach to his office. The president, wrote Reed, was "more interested in principles than in policies." To those who observed him at work he revealed a sense of "quietness inside," a certainty and order that manifested itself in calm efficiency, and in a disregard for the details of policy and administration. Knowing what he wanted to achieve in fundamentals, he was perfectly willing to compromise on details and to leave the running of day-to-day business in the hands of others. In his office, wrote Reed, "one heard scarcely a sound. . . . The window-curtains swayed slowly in a warm breeze; things were unhurried; yet the feeling in that room was of powerful organization, as if no moment were wasted,—as if an immense amount of work was being done."[1]

Wilson's inner certainty fitted him perfectly for the prime minister role he assumed in the new administration. At cabinet meetings he raised questions and subtly guided discussions to elicit information and build support for the policies he wanted. In dealing with Congress he "succeeded in taking his legislative leaders into partnership with him and . . . achieved the substance of cabinet government without constitutional amendment."[2] Feeling detached from the office he occupied, he was free of pomposity and able to treat members of Congress as equals, which made relations with the legislature more harmonious than they had been for many years. The setting of policy by "common counsel," one of Wilson's favorite phrases, did not preclude subtle direction of the process by the president.

Yet there were ways in which Wilson's detachment was a liability. Because his decisions were based on principle rather than being expedient reactions to immediate problems, he spent a great deal of his time alone, reading, thinking, and writing. Some people thought him cold and aloof. He had no social ambitions, did not entertain extensively in the White House, and seemed to avoid rather than to cultivate the social contacts with politicians that are the channels through which a great deal of public business flows in Washington. Enemies accused him of acting on intuition rather than information, and even House worried that he paid too little attention to facts. "The President is a peculiar man," wrote the colonel in his diary. "He never seems to want to discuss things with anyone, as far as I know, excepting me. Even his Cabinet bore him with their importunities, and he often complains of them. It is really a defect in his usefulness as an Executive, for the reason that he does not get many side lights on questions. He seldom reads the newspapers and gains his knowledge of public affairs largely from the matters brought to his attention, and his general information is gotten from a cursory glance at the Weekly Press."[3]

Reporters found Wilson hard to cover. Most knew that he had a sense of humor, loved limericks, was a talented mimic, knew a great deal about baseball, and enjoyed singing, but he almost never displayed any of these attractively human aspects of his personality in public. Although he instituted weekly press conferences, their topics were always official business. Moreover, even when the president talked to reporters, he was not always honest with them. He did not often lie outright, as he once told House he thought was "justified in some instances . . . where it involved the honor of a woman" or "matters of public policy," but he was a master of prevarication.[4] He could mislead or give only part of an answer in ways that led unfortunate reporters to totally false conclusions. Burned a few times, journalists became wary and less friendly.

Wilson's austere facade prevented him from getting the public affection he craved and made it hard for him to influence politicians and the press. Whether revered, admired, or hated, Wilson would always be "Woodrow" to Americans, never "Woody" or "Tommy." Ellen and House worked with some success to create the personal links to other leaders that Wilson could not establish, but they could not humanize him for the general public. Indeed, one of the secrets of House's remarkable influence was his ability to penetrate the president's reserve and respond to his hidden longing for love.

Yet if Wilson's personality was unusual among politicians and his style of leadership rare, he was no less effective than others. Exceptionally intelligent, he grasped the essentials of an issue rapidly and formulated his recommendations in broad terms that commanded wide support. He then presented his case to the public in powerful speeches that set the issue as a choice between good and evil, while in dealing with legislators he demonstrated an understanding of practical concerns like patronage as well as matters of morality. The result during his first term was "a spectacular, possibly unmatched, record of legislative and party leadership."[5]

The times, it must be admitted, were ripe for his triumph. Roosevelt had popularized the idea of progressive change and secured some notable achievements, but he had failed to provide tariff or currency reform or new antitrust legislation. The Democrats, out of power for sixteen years and eager to build a record, had been prepared by Bryan's leadership for action in all these fields. Where Roosevelt had had to poke and prod reluctant conservatives into action, Wilson found reform sentiment at the flood and labored more to control and direct it than to intensify it.

The first order of business was the tariff. Passage of the very high Payne-Aldrich Tariff in 1909 had angered many Americans and contributed to the Democrats' winning control of the House and increasing their strength in the Senate in 1910. The 1912 Democratic platform promised a reduction, and Wilson had made the promise a major campaign theme, so there was no doubt that the Democrats were committed to the principle of reduction. In practice, there were weak spots. The South wanted to protect its textiles, New England its shoes, and the West its sugar products. As President Taft had discovered in 1909, promised tariff reforms had a way of turning out to be tariff increases. Wilson's success or failure on this tough issue could be a measure of his presidency.

Wilson left drafting the tariff bill to Chairman Oscar W. Underwood and the members of his House Ways and Means Committee. The committee worked hard during January and February 1913, and on 17

March they sent a draft bill to Wilson, who responded by calling Congress into special session for 7 April. On 24 March he and Underwood spent four hours going over the details of the bill.

The president liked the Underwood bill in general, except for its continued protection of farm goods, sugar, wool, and leather boots and shoes. Those concessions to the products of strongly Democratic areas would have eased the passage of the bill through the House and assured support in the Senate, but Wilson feared any exceptions to the reduction principle would open the door to "log-rolling," the trading of protection clauses back and forth until everything was again protected. In a White House meeting with Underwood on 1 April he insisted that duties on food, leather, wool, and sugar be reduced. Because the sugar industry was heavily dependent on protection, he was willing to lower those tariffs over a three-year period, but even that concession was dependent upon a promise from Louisiana's representatives that they would support the rest of the bill. If Congress passed an unsatisfactory bill, Wilson threatened a veto.

Democratic members of the Ways and Means Committee grumbled at this executive meddling with their prerogatives, but they did as the president demanded. On 8 April Wilson broke more than a century of precedent by going personally before a joint session of Congress to urge the passage of the Underwood bill. "While the whole face and method of our industrial and commercial life were being changed beyond recognition," he pointed out, "the tariff schedules have remained what they were before the change began." That situation must be altered, he declared, so that "the object of the tariff duties henceforth laid must be effective competition, the whetting of American wits by contest with the wits of the rest of the world."[6]

In the House the matter was never in doubt. Democrats from Ohio objected to the wool schedules, and those from Louisiana opposed the sugar schedules, but an overwhelming majority of Democrats stood by the leadership. On 8 May the House passed the bill by 281 to 139, with only five Democrats, four of them from Louisiana, opposing. Two Republicans, two Progressives, and an independent joined the majority.

The Senate posed a more difficult problem. There the Democrats had a majority of only six, and there was a good deal of pressure on southern and western Democratic senators to reinstate protection for sugar and wool. Louisiana's senators were already pledged to oppose any bill including free sugar, and their defection opened the door to crippling deals and amendments. Moreover, although some Progressives were sympathetic to tariff reform, the fact that the Democrats had made the issue partisan meant that securing Progressive support was difficult. Sensing vulnerability, protectionists girded for battle.

Wilson fought back vigorously. On 9 April he again "jolted custom and woke up sleeping precedent" by going to the Capitol to confer with members of the Senate Finance Committee. "The net result of this meeting," he told reporters afterward, "is that we don't see any sort of difficulty about standing firmly on our party programme."[7] Later he followed up his initiative by writing and conferring privately with doubtful senators. In his press conferences during April he kept up the pressure, and on 1 May he met directly with six western Democratic senators who came out of the meeting promising to support the Underwood bill without amendments.

Yet despite the president's best efforts, he warned that an avalanche of advertisements, letters, and visits by lobbyists could bury reform. "This town is swarming with lobbyists, so you can't throw bricks in any direction without hitting one," he told reporters on 26 May, and later that day he issued a formal statement denouncing the activities of this "numerous," "industrious," and "insidious" group. They were, he charged, spending "money without limit" to defeat the tariff bill.[8]

Initial reaction to the president's charges was negative. The *New York Times* editorialized against any effort to block the use of "ordinary, usual, and perfectly legitimate measures . . . by protected interests to present their case to Congress."[9] Democrats in the Senate were obviously confused by the president's unexpected focus on lobbying, and Republicans thought he had blundered by making unprovable charges. Republican Senator Albert B. Cummins of Iowa gleefully introduced a resolution calling for the creation of a special committee to investigate lobbying, thinking thereby to embarrass Wilson.

When Wilson responded to this challenge by endorsing Cummins's resolution and offering to supply the names of lobbyists, Senate Democrats rallied. On 29 May they endorsed the Cummins resolution, changing it just enough to make it more respectful to the president and putting the investigation in the hands of the Democratically controlled Judiciary Committee. Five days later, on 2 June, a subcommittee of the Judiciary Committee headed by Senator Lee S. Overman of North Carolina opened hearings.

The Overman committee began by asking each senator to disclose his investments and financial holdings. As the revelations of preferred stockholdings in protected companies, of large acreages in sugar and cattle, of investments in textile and shoe factories piled up, it began to seem that Wilson's charges were not so farfetched after all. A good many senators, it appeared, stood to gain personally from continued protection. When reporters asked Wilson what he thought about the investigation, he replied drily that it was "very beneficial."[10]

A few days later, as the Overman committee turned its scrutiny directly on lobbying, he had more reason to be pleased. After a weak start, the committee unearthed a five-million-dollar lobbying effort by the beet sugar industry, which over the preceding twenty years had worked steadily to win the support of newspapers, legislators, and businessmen in the fight against free sugar.

Yet many of the Overman committee's results were negative from Wilson's point of view. The intensely protectionist lobbying by big business in earlier years had stopped, and one large industry, the Federal Sugar Refining Company, was actually proposing to reduce duties. Although no one in the administration recognized the significance of these findings, it is evident in retrospect that protectionism was becoming unnecessary for the largest American corporations.

Nevertheless, the glare of publicity created by the Overman committee's investigation quickly wilted opposition to tariff reduction. On 25 June the Senate Democratic caucus voted thirty-nine to six in favor of free wool and forty-three to two in favor of free sugar after three years. When on 7 July the caucus voted forty-seven to two to support the whole bill, it appeared that enactment of the measure would soon follow.

Republican leaders were determined to delay passage of the bill as long as possible, not because they felt strongly about the tariff, but because they wanted to obstruct currency and banking reform proposals, which were following hard on the heels of the tariff bill. Through the hot months of July and August they droned out endlessly technical speeches before an empty Senate chamber. Even Wilson, who had declared his intention of staying in Washington until currency reform came up, fled to the cooler climate of New Hampshire. Then, on 26 August, the Republicans stumbled onto a new approach that threatened the whole tariff measure.

The new attack came from Republican progressives, and it was fundamental. The authors of the Underwood bill, realizing that a sharp reduction of duties would cut government revenues, had taken advantage of the recently approved Sixteenth Amendment to the Constitution to include in the bill a federal income tax designed to raise a

107

hundred million dollars a year. Beginning with a levy of 1 percent on personal and corporate incomes of four thousand dollars or more a year and rising to a maximum of 3 percent on incomes over one hundred thousand, the tax was hardly burdensome. Yet when the income tax provision came up for debate, it permitted an unexpected attack on the whole bill. Led by Republicans William E. Borah of Idaho, Joseph H. Bristow of Kansas, and Cummins, progressives argued that the government should reduce the tariff even more and turn mainly to the income tax, because the tariff weighed on the rich and poor alike, while an income tax would shift the tax burden from the poor to the rich. On 27 August Senator Robert M. La Follette of Wisconsin introduced an amendment to the Underwood bill jumping the maximum tax rate to 10 percent on incomes over one hundred thousand dollars.

Democrats united to vote down the La Follette amendment on 28 August, but a few hours later some of them began to have second thoughts. During the evening of 28 August Senators Henry F. Ashurst of Arizona, James A. Reed of Missouri, William H. Thompson of Kansas, and James K. Vardaman of Mississippi met and demanded a special session of the Democratic caucus to reconsider the La Follette amendment. They insisted that a majority of the caucus would support it. Convinced of the seriousness of this insurrection, Democratic leaders agreed to a compromise raising the maximum rate to 7 percent and appealed to Bryan to hold his southern and western friends in line. On 5 September, after Wilson joined Bryan in endorsing the compromise, it was approved by the caucus.

The last challenge to the bill came on 8 September when the Senate voted down, fifty-eight to twelve, a proposal to add a heavy inheritance tax to the measure, and when it defeated, thirty-nine to twenty-nine, a Republican amendment calling for the reduction of duties on wool to 15 percent after 1 January 1916. The latter proposal, with its appearance of further reduction, was especially seductive, but approving it would have reopened every other schedule as well. A last minute plea for a change in the sugar schedule by Senator Joseph E. Ransdell of Louisiana aroused no support at all.

The following day, 9 September 1913, the Senate passed the bill by forty-four to thirty-seven, with only Senators Ransdell and John R. Thornton of Louisiana deserting the Democrats, while La Follette broke ranks to vote with the majority. "A fight for the people and for free business, which has lasted a long generation through, has at last been won, handsomely and completely," declared Wilson in a public statement.[11] On 3 October, after a conference worked out the differences between the House and Senate versions of the bill, the president signed the tariff bill into law.

The Underwood Tariff was a genuine attempt at reduction and reform. Under the Payne-Aldrich Tariff ad valorem duties had averaged 37 to 40 percent; the Underwood bill as passed by the House reduced them to about 29 percent, and the Senate, usually the bastion of protectionism, actually cut them further to about 26 percent. The bill was never intended to establish free trade, but in addition to cutting duties, it substantially enlarged the "free list" of items upon which no duties were charged. More important, it introduced the progressive income tax and set that tax on the road to replacing the tariff as the main source of government revenue. For all those reasons Democrats could and did take pride in the new tariff.

On the other hand, the absence of protectionist lobbying suggests that Wilson's hope that the bill would strike a major blow at the trusts was erroneous. Because World War I disrupted world trade patterns from soon after the passage of the bill until the Republicans restored protectionism in the 1920s, it is impossible to know what the Underwood measure might have accomplished in normal times, but contemporary businessmen did not share Wilson's conviction that it would have promoted competition and driven down consumer prices. Except for the sugar trust, no major corporation actively opposed tariff reduction. The attitude of most big business executives was exemplified by William E. Cody, former president of United States Steel, who said, "I approve of the Underwood bill and do not believe that it will affect business unfavorably in this country except in isolated cases."[12] During House and Senate hearings most testimony against the bill came not from the trusts but from small and medium-sized businesses, whose representatives insisted that the Underwood bill would ruin them by adding foreign to trust competition.

The attitudes of both big and smaller businessmen suggest that the Underwood Tariff was about twenty years too late to achieve what Wilson hoped. In the late nineteenth century while the trusts were still growing, lowered tariffs might have stimulated competition, but by 1913 most big corporations were in better shape to meet foreign competition than their smaller American rivals. Thus in normal times the Underwood Act might actually have reduced competition. Although the new bill obviously had some benefits, it was not the great reform measure that Wilson claimed and that many historians have thought it.

Congratulations poured in to Wilson after the passage of the tariff, but as usual his eye was fixed not on victory but on the next challenge. Even in his formal statement after the Senate vote he urged that currency reform be passed "with equal energy, directness, and loyalty to the general interest," and at the ceremony at the White House when he signed the bill on the evening of 3 October, he dwelt on the same theme.[13] "I feel tonight like a man who is lodging happily in the inn which lies half way along the journey," he said, and he urged the assembled legislators to "go the rest of the journey and sleep at the journey's end like men with a quiet conscience, knowing that we have served our fellow men and have, thereby, tried to serve God."[14]

Currency and banking reform were, however, no simple matter. They were, Wilson admitted, "not like the tariff, about which opinion has been definitely forming long years through." Instead, there were "almost as many judgments as there are men."[15] Understanding the complexities of the issues and reconciling varying opinions were among the most difficult tasks Wilson undertook.

Devised during the Civil War and modified only slightly thereafter, the nation's banking system, if it may be called that, consisted of about seven thousand independent banks loosely supervised by the comptroller of the currency. Only a primitive system existed for the maintenance and mobilization of reserves, and there was no uniformity in interest rates charged individual borrowers or discount rates that banks charged each other. Any attempt by bankers to get together on such matters was generally regarded by the public as a conspiracy, so anarchy reigned. Unable to support each other, even the soundest banks were vulnerable to recurrent bank panics, of which a recent and serious example had occurred in 1907.

The nation's monetary system was also a mess. In 1913 there were about $3.8 billion in circulation, consisting largely of gold and silver coins, gold and silver certificates, and national bank notes backed by government bonds. More or less adequate in normal times, this amount of money was insufficient to meet seasonal peaks in agriculture or industry and excessive in times of panic or recession. The country desperately needed some way to expand and contract the amount of money in circulation in proportion to the growth and contraction of the economy.

After the Panic of 1907 Congress created a National Monetary Commission headed by Senator Nelson W. Aldrich of Rhode Island to study monetary and banking problems and to report to Congress. Four years later, the Aldrich commission recommended the establishment of a privately controlled central bank, to be called the National Reserve Association, with fifteen branches around the country. The association was to act as a bank for other banks, not dealing with the public, but holding a portion of each member bank's reserves, setting discount rates, and issuing paper money based upon its gold reserves and upon commercial paper (promissory notes signed by businesses when they borrow). Since the volume of commercial paper increases when business is booming and decreases in slack times, the amount of money in circulation would also expand and contract in direct proportion to the state of the economy. According to the Aldrich plan, these national reserve notes would be an obligation of the association, not of the government; they would be, in effect, a privately issued currency.

Bankers and businessmen generally liked the Aldrich plan because it kept control over the banking business in private hands, but many reformers feared that would give bankers too much power and demanded that the system be publicly controlled. On this point William Jennings Bryan and Theodore Roosevelt found themselves in rare agreement.

Wilson's opinions on the subject, vague before 1913, rested on two convictions. The first was that financial power in the country had become too concentrated in a New York "money trust" that must be broken up so that credit would be "at the disposal of everybody upon equal terms."[16] His second belief was that when banking competition was restored, the system must be government supervised to protect the public interest. Although his analysis of the problem was probably wrong in that the banking system was more characterized by anarchy than excessive centralization, his attitude determined the administration's rejection of the private control feature of the Aldrich plan.

The aim of breaking up the alleged money trust was at the heart of a draft bill presented to the president-elect by House banking committee chairman Carter Glass, and the committee's expert adviser, H. Parker Willis, on 26 December 1912. Providing for a decentralized system of twenty or more privately controlled reserve banks, the bill sought to create regional financial centers that could compete with New York. Wilson applauded that aim but thought the system needed some sort of central body to coordinate it.

Glass disliked the idea of a central bank, but he made changes in the draft, and by May 1913 he had completed a bill that generally satisfied the president. Wilson then gave the draft to various members of the administration for comment. Both Bryan and Secretary of the Treasury McAdoo found it objectionable, but it was Bryan who led the attack. Charging correctly that the Glass bill was really nothing but a decentralized version of the Aldrich plan, Bryan demanded that all members of the central body, the Federal Reserve Board, must be government appointees, not chosen by the banks, and he insisted that currency issued by the board must be a government obligation. Failure to make those changes, said Bryan, "would be sure to arouse great opposition in the Democratic party and might jeopardize the passage of the tariff bill through the Senate." For his own part, he added, if he backed down on this issue, he "would forfeit the confidence of those who trusted me—this confidence being my only political asset, the loss of which would deprive me of any power to assist" the administration.[17]

When Bryan's genteel threats were backed by Senator Robert L. Owen of Oklahoma, chairman of the Senate banking committee, Wilson realized he was facing a serious rebellion. After conferring with Brandeis and finding that the lawyer agreed with Bryan, Wilson gave in and instructed Glass to alter the bill to give the bankers no control over board membership and to make Federal Reserve notes government obligations. Despite charges from bankers and the opposition press that the bill was "covered all over with the slime of Bryanism," the president, once convinced, made these provisions absolute requirements of the proposed legislation.[18] On 23 June 1913 Wilson again appeared before a joint session of Congress to urge immediate action on the Federal Reserve bill.

Bryan's objections now appeared to have been only the first gust of a major storm. During July and August southern and western Democrats in the House threatened to defeat the Federal Reserve bill altogether unless it were drastically revised to strike more forcibly at the "money trust" and to include the provision of short-term agricultural credit among the functions of the system. Wilson compromised on one of their demands by promising to ban interlocking bank directorates in forthcoming antitrust legislation but held out on other matters until mid-August, when it became obvious the agrarians would not be fobbed off. On 13 August the president issued a statement promising a future agricultural credit measure, but that also proved insufficient, and the next day Glass and House Democratic leader Oscar Underwood accepted an amendment to the bill making bills of exchange based on warehouse receipts for stored farm products eligible for rediscount by Federal Reserve banks along with commercial paper. Even that concession did not entirely satisfy the farm group, but when Bryan issued a strong statement a few days later urging all Democrats to "stand by the President," opposition collapsed.[19] On 28 August the House Democratic caucus voted overwhelmingly to make the bill a party measure. With party discipline restored, Glass pressed ahead with the bill, and on 18 September the House passed it 287 to 85. Only three Democrats, all Southerners, opposed it, and thirty-three Republicans and Progressives voted for it.

Outside of Congress there was considerable support for the Federal Reserve proposal among small businessmen and local bankers but strong opposition from the big banks. The convention of the American Bankers' Association in early October condemned the bill, and so did the United States Chamber of Commerce. Wilson would not have been concerned about such reactions, except that the situation in the Senate was very delicate. Of the seven Democrats on the Senate Committee on Banking and Currency, only four were reliable supporters of the administration. The other three, Gilbert M. Hitchcock of Nebraska, James A. O'Gorman of New York, and James A. Reed of Missouri, were troublemakers with grudges. Hitchcock was a bitter rival of Bryan's in Nebraska politics; O'Gorman and Reed were at odds with the White House over patronage and other matters. Shrewdly taking advantage of this split among the Democrats, Frank W. Vanderlip, president of the National City Bank of New York, suggested a substitute bill that would have created a privately owned national bank under strict federal control. Bankers liked the idea of a privately owned national bank; many progressives were attracted by the strong federal control in the Vanderlip plan.

For a time it looked as if the Vanderlip proposal might beat out the Federal Reserve bill. Wilson and Glass were convinced that it was only a "red-herring" intended to prevent the passage of any bill, but the proposal attracted enough support from both conservatives and progressives to make it a threat.[20] As the struggle grew more heated, Wilson leaped into it personally, summoning Democratic leaders to the White House to demand loyalty and flattering Reed and O'Gorman, who showed signs of coming back to the fold. Finally, on 7 November the committee took a vote and found itself tied—Hitchcock and the five Republicans against six Democrats. Two weeks later, unable to reach a compromise, the committee reported both the Federal Reserve and Vanderlip bills to the full Senate.

On the Senate floor the going was a little easier. After lengthy de-

bate during which conservatives predicted that this capitulation to Bryanism would ruin the country, the Democrats, minus Hitchcock,
united on 19 December to defeat the Vanderlip proposal forty-four to
forty-one, and to pass the Federal Reserve bill fifty-four to thirty-four.
In the end, even Hitchcock voted for the bill, and so did six Republicans and Progressives. Differences between the House and Senate versions were then straightened out, and Wilson signed the bill into law
on 23 December 1913. It was, he said, an example of "team work" not
only among Democrats but between Republicans and Democrats that
he believed would "secure us in prosperity and peace."[21]

The Federal Reserve Act was the most important piece of legislation passed by the Wilson administration. With some later modifica-
tions and improvements the Federal Reserve Board has continued to
manage interest rates, expand and contract the currency, and regulate
banks successfully for more than seventy years.

For the administration the Federal Reserve Act was also an important milestone. The bill Wilson and Carter Glass had shaped in May
1913 was significantly different from that passed in December, and its
changes reflected the administration's modification of the New Freedom. That program, as Wilson outlined it in 1912, was based on the
assumption that lifting artificial constraints from the marketplace would
create an ideal situation in which natural forces would regulate the
economy and competition would assure prosperity for all. With the
Federal Reserve Act, however, Wilson largely abandoned this classical
economic theory and moved toward accepting government as a partner
in regulation with business. In this instance he was pushed by the
Bryanites; urban progressives provided similar pressures in the future.
What was significant was not so much where the pressure came from as
that Wilson yielded to it, and that he was able to rationalize his change
of direction. Previously he had talked about conflicts with bankers and
about removing "some of the artificial obstacles to our prosperity." Now
he discussed "common counsel and the accumulating force of cooperation" between business and government.[22]

It would be a mistake to suggest that a philosophy of partnership
between government and business dominated Wilson's thought as it did
that of the Republican administrations of the 1920s. The history of
child labor legislation in these years demonstrates that Wilson did not
easily give up his old belief that government should stay out of the
economy, and it shows also that he could be pushed by the necessities
of politics into positions hostile to business.

For many years reformers and social workers had struggled to eliminate child labor through state legislation, but by 1913 they decided to try instead for a federal law. Early in 1913 the Supreme Court, in *Hoke v. United States,* seemed to affirm that Congress had broad powers to issue "police regulations" under the commerce clause of the Constitution, and reformers hoped that a child labor bill based on this interpretation would be found constitutional.[23] On 16 January 1914 Representative A. Mitchell Palmer of Pennsylvania introduced a bill drafted by the National Child Labor Committee, and a month later Senator Robert L. Owen of Oklahoma introduced the same bill in the Senate. The Palmer-Owen bill barred from interstate commerce any products manufactured by children under the age of fourteen or by children between fourteen and sixteen who had to work more than eight hours a day or forty-eight hours a week. All products of mines and quarries that employed children under sixteen were to be banned from interstate commerce.

Members of the national committee called on Wilson in February 1914 to ask his support for the bill but, reiterating his old states' rights beliefs, he told them, "in all frankness, that no child labor law yet proposed has seemed to me constitutional."[24] The most he would do was to remain silent, which meant that the bill would be considered in Congress only after administration-supported legislation was dealt with. Reported favorably by the House labor committee in August 1914, the bill did not come up for a vote until 15 February 1915, when it passed by 233 to 43. That was too late. By the time the bill was reported to the Senate on 1 March, Congress was on the verge of adjournment, and the bill died without a vote. Although legislators from southern textile-producing states had opposed the legislation, it was really Wilson's lack of support that doomed it.

During the next session of Congress, beginning in December 1915, the same child labor legislation was reintroduced as the Keating-Owen bill. Once again the House passed the measure, on 2 February 1916, and by an even larger majority, 337 to 46. In the Senate, however, southerners were able to use parliamentary devices to prevent the bill's coming up for a vote before the summer of 1916. Their efforts proved to be vain, for the Republican and Democratic presidential conventions both endorsed the bill in strong terms, and Wilson underwent a conversion. Warned by reformers that "action on the child labor bill will be regarded as a test of genuine interest in humane measures opposed by commercial interests" and reminded none too subtly that Republican presidential candidate Charles Evans Hughes had promised action, Wilson paid a surprise visit to Democratic Senate leaders at the Capitol on 18 July.[25] He reminded them of the party's platform promise and urged speedy action. Thus goaded, the leaders pressed the bill vigorously, and on 8 August the Senate passed it, fifty-two to twelve. After differences with the House version were reconciled, Wilson signed it into law on 1 September. Challenged by textile manufacturers, the law was found unconstitutional by a five to four majority of the Supreme Court in *Hammer v. Dagenhart* on 3 June 1918. Ironically, Wilson's original conservatism was upheld—in part by his own appointees to the court—after he had abandoned it.

Politics obviously played a role in Wilson's decision to support the Keating-Owen bill, but it would be erroneous to see his conversion as determined only by the close 1916 presidential race. As early as the autumn of 1913 his attitude toward the Federal Reserve Act revealed a shift away from the nineteenth-century liberal belief in restricted, nonregulatory government toward a twentieth-century definition of liberalism in which the government exercises a constant supervisory role in society and the economy. Indeed, even before 1912 he had favored "class legislation" to protect workers and other relatively weak members of society from oppression by stronger interests. By 1916, as other items of his agenda were completed, these concerns became more prominent, while the political pressures of various reform groups made it expedient for him to stress them. He gradually changed his mind about one such issue, woman suffrage, but other instances of apparent favoritism to particular groups, such as protection for seamen or exemption of farm groups from unreasonable interpretations of the Sherman Antitrust Act, were in harmony with long-standing convictions. Pragmatically, Wilson was seeking to build a government that could regulate without stifling, protect the helpless without suppressing initiative.

The most striking example of the degree to which Wilson's attitude about government's role in the economy evolved during his first term is in antitrust legislation. The theme of his 1912 campaign speeches had been that unfair competitive practices must be outlawed and corporate executives made legally liable for their behavior, but that continuous government oversight of the economy would be unnecessary if natural economic forces were allowed to operate freely. By 1914, however, Wilson's ideas on these matters had changed drastically, and that year's legislation reflected those changes.

Attorney General James C. McReynolds set the early tone of the administration's antitrust policy with a series of attacks on the so-called "Tobacco Trust," the Union Pacific Railroad, the United States Steel Corporation, American Telephone and Telegraph, and the New York, New Haven, and Hartford Railroad. His actions alarmed and angered businessmen and created an atmosphere of confrontation that was just the opposite of what Wilson wanted. Never antibusiness, Wilson had frequently said during the campaign that he wanted to reestablish competition, but to do it in such a way as to stimulate and energize business rather than to frustrate and antagonize businessmen. "I think it will be easily agreed that we should let the Sherman antitrust law stand . . . ," he said in his annual message to Congress on 2 December 1913, "but that we should . . . supplement that great act by legislation which will not only clarify it but also facilitate its administration and make it fairer to all concerned."[26]

As with the tariff and banking bills, Wilson was willing to work out details of legislation with appropriate members of Congress, provided they would let him set the overall direction. He conferred with leaders from both houses during late 1913 and then, during a Christmas vacation at Pass Christian, Mississippi, he drafted the speech with which he meant to present his plans to Congress. "The antagonism between business and government is over," he told a joint session on 20 January 1914, and "the Government and businessmen are ready to meet each other half way in a common effort to square business methods with both public opinion and the law."[27]

Wilson's soothing words were given substance during succeeding weeks with the introduction of three bills. The first, sponsored by Henry D. Clayton of Alabama, chairman of the House Judiciary Committee, prohibited interlocking directorates among banks, railroads, and large corporations so that, in Wilson's words, "those who borrow and those who lend" would no longer be "practically one and the same."[28] The Clayton bill also specified other unfair competitive practices, such as artificially lowering prices to destroy competition, or refusing to sell goods to some distributors; it made executives criminally responsible for violations of the Sherman Act; and it prohibited ownership of stock by corporations if the effect of that was to reduce competition.

A second bill, drafted by Representatives William C. Adamson of Georgia and James H. Covington of Maryland, Senator Francis G. Newlands of Nevada, and Attorney General McReynolds, proposed to create a bipartisan Interstate Trade Commission whose task it would be to advise corporations when they were violating antitrust laws and to help them comply with the law. In contrast to Roosevelt's call for a strong regulatory body, Wilson's ITC would attempt "to meet business half way in its processes of self-correction."[29] Wilson continued to believe, as he always had, that most businessmen were honorable, and that natural forces would regulate the marketplace once abuses were corrected.

The third element of the administration's program was the bill sponsored by Representative Sam Rayburn of Texas that gave the Interstate Commerce Commission power over new securities issued by the railroads. A response to a scandal involving the New Haven railroad, the Rayburn bill was never a major part of Wilson's program, and although it passed the House, it died in the Senate.

Businessmen who had awaited Wilson's antitrust program with apprehension were pleased by its conservatism, while progressives, including Brandeis, feared it was too weak. In the first few months, however, the sharpest attack on the proposed legislation came neither from businessmen nor from reformers, but from organized labor, which demanded total exemption from prosecution under antitrust laws as part of the new legislation. Wilson thought a complete exemption unreasonable and offered as a compromise a statement legalizing unions— that is, defining unions as not, in themselves, conspiracies in restraint of trade. Labor leaders were disappointed with that, pointing out that successive court decisions had already made the same point, but they could not muster enough votes in the House or Senate to win a broader exemption. In later years Samuel Gompers, president of the American Federation of Labor, frequently described the Clayton Act as "labor's Magna Carta," but at the time a spokesman for one of the country's leading antiunion organizations dismissed it as making "few changes in existing laws relating to labor unions."[30] The same charge—that the new legislation made little change in existing laws—might well have been leveled at the whole package that passed the House on 5 June 1914.

After their relatively easy passage through the House, Wilson's antitrust proposals ran into serious opposition in the Senate. The different treatment was not because of the nature of the two houses but resulted from the gradual coalescence of several groups into a strong opposition. Progressives and conservatives alike came gradually to the conclusion that the Clayton and Covington bills were unworkable and even possibly dangerous.

Small businessmen—the people Wilson most wanted to help—were alarmed by the personal guilt clauses of the bills, fearing that every business decision might send them to jail. Other entrepreneurs were as afraid of unrestrained competition as they were of monopoly and worried that the administration's program would reestablish the competitive jungle of the nineteenth century. Reformers, including Brandeis himself, despaired of ever being able to spell out all the ways businessmen and lawyers might be able to think of to restrain trade or compete unfairly.

Surprisingly, both conservatives and reformers agreed on what needed to be done. The pending legislation must be amended by abandoning the effort to specify in detail all unfair competitive practices. Instead "unfair" trade practices should be outlawed in general terms, with the specific interpretation of the generalizations and the day-to-day supervision of business practices left in the hands of a strong Interstate Trade Commission, which would have regulatory powers. In short, reformers, Brandeis, and conservative businessmen alike were all coming around to Roosevelt's point of view: the progressives, because they had found their original approach unworkable; the conservatives, because they hoped a strong ITC would make government policy predictable and enable them to plan ahead.

Wilson was impressed by the arguments against his legislative program but reluctant to reverse himself, especially since southern Democrats remained adamantly opposed to the Rooseveltian solution of the trust problem. Once the three bills were safely through the House, he called Brandeis, Representative Raymond B. Stevens and Senator Henry F. Hollis of New Hampshire, and George Rublee, a New York lawyer and friend of Brandeis who had been active in lobbying for effective antitrust laws, to a conference at the White House on 10 June. Stevens had introduced a strong ITC bill, and Rublee had suggested striking out the existing terms of the Covington bill and replacing them with the Stevens bill. Wilson, having changed his mind completely, agreed to this procedure and authorized Hollis and Brandeis to present it to the Senate Committee on Interstate and Foreign Commerce.

Both Democratic and Republican members of the Senate committee were delighted with Wilson's reversal and quickly took his advice. The new ITC was to be a nonpartisan, five-member body with sweeping investigative powers and authority to order termination of unfair competitive practices, enforcing its orders through the federal courts.

On the floor of the Senate the new measure aroused far more controversy than the old one. Conservatives blasted it as a "socialist" attack on private property, while radical progressives predicted that businessmen would capture control of the ITC and make regulation meaningless. This second charge must have stung Wilson, for he had said exactly the same thing about Roosevelt's proposed regulatory body during the 1912 campaign, but he stuck to his guns. When Senate leaders seemed willing to retreat toward yet another effort to define unfair competition, Wilson declared "very grave doubt" about the feasibility of any such course. What was necessary, he insisted, was "elasticity without real indefiniteness."[31] The president's intervention strengthened Democrats, and on 5 August they joined with many progressive Republicans to pass the bill, fifty-three to sixteen. During the conference to reconcile the radical differences between the House and Senate bills, Wilson again insisted on the Senate version, and the House obediently went along, making only one significant change, an amendment that broadened the powers of the courts to review and set aside ITC rulings. That amendment weakened the bill, but when Wilson signed it into law on 26 September 1914, it was essentially what he wanted, although drastically different from what he had originally proposed.

While the administration focused its attention on the ITC bill, the Clayton bill, originally the flagship of Wilson's program, was sucked into legislative whirlpools. Conservatives succeeded in striking specific definitions of illegal practices out of the bill, and criminal penalties for violations of antitrust laws were dropped. The completed bill did little or nothing to define "restraint of trade" and was essentially meaningless. Progressives appealed to the White House for help, but Wilson no longer cared. Senator James A. Reed declared bitterly that the bill ought to be entitled "An apology to unlawful restraints and monopolies," but an alliance of administration and conservative forces pushed it through, and Wilson signed it on 15 October 1914. It was, he admitted, "so weak you cannot tell it from water."[32]

The ITC and Clayton bills were a tacit admission that Wilson's original New Freedom program had been unworkable. The problem was not that he had lost faith in the self-regulation of the economy once abuses were rectified, but that it proved impossible to spell out and cure or prevent all possible offenses. The economy was not a machine subject only to mechanical laws; it was a human society vulnerable to all the stupid, selfish, ingenious, noble, and unpredictable things people do. In turning to the Rooseveltian solution to the trust problem Wilson was not only giving up the beautiful dream of a self-regulating economy, he was also admitting the essential hopelessness of all available solutions. For he had been right in 1912, when he argued that a strong regulatory agency would be captured by the businessmen it was supposed to control. Between 1915 and 1925 the ITC tried, against the opposition of many congressmen, the courts, and much of business, to do the job for which it had been created. Understandably, it was not very successful, but after 1925, when a majority of its members were appointed by Republican conservatives Coolidge and Hoover, it gave up even the attempt to regulate.

With the passage of antitrust legislation in the autumn of 1914 everything Wilson had promised in 1912 was completed. It was an astonishing record in so short a time, more for the way in which it was done than for the substance of the achievements. Incredibly, Wilson had kept Congress in continuous session for nineteen months without any national crisis to justify the extraordinary situation and had never lost control over the legislators. No other president has ever matched that record. Small wonder that Wilson told House in September 1914 that he was thinking of not running for reelection in 1916 because "he feared the country would expect him to continue as he had up to now, which would be impossible."[33]

As many experts have pointed out, "Wilson's performance of 1913–14 has become the classic example of presidential marshaling of support behind a predetermined program."[34] He stated his program clearly, developed public support for it, planned details in constant conferences with legislators, established clear priorities for various measures and scheduled them so as to avoid conflict, dramatized his case with personal appearances at the Capitol, used the power of his office to cajole, soothe, and pressure legislators, and proved willing to change his mind dramatically when persuaded his first approach was wrong. A master of both strategy and tactics, he demonstrated in the most convincing way that the American system could be effective and that as a leader within that system, he had no peer.

On the other hand, except for the Federal Reserve system, Wilson's stunning achievements have not had much lasting impact on the United States. Indeed, by the end of 1914, "Wilson faced a kind of ideological and policy bankruptcy. Where would the New Freedom Democrats go from there?" What he had accomplished thus far was a tribute to his personal leadership of "a patchwork collection of old Cleveland, anti-silver Democrats, city bosses, Bryan Populists, conservative Southerners, and a few urban, middle-class progressives," but there was little beyond what had been done that this coalition could agree upon, and in fact it was already coming apart under the strain of power.[35]

During the next two years Wilson moved toward acceptance of a more activist role for the government. As he actively supported measures like the Farm Loan Bank and the Agricultural Extension Service to assist farmers, the Adamson Act to require an eight-hour day for railroad workers, and the Keating-Owen child labor bill, it began to look as if he had either changed his opinions dramatically, or that he was opportunistically taking up such proposals in order to win support from progressives in the Republican party. By 1916, when he ran for reelection, he had the strong support of "virtually the entire leadership of the advanced wing of the progressive movement" plus even some radicals and socialists, as well as those ethnic and other groups for whom the peace issue was decisive.[36]

Although Wilson was certainly aware of the political benefits that might come from reform proposals that could broaden and strengthen the Democratic coalition, the directions of his program were not determined only by political considerations. He had been concerned about labor and farmers since 1912 and 1913 but had deferred reforms in those areas to give priority to other matters he thought more urgent. Moreover, as the evolution of the administration's antitrust policy demonstrated, the president was increasingly convinced that the federal government could and should take an active role. A genuine change of mind, plus the emergence of commitments that had always been present but submerged account for the impression that Wilson had altered dramatically by 1916. The transformation was more a matter of evolution than revolution.

We must also be careful not to overstate the extent to which Wilson had modified his views. He was neither a New Nationalist of Theodore Roosevelt's paternalistic stripe nor a welfare statist like Franklin Roosevelt. During World War I he resisted dramatic extensions of federal and executive power in favor of an attempt to mobilize the economy by voluntary cooperation among government, business, and labor. Elements of that policy were in fact evident even before the war in antitrust and banking policy and in his foreign policy in Asia and Latin America. Thus while Wilson rejected the passivity of classical economic thought, his ideas had more in common with those of Republican leaders of the 1920s like Herbert Hoover, who believed that an efficient, humane society could be achieved by cooperation between government and private interests, than with later twentieth-century liberals who saw the state as a broker among power groups. In the war that had already been raging in Europe for two years when Wilson was reelected in 1916 he would find the greatest test and opportunity for the ideas that had been developing out of his thought and experience as president.

8

LATIN AMERICAN AND ASIAN POLICY
1913–1920

During the 1912 campaign Wilson said little about foreign policy, but he laid down broad goals. "We must," he said on 2 November 1912 "shape our course of action by the maxims of justice and liberality and good will, think of the progress of mankind rather than of the progress of this or that investment, of the protection of American honor and the advancement of American ideals rather than always of American contracts, and lift our diplomacy to the levels of what the best minds have planned for mankind."[1] The "service of humanity is the best business of mankind," he repeated on 28 December, "and . . . the business of mankind must be set forward by the governments which mankind sets up, in order that justice may be done and mercy not forgotten."[2]

Although Wilson's statements revealed his conviction that service to others was a Christian's highest duty, his ideas also reflected America's changing relationship with the rest of the world. From the time of the nation's founding Americans had looked with a benign but usually passive sympathy on the struggles of other peoples for democracy and economic progress. The noble sentiments of the Monroe Doctrine and the Open Door policy embodied both good will and American self-interest in regard to Latin America and Asia, but neither policy produced much tangible action by the United States before the twentieth century. At the end of the nineteenth century, however, a reunited nation, muscled with new industrial and military strength, began to realize that its reach now extended to areas of the world where it had previously been unable to act effectively. The "impulse of expansion is the natural and wholesome impulse which comes with a consciousness of matured strength," said Wilson soon after the Spanish-American War, and his attitude was widely shared by other Americans.[3]

Wilson's assumption that the expansion of American influence into Asia and Latin America was inevitably "wholesome" was indicative of the naive arrogance of American policy. He and his contemporaries took it for granted that other peoples, regardless of their histories and traditions, would want to imitate the American political and economic systems if they could. Largely unaware of foreign nationalisms and innocently oblivious of the extent that their own self-interest motivated them, Wilson's generation welcomed America's new power because it gave them an opportunity—indeed seemed to obligate them—to set others on the road to freedom and prosperity. The nation's strength had grown faster than its understanding, and the result during the Wilson administration was a paradoxical combination of idealistic commitment to self-determination and intervention. "What a fine future of distinction and glory is open for a people who, by instinctive sympathy, can interpret and stand for the rights of men everywhere!" exclaimed Wilson in 1916.[4]

Warned soon after taking office that in some Latin American countries "a Democratic victory would be hailed by those seeking to foment revolution," Wilson quickly issued a statement stressing that the United States wished "to cultivate the friendship and deserve the confidence of our sister republics," but that it also believed that "just government" resting "upon the consent of the governed" was essential to harmonious relations, and he warned that the administration would "lend [its] influence of every kind to the realization of these principles in fact and practice."[5] These contradictory themes dominated Wilsonian policy in Latin America and Asia.

Further complicating the situation was the president's determination to pursue economic expansion aggressively. American business, he told an audience in October 1912, must break out of the "straightjacket" of dependence on domestic markets and "release our energies upon the great field which we are now ready to enter, and enter by way of conquest."[6] To implement his proposals, Wilson urged tariff reduction, which would compel American producers to become more competitive with foreign factories, supported a provision of the Federal

Reserve Act that permitted national banks to establish foreign branches, and encouraged the vigorous efforts of Secretary of the Treasury William Gibbs McAdoo and Secretary of Commerce William C. Redfield to open new fields of trade and investment overseas. Although Wilson saw no conflict between these activities and his concern for self-determination and promised never "to determine the foreign policy of [the] nation in the terms of material interest," he was also led inevitably to favor those nations "who protect private rights and respect the restraints of constitutional provision."[7] Assisted by the devastating impact of World War I on European economies, which sharply reduced competition, McAdoo and Redfield worked with striking success to turn an unfavorable balance of trade with Latin America before the war into a favorable balance by war's end. By 1919 Latin American nations were buying almost three times as many goods from American companies as before the war, and American direct investments in Latin America had more than doubled. In a pair of Pan-American financial conferences in 1915 and 1920 McAdoo sought to make these wartime gains permanent, and despite a postwar slump and the revival of European competition, he succeeded substantially.

It did not occur to Wilson and his aides that their efforts to open up trade and investment opportunities might be viewed with suspicion in Latin America. After all, Wilson had said in a speech in Mobile, Alabama, in October 1913 that the United States would "never again seek one additional foot of territory by conquest," and although he was suspicious of the imperialistic implications of foreign investments by Europeans, he was confident of his own ability to control American capitalists. As an earnest show of his good intentions, he adopted a proposal for a Pan-American nonaggression treaty that Colonel House suggested would "weld the Western Hemisphere together" and "serve as a model for the European Nations when peace is at last brought about."[8] Delighted with this idea, Wilson authorized House to open negotiations with the three largest Latin American nations, Argentina, Brazil, and Chile. But Chilean leaders, fearful that the treaty would force them to yield a border claim against Peru and concerned about a growth of American investments in Chile from $5 million in 1900 to $171.4 million by 1914, rejected the proposal, charging that Wilson "aims at United States domination in Latin America" and that the treaty's insistence upon "republican forms of government" would "tend to erect a United States tutelage over Latin America."[9] Subsequently Argentina, perhaps concerned by rapid growth of American investments during the war and by Wilsonian interventions in the Caribbean, also backed away from the treaty. Although the Americans continued to urge its approval, by the end of 1916 it was dead. Whatever Wilson might say, for Latin Americans intervention and economic power were dangerous symbols of a new imperialism.

Ironically, it was probably American intervention in Mexico in 1916 that finally put the kiss of death on the Pan-American treaty, yet from Wilson's point of view no aspect of his Latin American policy was more restrained and successful than that with Mexico. When Wilson took office in 1913 Mexican liberals had recently overthrown a forty-year dictatorship only to have their own constitutional regime ended by a military coup. Appalled by the murder of the constitutional president Francisco Madero by the military usurper Victoriano Huerta, Wilson refused to recognize the new government. Unmoved by threats to some $1.5 billion in American investments in Mexico, the president's instinctive concern was for the welfare of the Mexican people. "When will the poor land know what it can expect," he asked, "and have comfortable to-morrows?"[10]

At first Wilson assumed that the Mexican problem was entirely political. His 12 March 1913 statement denounced "personal intrigue and defiance of constitutional rights" and stressed the importance of "just government . . . based upon law."[11] During the summer and early autumn of 1913 he urged Huerta to call general elections and to promise to abide by their results. Not until October, when Huerta dissolved the legislature, arrested over a hundred members of the opposition, and assumed dictatorial powers, did Wilson give up on this approach.

Finding it difficult to secure reliable information about Mexican conditions, the president sent a journalist friend, William Bayard Hale, to talk to Huerta's opponents, a rebel group calling themselves the Constitutionalists. The name appealed to Wilson, and he must have been startled when Hale reported that the rebels rejected elections and believed that political democracy must be postponed until land reform was adopted and the power of the oligarchy of landowners, church, and military that had dominated the Mexican government for many years broken. Astonishingly, Wilson quickly understood and accepted this argument. Early in 1914 he told the British ambassador in Washington that "the real cause of the trouble in Mexico was not political but economic," and that "a radical revolution was the only cure." Nothing else could provide "a peaceful and permanent settlement."[12] On 3 February 1914 the president lifted an embargo imposed by Taft on the sale of arms to the rebels, and in April he took advantage of a minor insult by Mexican authorities to American sailors at Tampico to land American forces at the east coast port of Veracruz. "A psychological moment" had arrived, said Wilson, when American military intervention could help the rebels to topple Huerta and bring the revolution to success.[13]

Wilson successfully resisted strong pressure from military leaders to make the Veracruz landing the beginning of an all-out invasion of Mexico, but he was shocked by the desperate Mexican defense of the city in which 126 Mexicans and 19 Americans were killed, and stunned by the fury with which the American invasion was greeted by Mexicans of all political persuasions. As was too often the case, in his desire to be of service to other peoples, Wilson underestimated the force of nationalism. When Argentina, Brazil, and Chile offered to mediate the dispute, the president accepted.

On the surface, neither the Veracruz intervention nor the arbitration that took place at Niagara Falls, Ontario, during May and June 1914, were successful, yet Wilson skillfully used both to accomplish his broader goals. The American occupation of Veracruz deprived Huerta of arms and supplies, while American intransigence at the mediation sessions demonstrated that Wilson could not be talked out of his opposition to the dictator. In mid-July Huerta, his government and army crumbling, fled to Spain. American troops were quietly withdrawn from Veracruz in November.

With Huerta gone, Americans hoped for a speedy restoration of order in Mexico, but instead Constitutionalist leaders fell to fighting among themselves. After a long winter and spring during which foreigners and their property frequently became victims of the contending factions, Wilson warned the leaders on 2 June 1915 that if they could not compromise their differences, the United States would be forced to recognize and support one of them. Unsure of what would happen, the president hoped that his warning would "precipitate things (in the chemical sense) and open up either this or some other channel of action."[14]

By autumn the situation seemed to be clearing as the forces of one Constitutionalist leader, Venustiano Carranza, shattered those of his chief rival, Pancho Villa. Moreover, Carranza was promising constitutionalism, separation of church and state, public education, land reform by expropriation but not confiscation, and respect for foreigners' "liberty and their property."[15] On 19 October 1915 the United States joined with several Latin American nations in extending de facto recognition to the Carranza government. Confident that the Mexican problem was at last on its way to a happy solution, Wilson told a British diplomat that "he had no intention of intervening for he strongly entertained the opinion that every country had a right to struggle after liberty in whatever way it liked."[16]

Pancho Villa, on the run in northern Mexico with the remnants of his army, believed that the American policy had destroyed his chance to become Mexico's revolutionary chieftain. Hysterically, he denounced recognition as an "offense" to the Mexican people and an insult to their "national sovereignty" and accused Carranza of "the sale of the motherland" to the United States in return for an alleged half-billion-dollar loan.[17] Reports of his anti-American rantings panicked American border towns, and on 9 March 1916 their fear was justified when Villa led about five hundred men in an early morning raid on Columbus, New Mexico. For three hours they terrorized the town before being driven off by American cavalry. Behind them they left eighteen Americans dead, eight wounded, and almost a hundred of their own men killed.

Already under Republican attack for his allegedly weak policies toward Germany and Mexico, Wilson had to respond strongly to the Columbus raid or risk serious political damage in an election year. Also, seemingly authoritative reports reached Washington that German agents were encouraging Villa, and that he would continue to attack until stopped. Convinced that Carranza's forces could not do the job and that the Mexican government would not object to "hot pursuit by a punitive expedition" if it were clear no political intervention was planned, Wilson ordered General John J. Pershing to take five thousand men into Mexico to capture Villa and disperse his forces.[18]

The Pershing expedition turned out to be a dangerous failure. Tensions were high on both sides of the border as the U.S. unit crossed into Mexico on 15 March 1916. Carranza denounced the incursion at once, and as the Americans penetrated farther into Mexico without finding Villa, Carranza's forces converged on the American columns. Wilson began to think that he should have withdrawn the expedition "after it became evident that Villa had slipped through [Pershing's] fingers" and admitted he might have made "an error of judgment." Recognizing the danger of conflict between Pershing's and Carranza's forces, he called out one hundred twenty-five thousand National

Guardsmen to patrol the border but promised that even in the event of conflict there would be no "rearrangement and control of Mexico's domestic affairs by the U.S."[19]

Although neither government wanted war, Mexican pride and American stubbornness eventually led to a skirmish at Carrizal, Chihuahua, on 21 June 1916, in which nine Americans and thirty Mexicans were killed, twelve Americans and forty-three Mexicans wounded, and twenty-five Americans captured. Hotheads such as Theodore Roosevelt and Senator Albert B. Fall of New Mexico urged large-scale retaliation, but Wilson believed the nation wanted peace. "Do you think the glory of America would be enhanced by a war of conquest in Mexico?" he asked a New York audience. "No!" they roared, and the president's mail reflected a similar opinion.[20] When Carranza quickly released the American prisoners, Wilson forwarded to Mexico Lansing's suggestion for the creation of a joint Mexican-American commission to resolve the Carrizal incident and make general recommendations about the maintenance of order in the border region.

Carranza objected to having the commission even discuss what he considered Mexico's internal affairs, but he wanted no more incidents and so agreed to the American proposal. From early September 1916 to mid-February 1917 the Mexican-American commissioners met periodically without reaching any agreement, but the meetings at least reduced tension. On 5 February 1917, with German-American relations growing critical and Villa long gone, the last members of the Pershing expedition were withdrawn.

By this time the administration was eager to set Mexican problems aside, but on 23 February the British turned over to the United States an intercepted message from German foreign secretary Arthur Zimmermann to the Mexican government, proposing a German-Mexican-Japanese alliance in the event of war between Germany and the United States. If Mexico agreed, Germany promised financial support for a Mexican effort to reconquer "the territory lost by her at a prior period in Texas, New Mexico, and Arizona."[21] The Mexican government quickly denied any interest in this mad scheme when the Zimmermann telegram was published in the United States.

Behind the farce of the Zimmermann telegram and the tragicomedy of the Pershing expedition were serious Mexican-American frictions. For all Wilson's belief in self-determination, he still felt compelled to do what he could to promote democracy and constitutionalism in Mexico, and to safeguard American economic interests. Even as the soldiers of the Pershing expedition began to retreat toward the border, a revolutionary convention met at Querétaro between 20 November and 5 February to draft a new Mexican constitution. The Constitution of 1917 was central to the revolution because it provided for compensated expropriation of surface lands to permit land reform and limited subsurface mineral extraction to Mexican nationals or to foreigners who agreed to be bound only by Mexican law. For American business interests in Mexico the new constitution was the most serious threat thus far.

Led by oilmen who by 1914 had invested about $85 million in Mexican oil, American investors urged the administration to demand a treaty "protecting American interests against the objectionable provisions of the constitution." Secretary of State Lansing thought that proposal "admirable," but lobbyist Chandler Anderson warned the oilmen that Wilson seemed "to be wholly lacking in interest in the protection of property and material interests, and . . . chiefly concerned with the establishment of a stable government in Mexico, on the theory of serving humanity."[22] Whatever Wilson may have thought about the merits of the oilmen's concerns, Anderson correctly assessed the central aim of his policy as "trying to tide over the present critical situation [with Germany] without making an issue with Carranza."[23] Soon after Carranza began drafting a petroleum law that avoided challenging existing concessions, the administration extended full diplomatic recognition to his government on 26 September 1917.

Shaped by his commitment to self-determination and by his conviction that conflicts with Mexico must not divert energy from the European war, Wilson's Mexican policy was set firmly against intervention for the remainder of his term. He authorized the American ambassador to warn Carranza against arbitrary confiscation of American property but specifically admitted the right of compensated expropriation "for sound reasons of public welfare," insisted publicly that Mexican internal affairs were "none of our business," and told Gordon Auchincloss, in charge of the Mexican desk at the State Department, that "if we could not get the oil in a peaceful manner from Mexico, we would simply have to do without."[24] When Senator Albert B. Fall, representing oil interests, held a series of hearings during the autumn of 1919 that tried to play upon fears aroused by the domestic "Red Scare" to suggest a link between the Mexican revolution and Russian bolshevism in order to put pressure on the administration to defend American interests more vigorously, Wilson responded angrily.

Although paralyzed by a stroke on 2 October 1919, Wilson agreed to see Fall on 5 November in order to lay to rest rumors that his mind was damaged. "Well, Mr. President," said Fall as he was ushered into Wilson's carefully staged bedroom, "we have all been praying for you." "Which way, Senator?" Wilson shot back with one of his father's well-worn quips.[25] Subsequently, he made it clear to Fall and the Senate that he had no intention of allowing any change in his Mexican policy, and his belief that Lansing sympathized with Fall and Republican advocates of intervention was one cause for his firing the secretary of state early in 1920. Despite a new outbreak of disorder in Mexico leading to the assassination of Carranza and the dubious election of his principal opponent, Alvaro Obregón, later that year, Wilson refused to depart from nonintervention while he remained in office. He did not extend diplomatic recognition to Obregón's government, but he left the oil problem unresolved. His Republican successors grappled with the Mexican problem throughout the 1920s.

Wilson's Mexican policy drew attacks from several directions yet deserved less criticism than it received. Mexicans who denounced only its interventionist excesses gave the president too little credit for restraint in the face of considerable domestic and foreign pressure to intervene massively. Domestic critics who alleged that he failed to protect American interests in Mexico ignored or overlooked such facts as the growth of American oil investments in Mexico from $85 million in 1914 to $200 million by 1920 and grossly underestimated how costly and dangerous a Mexican war would have been. In dealing with Mexico at least, Wilson was surprisingly successful in combining respect for a neighbor's rights with the promotion of both short-term American economic interests and long-term interests in Mexican progress.

Convinced that his Mexican policy rested upon rectitude and justice, Wilson failed to appreciate how much its success required restraint by revolutionary leaders committed to the welfare of the Mexican people. Elsewhere in the Caribbean region where conditions were drastically different the same sorts of policies led to disaster.

That the administration meant well was evident from its willingness to negotiate a treaty with Colombia expressing regret for the 1903 American-aided revolution that turned Colombia's province of Panama into an independent nation and cleared the way for the building of the Panama Canal. Unfortunately, however, the administration found it almost impossible to win approval of the treaty in the Senate, where Theodore Roosevelt's friends objected strenuously to the implication the former president had done anything wrong. Equally futile were a series of bilateral investigation treaties negotiated by Secretary of State William Jennings Bryan with many Latin American nations. Reflecting Bryan's practical recognition that "friends are better customers than enemies" and the administration's desire to inaugurate a new era of honorable Pan-American relations, the treaties combined self-interest and idealism but were never used to solve any conflict.[26] Nor was Bryan successful in persuading Wilson that he should support a plan to relieve Latin American countries of the "oppressive financial agreement[s]" that the secretary believed "aroused [them] to revolution."[27] Bryan argued that the American government could borrow money at 3 percent, reloan it to the Latins at 4.5 percent, and use the profit to retire the loan, but Wilson, perhaps concerned about what would happen if a country defaulted on such a government-to-government obligation, rejected Bryan's proposal as too "novel and radical."[28]

One of the nations Bryan had wanted to help with his loan plan was Nicaragua, a debt-ridden country that controlled a route for a canal that might compete with the Panama Canal. Fearful the canal route might fall into foreign hands, Bryan first proposed to help through a loan, but when Wilson rejected that, negotiated a treaty purchasing an option on the canal route for the United States. The treaty was opposed by many Democrats because it authorized American intervention "for the preservation of Nicaraguan independence, the maintenance of a Government adequate for the protection of life, property and individual liberty and for discharging any obligation which it may assume or contract."[29] Wilson casually gave the draft his "entire approval," but the Senate would not assent to it until the intervention clauses were removed and worsening German-American relations in early 1916 made the administration's claims of a foreign threat more plausible.[30] As the treaty's opponents had feared, it was the first step in a series that led by late 1916 to interference in Nicaragua's political process and by 1920 to a virtual American protectorate. Wishing in a generalized way to be helpful and desiring at the same time to protect American interests, Wilson and his advisers were unable to devise a policy that could achieve both goals short of substantial intervention.

The same fatal combination of power and paternalism led to large-scale intervention and military control of Haiti and the Dominican Republic. In both nations the United States moved reluctantly but inexorably toward total control.

Although Haiti was the second oldest republic in the Western

Hemisphere, the fact that it was Negro and French-speaking had meant that relations with the United States were never close. On its north coast, however, lay a fine harbor, the Môle St. Nicholas, which American leaders feared might be taken over by a European power in partial payment of Haiti's enormous foreign debt. The Taft administration had urged American companies to invest in Haiti in order to enlarge American influence there, but with seven Haitian presidents assassinated or forced out of office between 1911 and 1913, the climate was hardly appealing to businessmen. With the Panama Canal due to open in 1914, Wilson feared that the fatal combination of foreign debt and political chaos would lead to German or French control of the Môle St. Nicholas.

Adding to the tension was the fact that the Germans and French frankly avowed their interest in setting up a foreign customs control arrangement in Haiti like that which the United States held in the Dominican Republic. Even after Germany and France were at war in Europe, rumors of "sympathetic cooperation" between them in Haiti continued to come to the State Department and to be viewed as "sinister" by the president.[31] That such an implausible threat was taken seriously reveals how little real thought Wilson gave the situation. As a memorandum by the chief of the Latin American division of the State Department in June 1914 argued, American leaders were convinced that political order could be assured in the Caribbean if economic order were established. Naively, they assumed that setting matters straight would be easy.

During 1914 and early 1915 the State Department proposed a customs control arrangement to a series of Haitian governments, but without success. Fiercely nationalistic, the Haitians spurned all interference but were unable to set their own house in order. Reluctantly, Wilson ordered the navy to prepare plans for a landing of marines. "I think . . . ," he wrote when Bryan told him about new rumors of Franco-German intervention, "that it is evident we shall have to take a very decided stand with the government of Haiti."[32]

In July 1915 events proceeded to a tragic climax. Haiti's president Vilbrun Guillaume Sam, facing a revolution, massacred nearly two hundred prisoners but was then hacked to pieces by a mob that invaded the French legation to get at him. Appalled, Wilson concluded, "I suppose there is nothing for it but to take the bull by the horns and restore order."[33] On 28 July 1915 about four hundred American sailors and marines commanded by Rear Admiral William B. Caperton occupied Portau-Prince and soon controlled the rest of the country. The very ease of the takeover contributed to Wilson's illusion that the reconstruction of Haitian society would be easy. Under the authority of a Haitian-American treaty signed on 12 September 1915, and a new constitution imposed on Haiti in 1918, the American military supervised Haiti's political and economic affairs, built roads, schools, and sewers, and created a constabulary to replace the Haitian military. Wilson, who paid little attention to the details of the occupation, doubtless believed that his goals of economic and political stability were being achieved, but when the occupation ended in the 1920s, the country fell back into its old patterns of political and economic turmoil.

At the other end of the island of Hispaniola, in the Dominican Republic, a similar tale of benevolent concern leading to intervention was being played out. Since 1905 the United States had run the Dominican customs service and exercised a general oversight of its political affairs. In 1911 the assassination of the Dominican president brought this placid period to an end, and when Wilson took office the country was being governed by a provisional president. Assuming that a return to orderly political processes would solve the problem, Wilson authorized the sending of election observers to oversee congressional elections in December 1913.

The elections only made the situation worse. The majority elected in December opposed the provisional president, who refused to give up his office. Encouraged by a crooked American minister who hoped to profit from concessions granted by the Dominican government, the provisional president demanded more money from the American customs collectorship, on the grounds that he could not hold a real election until order was restored in the country.

For a time Wilson went along with this implausible arrangement, but by the summer of 1914 the development of a rebellion made it obvious it would not work. Facing a deteriorating situation in which the United States had become a participant whether he liked it or not, the president on 27 July drafted a plan that called for an immediate ceasefire to be followed by the selection of a new provisional government (to be chosen either by the factions themselves or by the United States) whose only function would be to hold American-supervised elections. Once his plan was implemented, said Wilson, the United States would "insist that revolutionary movements cease and that all subsequent changes in the government of the republic be effected by the peaceful processes provided in the Dominican constitution."[34]

Under the guns of American warships the Wilson Plan was put into effect in the autumn of 1914, and in December a new constitutional president, Juan Isidro Jiménez, was elected. With unconscious arrogance Secretary Bryan proclaimed, "The election having been held and a Government chosen by the people having been established, no more revolutions will be permitted."[35] He had no idea that instead of being better, the Dominican situation had become significantly worse.

Throughout 1915 and into 1916 the American government pressed the Dominicans to agree to American supervision over their domestic finances as well as over the customs. Even if the Dominican president had been willing to accept such a plan, his Congress refused and threatened to impeach him if he acted alone. Caught hopelessly between the Americans and his Congress, in May 1916 President Jiménez resigned. Secretary of State Lansing and Wilson now grasped the nettle, ordering Admiral Caperton to land troops in the Dominican Republic as he had done a year earlier in Haiti. After a period of uncertainty Wilson decided in November "with the deepest reluctance" that a full military government would be "the least of the evils in sight."[36] As in Haiti, the military government in the Dominican Republic outlasted Wilson's term and failed to achieve his goals.

The Wilson administration's desire to assist Latin American nations to secure economic stability and constitutional democracy was not a new impulse in American diplomacy. What was new was the amount of American economic and strategic involvement in the Caribbean, which made events there of pressing concern to Washington, and the availability of military force that could carry out the president's wishes with seeming ease. Largely ignorant of local conditions and confident of the rectitude of their own intentions, Wilson and most other Americans overestimated what intervention could achieve and underestimated its cost to all concerned. Where prudence limited intervention and local forces sought genuine reforms, as in Mexico, Wilson's approach had limited success; where intervention was unlimited and local forces uncommitted to reform, the result was disaster.

Many of the same motives dominated American policy toward Asia, but distance and a smaller number of specific interests reduced Wilson's willingness to become involved deeply. Nevertheless, as in the Caribbean, the president's hopes for the future rather than his recognition of the realities of the present frequently shaped policy. Thus China, where American economic involvement had never realized optimistic predictions, dominated administration thought because they believed it was on the brink of becoming democratic and Christian. Japan, on the other hand, already America's fourth largest trading partner with a volume of trade more than three times as great as that with China, was treated as an enemy.

The dream of seeing China become Christian and democratic appealed to Wilson and Bryan partly because both had strong ties to the Christian missionary movement in China. In the State Department important second-rank posts were filled by men who had been missionaries or were close to them, and frequently Wilson and Bryan based actions on information about China that came directly from missionary sources. Indeed if the president and secretary had had their way, the American minister to China would have been John R. Mott, head of the YMCA, and described by one historian as a "spiritual social worker" in close harmony with "the practical missionary mood" of the administration.[37] Unable to secure Mott, Wilson instead appointed Paul S. Reinsch, a University of Wisconsin political scientist who had written several books about East Asia and who believed that it was "incumbent" on the United States "to do her share independently and to give specific moral and financial assistance" to China.[38]

Symbolic of the administration's attitude was Wilson's decision a few days after inauguration to terminate American participation in an international financial consortium organized in 1911 to loan money to China for internal development. Believing that the loan conditions proposed by the consortium would "touch very nearly the administrative independence of China" and that "we ought to help China in some better way," Wilson urged American bankers to withdraw from the consortium.[39] Because he saw the issue as a matter of principle rather than a practical issue, he announced his decision without consulting either the experts in the State Department who had negotiated the consortium agreement or the other governments that were parties to it.

Equally revealing of the administration's attitude was Wilson's decision to extend diplomatic recognition to the new Chinese republic, organized in 1912 but not yet recognized by any Western nation. Convinced that other nations, and especially Russia and Japan, were withholding recognition to extort commercial or territorial concessions from China, Wilson told a cabinet meeting on 1 April that he intended to act at once "because he wished to see China establish a stable government and he was afraid that certain great powers were trying to prevent her from doing so."[40] Learning from the criticism that had followed his independent withdrawal from the consortium, Wilson told the other nations of his intention and offered them a chance to join the United States, but when they refused, on 2 May he acted alone. In China and the United States his decision was widely praised, but in Europe, and especially in Japan, it was viewed with suspicion and hostility as an American effort to secure special preference in China.

Further complicating the Japanese situation was the fact that the United States was then embroiled in a controversy with Japan over land ownership by Japanese aliens in California. On the West Coast Japanese residents had long been resented for their mastery of the Yankee virtues of thrift and hard work. Originally brought in to help build railroads, by the late nineteenth century Orientals became targets of racial discrimination and mob violence. Successive American administrations restricted immigration, but racial and economic tensions built anyway. In California Progressive governor Hiram Johnson saw Wilson's election as an opportunity to strike a blow at both Orientals and Democrats and supported a bill in the California legislature declaring that aliens "ineligible to citizenship" (i.e., Orientals) could not own land in California. Although the Japanese denied *all* foreigners the right to own land in Japan, they bitterly resented this pointed discrimination against Orientals in the United States.

Facing strong protests from Japan but limited by his own belief that he "had no right to intervene in the business against the undoubted constitutional powers of the State of California," Wilson sent Secretary of State Bryan to Sacramento to seek a compromise.[41] When Bryan failed and the Japanese complained bitterly that the California law was "unfair and discriminatory," "unjust and inequitable," and rumors that Japan might attack the Philippines in retaliation began to come in, Wilson faced a difficult decision.[42] On 14 May the Joint Board of the Army and Navy, the combined planning committee of the two services, assessed the situation and recommended reinforcing the Philippines with three gunboats from China. At a meeting on 16 May the cabinet divided evenly on the recommendation, and it was left to Wilson to make the choice. He did not hesitate. "We must not have war except in an honorable way," he told Secretary of the Navy Josephus Daniels, "and I fear the Joint Board made a mistake."[43] A few days later Secretary Bryan assured the Japanese ambassador that "there is nothing final between friends," and the willingness of the administration to continue negotiating in the hope of finding some satisfactory resolution of the dispute cooled war fever in both countries.[44] Nevertheless, Wilson's inability to offer any real concessions on the land issue remained a significant irritant in Japanese-American relations.

The 1913 war scare lent urgency to the redemption of a long-standing Democratic promise of independence for the Philippines, but that pledge would have had a high priority even without the crisis. Bryan had always opposed imperialism, and Wilson had gradually moved away from his own half-hearted expansionism of the early 1900s. Although he had written in 1900 that it was "the duty of the United States to play . . . a leading part . . . in the opening and transformation of the East" toward democracy and Christianity and said as late as 1911 that he did "not believe that the inhabitants of the Philippine Islands are prepared for independence," he had never wanted the United States to hold the islands permanently.[45] While president-elect he sent an old friend, Princeton professor Henry J. Ford, to investigate conditions in the islands, and on the basis of Ford's report and another by a young War Department lawyer, Felix Frankfurter, he decided to move rapidly toward Filipino self-government and eventual independence. As a first step he appointed a new governor of the islands, Francis Burton Harrison, who was instructed to give Filipinos majorities in both houses of the legislature and to determine his actions according to the will of the legislative majority. A second, more decisive step came in August 1916 with the passage of the administration-supported Jones Act promising Philippine independence "as soon as a stable government can be established."[46] To the delight of both antiimperialists and those concerned about American security, an old promise had been honored.

Of course the promise that the islands would be freed eventually did not eliminate concerns about frictions with Japan, which worsened with the beginning of World War I in the summer of 1914. When war began, the Japanese used the excuse of a 1902 alliance with Great Britain to justify declaring war on Germany and seizing German holdings in China. As one Japanese diplomat explained frankly, "When there is a fire in a jeweller's shop, the neighbours cannot be expected to refrain from helping themselves."[47] British leaders were no happier about this situation than the Americans, but as the foreign secretary pointed out, there was not much they could do: "To explain to an Ally that her help will be welcome, but that you hope it will not be made inconvenient, is a proceeding that is neither agreeable nor gracious."[48] If the Americans wanted to act, they must do so alone.

That was a sobering thought, and on 4 November 1914 the State Department explained to Minister Reinsch that "it would be quixotic in the extreme to allow the question of China's territorial integrity to entangle the United States in international difficulties."[49] Plainly, for all its talk about assisting China on its way to democracy, self-determination, and Christianity, there were definite limits on what the administration was willing to do. Even when, early in 1915, reports began to arrive from China that Japan had delivered a series of secret demands that would have turned much of China into a virtual Japanese colony, Secretary Bryan reacted with utmost caution. After several months of discussion, the secretary sent the Japanese a note that objected mildly to some of the more outrageous of the Twenty-One Demands but concluded limply that "territorial contiguity creates special relations between Japan and these districts."[50]

The 21 March 1915 Japanese reply to the American note made use of the unfortunate "territorial contiguity" phrase to justify Japanese claims and attempted to pass off the "demands" as mere "requests." Bryan was inclined to accept this explanation, but Wilson overruled him. While admitting that there were problems in Sino-Japanese relations, he argued that "the remedies and safeguards proposed in the 'requests' go too far. Whatever the intention, they do, in effect constitute a serious limitation upon China's independence of action, and a very definite preference of Japan before other nations, to whom the door was to be kept open."[51] In mid-April, as Reinsch sent new information confirming the suspicion that the Japanese government had "systematically and deliberately sought to deceive the American Government," Wilson ordered Bryan to tell the Japanese ambassador informally that the United States considered the demands *and* requests "incompatible with the administrative independence and autonomy of the Chinese Empire and with the maintenance of the policy of an open door to the world."[52] "We shall have to be very chary hereafter about seeming to concede the reasonableness of any of Japan's demands or requests," he added two days later.[53]

By this time Wilson had become so convinced that yielding anything to the Japanese was a mistake that even after the Japanese on 30 April submitted to the Chinese a revised list of their proposals that had been extensively modified to meet American objections, he and Bryan went ahead in drafting a sharp protest which the secretary handed to the Japanese ambassador on 5 May. Not only did the note object to almost every concession still requested by the Japanese, but it challenged some concessions the Americans had accepted in their note sent in March.

Dramatic as the American note was, it did not affect Japanese policy. On 4 May the Japanese, reacting to an internal power struggle and to warnings from England, had decided to soften substantially their demands on China. Disguised for face-saving purposes as an "ultimatum," their revised offer was sent to Peking on 7 May and accepted with relief by the Chinese on 9 May.

Ignoring this resolution of the crisis, Wilson decided on 10 May to send a note that had been drafted by State Department counselor Robert Lansing several days earlier when it still appeared that Japan might use force to compel acceptance of all the demands. "It will not do," wrote the president, "to leave any of our rights indefinite or to seem to acquiesce in any part of the Japanese plan which violates the solemn understandings of the nations with regard to China."[54] The United States, declared the note sent on 11 May, would not recognize any agreement between China and Japan that violated "the treaty rights of the United States and its citizens in China, the political or territorial integrity of the Republic of China, or the international policy relative to China commonly known as the open door policy."[55]

Despite the note's harsh tone, its meaning and purpose were obscure. Obviously it reflected Wilson's hardening attitude toward Japan, but as a method of defending the Open Door, its nonrecognition threat was weak. Mystified as to the note's meaning but infuriated by its tone, the Japanese bided their time, awaiting a moment when they could compel the Americans to accept their rights and status.

As the Japanese suspected, Wilson's 11 May note expressed a major change in American policy. His decision to withdraw from the loan consortium and to recognize China unilaterally had implied a confidence that Americans could compete economically in China and could influence Chinese development without the support of other western nations, but by 1915 that confidence was disappearing. At home his belief in competition as a panacea was waning, while the withdrawal of the European nations from China as a result of the war revealed that despite America's allegedly independent course, its ability to compete in China really had rested on a now disrupted balance of power. Suddenly, American businessmen in China were fully exposed to Japanese

competition they could not meet. The 11 May note was a symbolic announcement that the United States government would in future give
businessmen more active support in China.

The implications of this change became clearer in 1916 when the
State Department reversed previous policy and began to explore the
possibility of having American bankers rejoin the international loan
consortium they had left in 1913. For a variety of reasons these efforts
did not bear fruit until the summer of 1918, when a new consortium
was announced. Wilson promised that the new agreement would be significantly different from the old one and that "everything necessary
would be done to protect the Chinese Government against such uncon-
scionable arrangements as were contemplated by the former Consortium," but in reality the project was a failure from the start.[56] Despite
vigorous American efforts, the Japanese refused to open their concessions in South Manchuria and Inner East Mongolia to consortium activities. When the Japanese finally entered the consortium in May 1920
after almost two years of negotiations they kept for themselves exclusive
rights to railway loans in their sphere and a tacit right of veto over
other types of loans as well. As a result of continuing frictions among
its members, the new consortium never made a loan of any kind. Its
failure not only revealed that the president's faith in American businessmen's ability to compete in China without government backing
and his belief in the efficacy of example to shape political events there
had been naive, but also showed that exercising economic and political
influence in Asia would require much more governmental commitment
than even Wilson's Republican predecessors had imagined.

Concerned and uncertain about the new American activism in
Asia, the Japanese seized the opportunity presented by American entrance into the war in 1917 to try to solidify their position. Already
promised postwar title to German islands in the North Pacific and to
German concessions in Shantung Province of China by secret treaties
with Britain, France, Italy, and Russia, the Japanese dared not ask Wilson for explicit recognition of such claims, but they hoped at least for
a general guarantee of their interests. In June 1917 they proposed a
public affirmation of Japanese rights in China, which had been accepted in the State Department's 13 March 1915 note but later questioned in the note of 11 May 1915. Alarmed, Wilson and Lansing
quickly rejected their proposal, explaining that there was no inconsistency between the two American notes. The United States, wrote Lansing, recognized "special relations between Japan and the districts of

Shantung, Southern Manchuria and East Mongolia," but it "might . . . in the future be justified in expressing its views in regard to Chino-Japanese relations involving even these districts."[57]

Soon after Lansing sent this frosty message to Tokyo, a crucial shortage of merchant and antisubmarine vessels in the North Atlantic led the administration to reconsider its position. Since American ship-yards could not build both the smaller vessels and large warships at the same time, American leaders felt they had to reduce the danger of con-flict with Japan. When the British rejected an American proposal that England sell the United States warships after the war in order to build up the Pacific fleet rapidly, Wilson had little choice but to seek a diplo-matic accommodation with Japan.

In September 1917 a special Japanese delegation, headed by former foreign minister Viscount Kikujiro Ishii, arrived in the United States. Although personally friendly to the United States, Ishii was under or-ders to secure a promise that it would not attempt to influence China against Japan and would respect Japan's sphere of influence in South Manchuria and Inner East Mongolia; he was also to seek a treaty assur-ing Japanese residents in the United States the same rights as other aliens. On the American side, Wilson ordered Lansing to insist that Japan give up all special interests in China and reaffirm its acceptance of the Open Door policy. Long gone were the president's illusions that he could safeguard China and American interests by declarations of principle.

Nevertheless, neither Japan nor the United States was eager to bring their differences to an open break. In a series of meetings between 6 September and 2 November 1917 Lansing and Ishii labored to find a formula that would conceal differences and present the impression of harmony. The resulting memorandum of agreement, signed on 2 No-vember, reiterated both governments' adherence to the Open Door but declared also that "territorial propinquity creates special relations be-tween countries" and stated that the United States recognized that Ja-pan had "special interests in China, particularly in that part to which her possessions are contiguous." Nevertheless, the memorandum con-tinued, the United States had "every confidence in the repeated assur-ances of the Imperial Japanese Government that . . . they have no de-sire to discriminate against the trade of other nations or to disregard the commercial rights heretofore granted by China in treaties with other Powers."[58]

The double-talk of the Lansing-Ishii agreement left each side free to interpret it according to its own interests. In Tokyo the Japanese foreign minister told the Russian ambassador that the United States had recognized Japanese "special interests" throughout China, and Minister Reinsch asked for an explanation of the agreement, "which at first sight appears a reversal of American policy in China."[59] Wilson, however, denied any concessions to Japan. "There has not only been no change of policy," he wrote, "but there has been a distinct gain for China," and Lansing assured Reinsch that the memorandum meant that Japan had agreed not "to take advantage, commercially or industrially, of the special relations to China created by geographical position."[60]

Yet whatever the Americans might say or believe, the Japanese were in a position to enforce their interpretation of the agreement. Late in 1917 they tightened their hold over Shantung and in 1918 offered loans to the Chinese government in return for further concessions. Each time they justified their actions in terms of the Lansing-Ishii agreement. The necessity of wartime cooperation compelled Washington to accept this argument, particularly after the Bolshevik Revolution took Russia out of the war against Germany, which offered Japan the same opportunity to establish influence in Russian Siberia by making alliances with local leaders as they had earlier exploited skillfully in securing power in Manchuria and Mongolia. If the United States were to have any success in restraining Japanese ambitions in Siberia, it was essential to maintain the illusion of harmony, even while taking steps to curtail Japanese expansion. As Lansing lamented, the East Asian situation had become "the hardest and most complicated of all our problems."[61]

Early in 1918, when the Russians began separate peace negotiations with the Germans, the Asian situation became acute. The British and French were hostile to the Bolsheviks and desperate to restore an eastern front by getting Russia back into the war. They urged the Americans to agree to support Japanese intervention in Siberia, which they believed might somehow achieve that aim, although the Japanese had little interest in either the eastern front or the civil war in Russia.

Lansing, who was strongly anti-Bolshevik, favored the Allied proposal, but Wilson opposed it. In his 8 January Fourteen Points address he described "the treatment accorded Russia by her sister nations" as the "acid test" of Allied commitment to principle rather than self-interest and later explained to British and French leaders his conviction that trying "to stop a revolutionary movement with ordinary armies is like using a broom to sweep back a great sea. . . . The sole means of acting against Bolshevism is to make its causes disappear."[62] Nevertheless, his opposition was gradually worn down by incessant British and French pressure and by the fear that Japan might act on its own and use intervention to seize territory.

In the end the president consented to intervention, partly because of his concern about the Japanese and partly because he and other Allied leaders were eager to see about sixty thousand members of the Czech Legion, formerly reluctant soldiers in the Austro-Hungarian army and now interned in Russia, freed for service on the western front against Germany. Since the Czechs could not go west across Germany, their only route to the front lay eastward, across the Trans-Siberian Railroad to Vladivostok, and then by ship around the world to France. As they attempted to make this arduous journey, however, they were impeded by the turmoil of the civil war and came under attack by former German prisoners-of-war, recently freed in Russia by the Treaty of Brest-Litovsk. Wilson was as eager as the British and French to see the Czechs on the western front, and in July 1918 he agreed to send seven thousand American soldiers to guard the Trans-Siberian line, despite his belief that the Japanese "had more in mind than merely assisting the Czechs." Nor did he trust the Europeans, whom he suspected of wanting to turn limited intervention "into an anti-Soviet movement and an interference with the right of Russians to choose their own form of government."[63] Secretary of War Newton D. Baker's orders to the American commander, General William S. Graves, warned him of probable Japanese ambitions and instructed him to avoid interference in Russia's internal affairs.

The intervention bore out many of Wilson's fears and was a constant frustration. The main function of the American troops was to oversee the operation of the railroad, which brought them into conflict with everyone, since the railroad was the only transportation in the region. The British and French urged the Czechs to go west rather than east in hopes of somehow reestablishing the eastern front, probably by supporting Russian opposition to the Bolsheviks, while the Japanese constantly reinforced their troops in Siberia on the pretext of defending China against phantom attacks by German and Austrian former prisoners-of-war. By November 1918 the Japanese had about seventy thousand troops in Siberia, and despite the war's end, they showed no desire to leave. Forced into intervention against his better judgment,

Wilson now found he could not escape it. American withdrawal would leave the Europeans free to meddle in the Russian civil war and the Japanese at liberty to gobble up Siberia.

Ultimately the Americans were able to leave Siberia when the growing strength of the Bolsheviks faced the intervening powers with the choice of withdrawing or fighting a major war with the Red army. Losing their enthusiasm for intervention, the Europeans withdrew in 1919, and on 9 January 1920, despite his illness, Wilson personally approved a note to the Japanese announcing American withdrawal. The last American left Vladivostok on 1 April 1920, and the Japanese, after pulling back slowly and reluctantly, finally left at the end of October 1922.

In Siberia as in the Caribbean region, Wilson found that it was easier to begin intervention than to use it effectively for specific purposes, or to bring it to an end. Although the president had a keen instinct for the importance of keeping intervention limited in scope and closely restricted to specific and practical goals, he constantly underestimated the hostility it provoked and overestimated what the United States could achieve in the internal affairs of other nations. Wilson's motives were benevolent, his sense of the limits of force sound, yet the growth of American military and economic power constantly tempted him to attempt more than even he, in his wisest moments, believed could be achieved. "Political growth refuses to be forced," Wilson had written in *The State* in 1889, but neither he nor other Americans could resist the temptation to try.[64] The most basic criticism of his Latin American and Asian policies was neither that they were imperialistic nor naive, but that they were attempting something that Wilson knew in his own heart was impossible.

Wilson was the first president to hold office in a time when Americans generally had become aware of their nation's global reach. Like his successors, he struggled to balance the protection of national interests, the rights of other peoples, and the promotion of national ideals in a world being radically transformed by war, revolution, and nationalism. His policies played a part in the breakdown of the old order, and his ideals contributed to the development of the new one, but he could command neither the forces of destruction nor of construction. Flawed though his policies were, American leaders since his time have found few better ways to achieve the purposes entrusted to them.

Joseph Ruggles Wilson. *Courtesy of the Wilson Collection, Princeton University Library.*

Janet Woodrow Wilson, *Courtesy of the Wilson Collection, Princeton University Library.*

Wilson as he looked at the time of his marriage and first job in the mid-1880s. *Courtesy of the Wilson Collection, Princeton University Library.*

Members of the Wilson family on the steps of Dr. George Howe's house in Columbia, South Carolina, in the 1880s. Front row, left to right: Wilson Howe and George Howe (Woodrow's nephews). Second row: Dr. George Howe, Jessie Howe. Third row: Woodrow Wilson, Annie Wilson Howe holding "Little Annie" Howe, Joseph Ruggles Wilson, Marian Wilson (Woodrow's sister), Joseph R. Wilson (Woodrow's brother). Standing: Nannie, Minnie. *Courtesy of the Wilson Collection, Princeton University Library.*

The Wilson family at Cornish, New Hampshire, in the summer of 1913. Left to right: Margaret, Ellen, Eleanor, Jessie, Woodrow. *Courtesy of the Library of Congress.*

Wilson campaigning from the rear platform of a train in 1912. *Courtesy of the Library of Congress.*

Wilson's inaugural address, 4 March 1913. Despite his plea for simplicity, huge crowds of Democrats came to Washington, D.C., to celebrate the party's return to power after sixteen years. *Courtesy of the Library of Congress.*

HE HAD EXPECTED TO FIND THE PRESIDENT ALONE.

William Allan Rogers's cartoon of German Ambassador Bernstorff delivering a note explaining the German sinking of the liner *Lusitania* well illustrates American anger at German submarine warfare. *Courtesy of the Library of Congress.*

"Drifting," a cartoonist's satirical comment on Wilson's neutrality policy in 1915.
Courtesy of the William H. Walker Cartoon Collection, Graphic Arts Collection, Princeton University Library.

Wilson's first grandchild, Ellen Wilson McAdoo, was born at the White House on 22 June 1915. *Courtesy of the Library of Congress.*

President Wilson with his second wife, Edith Bolling Galt Wilson, whom he married in Washington, D.C., in December 1915. *Courtesy of the National Archives.*

"Choosing a Fall Model." Women's suffrage was an important issue in the 1916 presidential election. Here Wilson and his Republican opponent, Charles Evans Hughes, model their proposed policies for a suffragette. *Courtesy of the William H. Walker Cartoon Collection, Graphic Arts Collection, Princeton University Library.*

Wilson addressing Congress to explain his decision to sever relations with Germany as the result of submarine attacks on American ships, 3 February 1917. *Courtesy of the National Archives.*

Crowd welcomes Wilson to Paris upon his arrival in December 1918. *Courtesy of the Wilson Collection, Princeton University Library.*

An enormous throng of Parisians turned out to welcome President Wilson to France on 14 December 1918. In the center of the picture his carriage may be seen passing the Arc de Triomphe. *Courtesy of the National Archives.*

Wilson speaks (without amplification) to an audience of 20,000–30,000 in support of the ratification of the Treaty of Versailles, 13 September 1919. *Courtesy of the Library of Congress.*

Following his massive stroke on 2 October 1919, Wilson was an invalid for the remainder of his presidency. This meeting with his cabinet was arranged for the press on 15 February 1921, but it lasted only a few minutes. *Courtesy of the Library of Congress.*

Wilson on his sixty-seventh birthday, 28 December 1923. It is obvious how little he had recovered from his stroke of October 1919. *Courtesy of the Library of Congress.*

The scene across the street from Wilson's house on S Street on Sunday morning, 3 February 1924, just after the news of his death was announced. *Courtesy of the Library of Congress.*

9

WAR AND NEUTRALITY
1914–1917

In the summer of 1914 Americans celebrated the opening of the Panama Canal and rejoiced that there had been no major war for a hundred years. Many believed that war had been forever banished from the world, and they were confident that at the very least conflicts elsewhere would never affect America. They were appalled but complacent when the assassination of an Austrian archduke triggered a chain of mobilizations and declarations of war in Europe.

The beginning of war that summer came during a terrible personal turmoil for Wilson. He had been well during his first year in the White House, but ironically, Ellen, who had so long nursed everyone else in the family through physical and emotional illnesses, fell gravely ill. Declining rapidly during the spring of 1914, she died on 6 August 1914, at almost exactly the same moment that war swept Europe.

The Wilsons had never enjoyed the social aspects of the presidency. They much preferred to dine and spend the evenings with family or a few close friends rather than to attend official dinners and receptions. Recognizing that ceremony was a necessary evil, Ellen had managed it as she had while Woodrow was president of Princeton, but the effort tired her more than in the past, and during the summer of 1913, which she spent with the girls at Cornish, New Hampshire, she was unusually exhausted. That autumn she returned to Washington to take up her duties and to plan for the White House marriage of Jessie to Professor Francis B. Sayre of Williams College on 25 November 1913. Soon after the wedding the family was greatly upset when Nell announced her engagement to Secretary of the Treasury William Gibbs McAdoo, a widower twenty-six years her senior. Nell and "Mac" were married in a modest White House ceremony on 7 May 1914.

By the spring of 1914 it was obvious that Ellen was seriously ill. Suspecting the problem, White House physician Cary T. Grayson called in consultants, and they confirmed his diagnosis, a form of cancer known as Bright's Disease. At first Grayson told none of the Wilsons how serious the situation was, but soon after Nell's wedding in May Ellen took a turn for the worse. Each night at 3:00 A.M. Wilson arose to go into her room and see how she was. During the day he often sat beside her bed for hours as she slept, sometimes holding her hand in one of his while he wrote with the other. When at last Grayson informed him that the situation was hopeless, he insisted that the doctor must each morning inform him absolutely frankly of her condition, but he refused to give in to despair. "We must be brave for Ellen's sake," he told Grayson.[1]

Wilson's job gave him little time for brooding. After the first year's legislative successes, the two houses of Congress were at odds over antitrust legislation, and Senate progressives gave the president a sharp rebuff by forcing him to withdraw the appointment of his old friend Thomas D. Jones, a director of the International Harvester Company, as a member of the new Federal Reserve Board. In Colorado a bitter strike in the coal mines culminated in the Ludlow Massacre of April in which state troops burned strikers' tents and killed eight strikers, two young mothers, and eleven children. Despite the administration's pleas and pressures, mine owners led by John D. Rockefeller, Jr., stubbornly refused to meet with the United Mine Workers, even after Wilson sent federal troops to occupy the region. In December the strike collapsed, the union defeated. Meanwhile, the economy sagged in recession, while the Mexican and Japanese crises constantly threatened to become unmanageable. Small wonder that in that summer of 1914 Wilson asked himself, "Why was I so imprudent as to choose this particular term of office?"[2]

At the beginning of August the doctors warned Wilson that Ellen could not live long, and he summoned members of the family to the White House, where they were gathered at her death on 6 August. With her to the end, the president "gently folded her hands across her breast, walked to the window, and broke down, sobbing like a child."[3] Desolated, he accompanied her body to Rome, Georgia, where she was buried next to her father and mother.

For two weeks Wilson was "nearly paralyzed," scarcely able to turn his attention to crucial decisions forced upon him by the war in Europe, unable even to talk about Ellen to family and friends.[4] "Whenever I tried to speak to those bound to me by affection and intimate sympathy," he said later, "it seemed as if a single word would open the floodgates and I would be lost to all self control. . . . Business, the business of a great country that must be done and cannot wait, the problems that it would be deep unfaithfulness not to give my best powers to because a great people has trusted me, have been my salvation; but, oh! how hard, how desperately hard, it has been to face them, and to face them worthily!"[5]

With time, of course, Wilson learned how to go on. Dr. Grayson insisted that he play golf and take automobile rides to escape the cares of office, and in December 1914 he even summoned the courage to put up a Christmas tree in the White House for the pleasure of a young niece. Only those closest to him realized how little anything meant to him, what a great void there was at the center of his life.

Then one day in March 1915 Wilson and Grayson broke off their golf game because the course was muddy and returned early to the White House. Rounding a corner by the elevator on the second floor, they came suddenly face to face with two equally mud-spattered ladies, just back from a walk in Rock Creek Park. One, small, dark, and pretty, was the president's cousin, Helen Bones, who had been serving as his secretary and hostess since Ellen's death. The other, tall and imposing, but with a lovely broad smile and a gay laugh, was Edith Bolling Galt, a forty-three-year-old widow of a Washington jeweler. Grayson and Helen had thought for some time that Woodrow and Edith might like each other, and this chance meeting brought them together in an easy way. After separating briefly to clean up, the group reunited for tea, and to everyone's pleasure, the president and widow took to each other immediately. This first meeting led to others, and on 23 March Woodrow invited Edith to dinner at the White House where, around the fireplace, for the first time in months he began to return to normal, telling some of the funny stories he loved and reading aloud from his favorite poems.

Edith Bolling was born in 1872 into a prominent family in Wytheville, Virginia. In 1896 she married Norman Galt, who became the owner of a well-known Washington jewelry store, and after his death in 1908, she managed the business successfully herself. Self-educated and well traveled, she enjoyed books and the theater, relished conversation, and loved a well-told story, even, as was soon the case with Woodrow, if she had heard it many times before. Although always fashionably dressed, she cared no more about Washington society than Ellen had. Like the other women to whom Wilson was attracted, she was charming, intelligent, and above all, capable of extraordinary devotion.

On 4 May, hardly two months after meeting Edith, Woodrow told her that he loved her and implored her to marry him. She had been unhappy in her first marriage, but his ardor burned away her doubts and she agreed. On 6 October 1915, the president's engagement was announced, and on 18 December he and Edith were married. Their relationship sustained him through the desperate war years and through four and a half years of invalidism. The Washington scandalmongers who gossiped about the president's quick remarriage understood neither his dependence upon a woman's support nor Edith's commitment to Woodrow Wilson the man, not the president.

Yet because Wilson was president when he and Edith met, and because the country was enmeshed in a crisis with Germany over submarine warfare, their relationship inevitably had a political dimension that Woodrow's and Ellen's had lacked. He showed her notes to and from Germany, talked about the impending resignation of Secretary of State Bryan, asked whom to appoint in Bryan's place; she was flattered by his confidences as well as enchanted by his passion. Colonel House, who had so long filled the role of political confidant, now found himself edged away from the center of the president's intimacy. For obvious reasons, House never liked Edith as well as Ellen, and a subtle rift began to open between the two men; it later became an impassable chasm.

None of that was evident in the summer of 1914, however, when it seemed that House was the president's alter ego. Even as Ellen was dying, the Texan was in Europe seeking an understanding among the British, French, Germans, and Americans that might avert war. Such a mission, of course, violated the United States's traditional policy of avoiding involvement in purely European problems, but it was even more remarkable because House had no official position or standing. He was received and listened to by European leaders simply because of his personal relationship with the president, which was so close that in this case Wilson allowed his friend to undertake the trip even though the president did not fully share House's alarm about the European situation.

Early in July House returned to the United States, confident that he had made significant progress toward his goal and unaware that the assassination of the heir to the Austro-Hungarian throne by a Serbian nationalist on 28 June had doomed his hopes. Nor was Wilson any more sensitive to the crisis. "It is perfectly delightful to read your letters and to realize what you are accomplishing," he wrote House on 9 July. Even when, two weeks later, American diplomats in Europe began to send warnings of mobilization and war, he seemed relatively unconcerned. "The United States has never attempted to interfere in European affairs," he told reporters on 27 July.[6]

Within a few days his complacency vanished as Russia, France, and England declared war against Austria-Hungary and Germany, and as German troops marched through Luxembourg and Belgium on their way into France. Alarmed, Wilson wanted to help but was unsure of what to do and afraid to commit America's prestige to a futile gesture. When at last on 4 August he sent a message to the European leaders offering America's good offices in the interest of peace, it was too late, if indeed there had ever been any hope of halting the crisis.

American reactions to the war in Europe, writes one historian, "were as uniform and diverse and as naive and sophisticated as the American people themselves; and this was as true of the administration in Washington . . . as it was of the so-called masses of people across the American continent."[7] Yet it was the duty of the president, despite grief and his own confusion, to enunciate a national policy. He must set aside the memory of the happy months he had spent bicycling through England and walking in the Lake Country; he must put away his admiration for British writers and statesmen; he must turn away even from his Christian desire to serve the suffering; he must think coolly and dispassionately about the best course for the United States.

Of course such detachment was beyond Wilson's ability as it was beyond that of most Americans, but it remained his goal until 1917. In an appeal to the American people issued on 18 August he acknowledged the "variety of sympathy and desire" among Americans and warned that it would be "easy to excite passion and difficult to allay it." Divisions, he warned, would "be fatal to our peace of mind and might seriously stand in the way of the proper performance of our duty as . . . the one people holding itself ready to play a part of impartial mediation." For all those reasons he urged Americans to strive to be "neutral in fact as well as in name . . . , impartial in thought as well as in action."[8]

Some bitter partisans of one side or the other rejected Wilson's appeal, but most Americans welcomed it. Many people believed that the conflict had nothing to do with America and was the result of rivalries and alliances with which the United States had and should have no connection. Others saw the logic of Wilson's argument and tried to rise above their own allegiances, as he did. On both sides the belligerents tried to influence American opinion through propaganda, but their efforts had less effect than the events of the war itself, which forced Germany to take actions that injured Americans in ways the Allies could avoid. Although over time those events on the seas and battlefields of Europe eroded Wilson's hopes for neutrality, at the beginning of the war his words reflected most Americans' wishes.

Characteristically, once he had found basic principles to guide American policy, Wilson felt no need to keep agonizing over specific issues and incidents of the war. House complained that the president seemed "singularly lacking in appreciation of the importance of this European crisis," but Wilson believed he must stay above details in order to maintain "the fine poise of undisturbed judgment, the dignity of self-control, the efficiency of dispassionate action" that would enable America to promote peace.[9] Moreover, having concluded that no nation bore the sole responsibility for war, Wilson quickly came to believe "that the chance of a just and equitable peace, and of the only possible peace that will be lasting, will be happiest if no nation gets the decision by arms; and the danger of an unjust peace, one that will be sure to invite further calamities, will be if some one nation or group of nations succeeds in enforcing its will upon the others." Only if a compromise peace proved out of reach, he added, might he favor a victory for England and France, for in such a victory he thought there would be less risk for the United States than if Germany dominated Europe.[10] Thus early in the conflict did Wilson make what he would later call "peace without victory" the goal of his diplomacy.

The most serious threat to American neutrality was economic. Because the United States was in a recession when the war began, manufacturers and farmers were eager to sell goods to the belligerents. The British and French, less well prepared for war than the Germans, desperately needed American goods and began sending purchasing missions to the United States in October 1914. By late 1916 and early 1917 "fully 40 percent of British war expenditure was devoted to North American supplies," nearly sixteen hundred British agents were buying supplies in the United States, and those agents were spending $83 million a week purchasing agricultural and manufactured goods.[11] Such enormous expenditures by one side inevitably undermined American impartiality.

In the long run Britain's wartime dependence on American supplies meant "the passing of hegemony from Britain to the United States," a fact of which many administration leaders were early aware, but in the short term it involved the United States with the Allied cause and eroded neutrality.[12] When the war began Secretary Bryan, fearing the impact economic ties could have on policy, recommended using the government's "influence against the enlistment of the nation's dollars in a foreign war" by discouraging private loans to the belligerents. "We are the one great nation which is not involved and our refusal to loan to any belligerent would naturally tend to hasten a conclusion of the war," he argued, expressing a belief common in the peace movement that modern war was too expensive for any nation to sustain long.[13]

Wilson shared his view, and when J. P. Morgan and Company asked the State Department about the propriety of a loan, they were requested not to make it. If the belligerents wanted to buy American goods, they had to pay in gold or dollars, which necessitated the sale of American securities held by private citizens in Europe. Such arrangements soon proved too clumsy, slow, and insufficient for the volume of trade, and in October 1914 Wilson and State Department counselor Robert Lansing faced up to the reality that the loan ban would strangle the war trade. They agreed to keep the loan ban in force because they feared that direct loans would involve the emotions of the bondholders, but they decided that there would be no objection to allowing banks to grant "credits" as "a means of facilitating trade."[14]

The decision opened the floodgates. Between October 1914 and March 1915 credit amounting to over $80 million was extended to the Allies by New York banks, but even that was not enough, and in October 1915 the loan ban was dropped completely. Failure to do so, Lansing warned, would mean "restriction of outputs, industrial depression, idle capital and idle labor, numerous failures, financial demoralization, and general unrest and suffering among the laboring classes."[15] As a result of its economic entanglement with the Allies, one historian argues that by April 1915 "the United States was no longer entitled to the legal status of 'neutral.' "[16]

Whether or not that conclusion is overstated, there is no doubt that concern about trade influenced most aspects of American neutrality policy from the outset. On 6 August 1914, just after the beginning of the war, Secretary Bryan sent a note to the belligerents asking that they follow the rules of naval warfare laid down in the Declaration of London of 1909. The product of an international conference in 1908–9, the declaration was desirable from the American point of view because it maximized neutral rights and minimized those of the belligerents. The Germans also liked it because they had only a small navy and did not expect to do much fighting at sea, but the British, who anticipated using their fleet to wage economic warfare by blockading Germany, rejected the American proposal.

Wilson found himself in a dilemma. Perhaps a trade embargo would force the Allies to accept the Declaration of London, but it would infuriate American producers and deprive the British of their best weapon in a decidedly unneutral fashion. On the other hand, if the administration let the British stop the sale of American food, cotton, and raw materials to the Central Powers, Democrats from the West and South would be furious. Accordingly, at the end of September Lansing, Wilson, and House drafted a note that demanded the British accept the Declaration of London but hinted that the United States would not protest if the British expanded the definition of blockade far beyond its usual meaning to include blockade of neutral ports through which food and raw materials were reaching the Germans. In essence, the Americans were "telling the British government that if it adopted the declaration in form it need pay no attention to it in fact."[17]

Although the British object was "to secure the maximum of blockade that could be enforced without a rupture with the United States," they dared not accept this offer.[18] The danger was that British prize courts (the special courts that decided the fate of ships and cargoes seized for blockade violations) would take the declaration at face value and thus rule subsequent expansions of the blockade illegal. Despite the risk to Anglo-American relations, the British rejected the declaration. They could only hope the Americans would not push the matter to a break.

The British position forced Wilson to confront himself. In his heart he believed that German militarism jeopardized the democratic values and aspirations for peace that were the hope of the world. He dreaded being forced into war with Britain, as Madison had been in 1812, and he realized that American economic interests lay in the growing trade with the Allies rather than in the negligible trade with the Central Powers. Allied dependence on American trade provided a whip with which to force the British to heel, but the risks in terms of possible Allied defeat and damage to the American economy were too great. The president accepted Lansing's recommendation that the Declaration of London be dropped and American policy be based on traditional international law. In practice, the Americans tacitly accepted the British blockage as legal, and the State Department spent the last months of 1914 discussing with American companies how to adjust to it. Since the British wisely avoided adding cotton to the list of prohibited items at this point, and since the Germans wanted little while the Allies were rapidly increasing purchases, practical problems were few. Without realizing it, the Americans had let trade reshape their neutrality so that it favored the Allies.

Resolution of the Declaration of London issue did not, however, end trade problems. It was fine to talk about increasing trade, but how were goods to be gotten to market? When the war began, the United States had virtually no merchant marine, a problem about which Wilson had repeatedly warned during the 1912 campaign. Of the approximately 5.5 million gross tons of American merchant shipping, almost 4.75 million were on the Great Lakes, and only fifteen ships, nine of which were non-cargo-carrying passenger vessels, were oceangoing. With German merchant vessels driven off the seas by the British, shipping space became scarce and costs shot up. The shortage threatened to strangle America's wartime trade in its infancy.

Even before the war began Wilson foresaw this problem and on 31 July 1914 proposed to Democratic congressional leaders that they introduce legislation making it easy for foreign owners to transfer their ships to American registry. They did so, and the bill quickly passed Congress, but it did not solve the problem, largely because German shipowners did not take advantage of it, realizing that a wartime transfer of registration to a neutral would not protect their ships from seizure under international law. Disappointed, Wilson and Secretary McAdoo conferred about the problem and agreed on a much more drastic step, a bill creating a government-owned corporation that would buy and operate merchant vessels.

The Ship Purchase bill immediately aroused major opposition;

from some who denounced it as socialist, from others who feared that having government-owned ships in war zones would jeopardize neutrality, and from still others who objected that the British would seize former German ships even if they were owned by the American government. With most of the leaders of his own party opposed to the bill, Wilson was forced to give it up in 1914, but he warned Congress that he meant to renew the fight in 1915. When he did so, he was able to get the House to pass the bill, but in the Senate a Republican filibuster and Democratic defections doomed it despite all the president's efforts. It was probably just as well, for the British were determined to seize any German ship transferred to American title or registry. The shortage of merchant tonnage thus remained a problem throughout the period of American neutrality and into the war. Not until 1918 did the United States Shipping Board's Emergency Fleet Corporation succeed in producing 3 million tons of shipping, as much as had been built in the whole world in any prewar year, but that triumph did not come until the war was almost over.

In 1915 problems with Germany began to overshadow those with the Allies. The cause of these problems was Germany's decision to begin submarine warfare. At the beginning of the war the Germans had only twenty-five seagoing submarines, of which only ten were diesel powered and capable of long cruises, but despite this small fleet, German naval leaders believed they could blockade the British Isles and defeat the Allies before the United States and other neutrals could come effectively into the war. German civilian leaders were skeptical of these claims, but the stalemated land war in France alarmed them because Germany was unprepared for a long war, and German public opinion was enthusiastic about anything that might strike at the hated British. Little by little the navy wore down the civilians, and on 4 February 1915 the German government declared that the waters around Great Britain would become a "war zone" in which enemy vessels would be sunk on sight and neutral vessels exposed to grave danger because British ships often flew neutral flags as disguises.

Because the American ambassador's report from Berlin was delayed in transmission, Wilson read about the German decision in his morning paper on 5 February. He could hardly believe his eyes. The German action seemed so deliberately provocative that in his cabinet meeting that morning the president compared it to boys drawing lines in the sand and daring each other to cross. Shocked by the idea that Germany would abandon universally accepted rules of international law that a belligerent could seize vessels and cargoes on the high seas only under very specific conditions and must never sink merchant ships without warning or without providing for the safety of passengers and crew, Wilson described the German policy as "unprecedented in naval warfare." Finding it hard to imagine that Berlin would follow through on its announcement, the president nevertheless authorized Counselor Lansing to warn the Germans that the United States would "hold the Imperial German Government to a strict accountability" for injuries to Americans or damage to their property.[19] At the same time, in an effort to maintain impartiality, a second note requested that the British government discourage the use of neutral flags on their ships, although the note admitted that such a *ruse de guerre* was acceptable under international law.

As it turned out, the German announcement was premature. Germany did not have enough submarines to curtail Allied trade significantly, but the flagrant illegality of their action justified British retaliation in the form of only slightly less illegal countermeasures. From the standpoint of the United States and other neutrals, both belligerents were behaving atrociously, but there was an important difference in that German policy threatened lives while Allied action only jeopardized property. For the sake of a dubious military advantage, Germany risked drawing the United States into the war.

Although the submarine campaign began in late February under strict (but secret) order to captains to avoid attacking neutral vessels, those limits did not assure Americans' safety. On 28 March 1915 the first American, mining engineer Leon C. Thrasher, was killed when the British liner *Falaba* on which he was a passenger was torpedoed and sunk. The Thrasher case was difficult because, as Secretary Bryan pointed out, the engineer had exposed himself to danger by traveling on a belligerent-owned vessel in the war zone. Wilson agreed that the case posed "disturbing possibilities," but the central point seemed to him that the United States must "insist that the lives of our citizens shall not be put in danger by acts which have no sanction in the accepted law of nations."[20]

Bryan believed that neutrals had an obligation to avoid excessive risks and would have reserved claims until after the war; Wilson, although still uncertain, was moving toward the position that defense of American rights was essential. Because Bryan's willingness to curtail travel in the war zone would necessarily have meant loss of trade, the difference between the two men had important economic ramifications as well as reflecting disagreement over more abstract rights. Whereas Bryan's position could be defined as "practical" in that it would minimize dangerous incidents and conflicts with Germany, Wilson's was equally practical in that it safeguarded the trade that had become vital to the American economy.

Recognizing that the Thrasher case was a poor basis for a major protest, throughout April administration officials debated the issues without resolving them. On 29 April an American ship, the *Cushing,* was slightly damaged by a German bomb, but as there were no injuries, the attack did not change the situation. Two days later, however, on 1 May, the American tanker *Gulflight* was torpedoed with the loss of three lives, and the issue was suddenly clear. This time Americans had been killed during the sinking of an American ship.

It is impossible to know how far Wilson might have gone in protesting the *Gulflight* sinking because on 7 May there occurred a far greater catastrophe. The German submarine *U 20*, nearing the end of a routine patrol, sighted and torpedoed the giant British passenger liner, *Lusitania.* Within a horrifying eighteen minutes the ship exploded and sank, carrying to their deaths 1,201 passengers and crew, including 128 Americans.

With a sort of grotesque irony, the very morning of the sinking Colonel House, in London on a peace mission for the president, had been speculating with Sir Edward Grey about what would happen if a liner were sunk by a submarine. "I told him," House wrote in his diary that day, "if this were done, a flame of indignation would sweep across America, which would in itself probably carry us into the war."[21] And as the news reached the United States, Americans did indeed burn with a fiery anger that made House's prediction seem all too likely.

At the White House Wilson canceled a golf game to await the slow trickle of tragic news that came from the Irish coast near where the ship had gone down. Outside the day darkened and a gentle rain began. At about eight o'clock after learning that the loss of life would probably exceed a thousand, the president suddenly leaped to his feet, and before his Secret Service agents realized what had happened, strode out the door into the rainy twilight. For an hour he walked the streets of Washington, alone with his responsibility and with the terrible visions of suffering and death at sea.

The next three days Wilson spent virtually in seclusion, avoiding reporters, refusing to meet with members of Congress or the cabinet, pouring out his troubled thoughts only to Edith Galt, and searching as

158

he always did for the central principle upon which to base action. The depth of his struggle for calm in these days of crisis was suggested by some lines he inserted on the spur of the moment in a speech to newly naturalized citizens in Philadelphia on the evening of 10 May. "The example of America must be a special example," he said. "The example of America must be the example, not merely of peace because it will not fight, but of peace because peace is the healing and elevating influence of the world, and strife is not. There is such a thing as a man being too proud to fight. There is such a thing as a nation being so right that it does not need to convince others by force that it is right."[22] Carried away by the moment, the president had rashly revealed only one side of his thoughts with the "too proud to fight" phrase, and almost before it was out of his mouth he wished he had not said it. Seized upon by the press and jumped on by critics, it made Wilson sound as if he thought the United States should not fight regardless of provocation.

For all the depth of his commitment to peace, on the very day of the "too proud to fight" speech Wilson had spent much of his time drafting a sharp protest to Germany that revealed he had found the principle for which he had been searching and upon which he would stand, even at risk of war. Read to a cabinet meeting on 11 May, the president's draft pointed out the simple fact that submarines could not assure the safety of passengers and crew as international law required and concluded that Germany must therefore give up submarine warfare. Although he wrote to Bryan that he had "unaffected misgivings that I may be wrong," Wilson had in fact clarified the issues in his own mind in such a way as to foreclose any substantive debate about them in future.[23] After a month of futilely battering his own arguments for a different course against the president's determination, Bryan admitted defeat and on 8 June resigned from the cabinet.

The principle upon which Wilson would stand inflexibly was set out in his 11 May 1915 draft of a protest about the *Lusitania* sinking. It was that "the lives of non-combatants, whether they be of neutral citizenship or citizens of one of the nations at war, cannot lawfully or rightfully be put in jeopardy by the capture or destruction of an unarmed merchantman," regardless of "whether a suspected merchantman is in fact of belligerent [sic] ownership or is in fact carrying contraband of war under a neutral flag."[24] In short, the United States insisted that Germany must obey traditional rules of warfare or give up submarines as weapons. Impeccable legally and practical from the standpoint of maximizing American trade opportunities, Wilson's position ignored the reality that technological change had altered the rules of warfare.

Wilson's policy in effect turned over to the German government the decision whether or when the United States would enter the war. Recognizing this, Bryan resigned from the cabinet in protest and Wilson appointed Counselor Robert Lansing to succeed him. In Germany the American note caused some consternation. The Germans now had forty submarines and were rapidly building more, but civilian leaders dreaded American intervention and persuaded the navy to order submarine commanders secretly to avoid torpedoing passenger vessels. In a tragic irony, both that order and its inadequacy became public knowledge only after the British liner *Arabic* was torpedoed without warning with the loss of two more American lives on 19 August 1915. On 7 November and 30 December two more passenger vessels, the *Ancona* and the *Persia*, were also torpedoed with further losses of American lives, although in questionable circumstances that made protest difficult. For all Wilson's clear stand on principle, German half-concessions and ambiguous incidents made it difficult to act decisively.

By the autumn of 1915 the president realized that his failure to force Germany to abandon submarine warfare necessitated a change of policy. Although he had previously opposed building up armaments as likely to cause rather than prevent war, on 4 November he announced a program of naval expansion and a plan to raise a four-hundred-thousand-man army. Describing his proposal as preparation "not for war, but only for defense," Wilson tried to distinguish it from bellicose "preparedness" plans being pressed by Theodore Roosevelt and others, but many Democrats were alarmed by his reversal.[25] Particularly in the South and West, many people regarded a naval buildup as justifiable, but the idea of a large army terrified them. With no threat of invasion, the army seemed pointless unless the president contemplated intervention in Europe.

Obviously this was a possibility that was beginning to haunt Wilson's nightmares, but he still hoped that it might be possible to bring the war to an end before it happened. Seizing upon a hint in a letter from Sir Edward Grey in late September that Britain might accept American mediation if the United States would join a postwar "League of Nations" that would bind its members to unite against any nation that violated a treaty or broke international law, Colonel House advanced a radical proposal. He believed that England might be willing to agree to mediation and might accept real arms reduction in return for collective security agreements, and he proposed bringing pressure to bear on Germany for similar concessions. The United States, he suggested, should call for an end to hostilities to be followed by military (i.e., German) and naval (British) disarmament. Assuming the Germans would oppose anything they thought the British favored, he proposed deceiving Berlin into agreement by indicating to them that the Allies opposed the proposal, while at the same time promising the Allies that if Germany "were still obdurate, it would be necessary for [the United States] to join the Allies and force the issue." To this bizarre and devious scheme Wilson assented, with the single qualification that he insisted on adding the word "probably" before the phrase "be necessary."[26] With the improbable hope of bluffing both belligerents into peace talks, House set out for Europe once again on 28 December 1915.

On 22 February 1916 House and Sir Edward Grey initialed a memorandum agreeing that when the Allies thought the moment appropriate, the United States would call a peace conference, and if the Germans refused to participate, would *probably* enter the war on the side of the Allies. If the conference failed, the memorandum continued, the United States would also enter the war on the Allied side, a promise to which Wilson later added the word "probably" also.[27] Astonishing though the House-Grey Memorandum seems, in reality it was meaningless. All it said was that if the war continued, the United States might at some unspecified time be forced to enter on the Allied side. By 1916 the danger that America would be dragged into the conflict was obvious to everyone, while emotional and economic ties and the outrages of submarine warfare made joining the Allies the only possible course. Essentially the memorandum sought to recommit the British and French to peace terms they had earlier announced but were now backing away from in hopes of defeating the Central Powers and imposing a much more severe settlement.

Wilson and House knew perfectly well that honoring the memorandum's conditional promise would require a congressional declaration of war. They also knew in the spring of 1916 that Congress was in no mood to declare war. Lansing warned Wilson that Senator William J. Stone, chairman of the Foreign Relations Committee, had pro-German sympathies that would "make it difficult for him to deal with our foreign affairs in a way that will strongly support the Administration and carry through its policies."[28] In the House the situation was even more difficult. There several Democratic leaders, cheered on by William Jennings Bryan, introduced the McLemore Resolution calling on the State Department to deny passports to anyone traveling on belligerent-owned vessels. Alarmed by the Speaker's report that the resolution commanded overwhelming support in the House, Wilson put heavy pressure on the Senate to defeat a parallel resolution sponsored by Senator Thomas P. Gore and succeeded, but it was obvious that a declaration of war was out of the question.

The British, for their part, had no interest in invoking the House-Grey Memorandum. They did not want a compromise peace if they could have victory, and in March of 1916 they hoped to win without the United States and without having to make any embarrassing promises of restraint at the peace table. Indeed, it seemed possible that German submarines would force the United States into war without any British actions. When on 24 March 1916 a German submarine torpedoed the channel steamer *Sussex* killing eighty passengers and injuring several Americans, there was outrage in the United States. Wilson and Lansing agreed that unless Germany agreed to "abandon its present methods of submarine warfare against passenger and freight-carrying vessels," the United States would have to "sever diplomatic relations," and on 18 April a note was sent to Germany with this message.[29]

Having in the spring of 1916 only fifty-two submarines, of which about eighteen could be at sea at any one time, the Germans decided the risks of American hostility outweighed the benefits of putting pressure on the British. On 4 May Berlin issued the "*Sussex* Pledge," promising not to attack unresisting merchant vessels without warning, *provided* the United States could make the British loosen their blockade of Germany. Wilson embraced the promise and conveniently ignored the condition, which Lansing dismissed as a " 'gold brick' swindle with a decidedly insolent tone."[30] From the American point of view British offenses were simply not to be equated with those of Germany. "If some one murdered my sister I would probably pursue him first in preference to a small boy who had stepped on my flower beds," declared the American ambassador to Germany, accurately reflecting the administration's fury at the idea of any deal with Berlin.[31] "Responsibility in such matters is single, not joint or conditional, absolute, not relative," said Wilson flatly.[32]

Yet despite American annoyance at Germany's proposed blockade deal, German-American relations improved in the months after the *Sussex* Pledge, while Allied-American relations deteriorated. Americans in general were appalled when the British brutally put down the Irish rebellion in the spring of 1916, and Wilson was constantly annoyed at London's refusal to call for a peace conference as promised in the House-Grey Memorandum. The "last straw" from the president's point of view came in July, when the British government announced a "blacklist" of eighty-seven American companies it accused of trading with the Central Powers and ordered its citizens not to do business with those companies. About to begin his reelection campaign, Wilson was troubled by indigestion and fatigue, frequently in the past symptoms of severe emotional distress.[33]

Since British actions were technically legal, there was little the president could do except complain in public and mutter in private about the "boobs" in London.[34] His gradual drift toward the Allied side was arrested temporarily, and his commitment to an independent, neutral policy for the United States was reinforced. As the war in the European trenches settled into a stalemate of slaughter during the summer of 1916, Wilson rejoiced when Congress passed the Naval Act of 1916. He had earlier described the measure as essential not only to American defense but also as crucial to American participation in a future "joint effort to keep the peace," which he felt must ultimately rest upon the "application of force" or at least the threat of it.[35] He believed the war must be brought to an end and that the United States must be strong enough to insist that its values and standards determine the future structure of peace. When Wilson campaigned that autumn on the slogan "He kept us out of war," he was not calling for isolationism but for a national stand above the issues of the European war and for a long-term commitment to building an international structure that would make war impossible.

Unfortunately, the president's position was indistinguishable in America from isolationism, and the closeness of the election made it impossible for him to act boldly on his ideas in Europe. He was reelected with a substantially larger popular vote than he had in 1912, but the outcome depended upon his carrying areas of the South, Midwest, and Far West where it would have been politically risky to hint that the United States might join an international organization. Unwilling to take chances, Wilson did nothing during the early autumn to follow up on German hints of interest in a peace conference.

Once the election was successfully passed, Wilson began to draft a call for a peace conference, completing it about 25 November. Fearing that the British would resist, he suggested that the Federal Reserve Board tighten up on short-term credits to the Allies, knowing that in so doing he would be putting enormous pressure on them, since access to American credit had become vital to their survival. By the beginning of December he hoped that the long-awaited opportunity was at hand.

Then everything fell apart. American public opinion was outraged when the Germans deported several thousand Belgians to work in Germany, and Wilson declared that their action had been a "great embarrassment" to his plans.[36] While he was waiting for the furor to die down, the German government issued a statement on 12 December indicating its willingness to discuss peace terms. Although the German announcement was encouraging from one standpoint, Wilson was afraid it might give the Allies the impression that there was collusion between Berlin and Washington if he followed it with his own call for a conference. For almost a week the president hesitated before deciding to continue. On 18 December 1916 he sent identical notes to the Allies and Central Powers, inviting each to state its war aims fully and frankly as a first step toward negotiations.

In his note Wilson observed that publicly stated objectives of both sides were "virtually the same" in that both claimed to seek security for weaker states and for themselves and a stable order that would eliminate future wars.[37] There was a double purpose behind this statement. One was to undercut secret agreements among the Allies for a division of the spoils if the Central Powers were defeated. The other was to force both sides to state goals in such a way as to maximize the chance of agreement.

Wilson had counted on the British seeing the situation much as he did and had not bothered to check his language with House before sending the note. Too late, he heard from House that the British had become "as war mad as Germany was . . . in 1914, and we can no longer count upon their looking at things from the same viewpoint as heretofore." Privately, House thought that Wilson's statement would arouse so much hostility in the Allied countries that it had "nearly destroyed all the work I have done in Europe."[38] Ambassador Walter Hines Page in London reported that the king had wept publicly at the idea that Wilson might think "the allies and the central powers on the same moral level," while in the British press reactions ranged from anger to disappointment.[39] James Bryce, former British ambassador in Washington, and an old friend of Wilson's, wrote bitterly that "German faithlessness, and unblushing disregard of honour and the principles of right, have made it impossible for us to attach the slightest value to any protestations she utters or any promises she makes."[40]

Distressing as the British reaction was to Wilson, it was no less so than that of the secretary of state. On 21 December Lansing issued a statement to the press in which he explained, without consulting the president, that the reason for Wilson's note to the belligerents was "*that we are drawing nearer to the verge of war ourselves,* and therefore we are entitled to know exactly what each belligerent seeks in order that we may regulate our conduct in the future."[41] Wilson was furious, for Lansing's statement implied that the American note was not intended to promote peace but to prepare the way for American entry into the war. Icily, he directed the secretary to issue another statement correcting the false impression. Later he told House that he had been on the verge of asking for Lansing's resignation. Perhaps he should have done so, for Lansing had decided that the United States "*must* go in on the side of the Allies," and his statement *was* intended to undercut the president's peace effort.[42] His opinion was no secret to the British and French.

Even without Lansing's sabotage Wilson's proposals had no chance in Britain or France, and little in Germany. By the beginning of January the president was thinking of an entirely different approach. Perhaps, he suggested to House, he might himself propose "the general terms of settlement . . . , making the keystone of the settlement arch the future security of the world against wars, and letting territorial adjustments be subordinate to the main purpose."[43] When it became obvious that the belligerents would not state reasonable peace terms, he decided to proceed with this plan, and on 22 January he went before the Senate to lay out peace proposals in what has come to be known as his "Peace without Victory" speech.

"Only a peace between equals can last," he said. "A victor's terms imposed upon the vanquished" would "rest, not permanently, but only as upon quicksand." To avoid such a situation, he proposed that the United States "join the other civilized nations of the world in guaranteeing the permanence of peace based upon" mutual guarantees of territory, a concert of power in place of alliances, governments based upon the consent of the governed, freedom of the seas, and restriction of armaments. He believed that settlement would "win the approval of mankind" and so commend itself to the American people that they would give up the tradition of a century and a half and "add their authority and their power to the authority and force of other nations to guarantee peace and justice throughout the world."[44]

In 1908 Wilson had written that "one or two Presidents of unusual political sagacity" had been wise enough to avoid conflict with the Senate over foreign policy by conferring with its leaders at every stage instead of laying completed projects before that body "to be accepted or rejected."[45] In part, his Peace without Victory speech was an effort to open such a dialogue about abandoning isolationism in order to "lay afresh and upon a new plan the foundations of peace among the nations."[46] Only a national debate that went beyond immediate issues and grievances and explored the opportunity for a new kind of peace might persuade Americans to alter traditional policy and accept a role of world leadership.

It was not to be. Although the Allies were dependent on American money by this time, the Germans did not believe that Wilson could force the Allied leaders into serious negotiations and so yielded to public and naval pressure to stake everything on one last great gamble. On 6 January an imperial conference approved unrestricted submarine warfare in a zone around the British Isles. The Germans realized their decision meant war with the United States, but they hoped they could starve Britain into defeat within six months, long before the Americans could make any difference. Even as the echoes of applause for Wilson's speech were dying away, on 31 January the German ambassador delivered to the State Department a note announcing the new policy and warning that no ships, including those of neutrals, would be spared. "As usual," wrote a British embassy official from Washington, the Germans had been "more stupid than ourselves in our dealings with the U.S."[47]

Stunned, Wilson told House that he felt as if the rotation of the earth had suddenly reversed itself, "and that he could not get his balance."[48] Yet despite the shock, what must be done was obvious. So quickly did House and Wilson agree on breaking off relations with Germany that they found themselves with nothing more to say. Restless and unhappy, the president wondered if it would be improper to play a round of golf but decided to play a game or two of pool inside the White House instead. The following day the cabinet overwhelmingly if sadly endorsed an immediate rupture in relations, and in the evening a small group of Democratic senators met with the president and also reluctantly assented. Their concern, of course, was with the prospect of war, not about the peace that might come later; discussion of that issue had been cut off before it started.

What one senator described as "an insolent threat of ferocious terrorism" seemed to most Americans reason enough for breaking off relations, and many assumed that war would soon follow.[49] Wilson, however, was still determined to avoid that if possible. To House he

166

"reiterated his belief that it would be a crime for this Government to involve itself in the war to such an extent as to make it impossible to save Europe afterward."[50] And in announcing to Congress on 3 February the severance of relations with Germany he declared that he could not imagine that Germany would actually do as it said and announced that no further actions would be taken unless overt attacks on American ships took place.

The next month was agonizing. During February the Germans avoided attacking American ships, but most American shippers refused to enter the war zone, and mountains of goods piled up on the wharves. Then on 24 February the British turned over to the Americans an intercepted telegram from German foreign secretary Arthur Zimmermann to the Mexican government proposing a German-Mexican-Japanese alliance against the United States in the event of war. Almost as infuriating as the fantastic scheme itself (which the Mexicans and Japanese repudiated) was the fact that the offer had been sent over official State Department telegraph wires, using a cipher for which the Americans had, out of courtesy, not asked for a key. Angry and depressed, Wilson went before Congress again on 26 February to ask for authority to arm American merchantships, and two days later he released the Zimmermann telegram to the newspapers.

The House responded to the publication of the Zimmerman telegram by passing the Armed Ship bill on 1 March by 403–13, but in the Senate a filibuster by eleven antiwar senators prevented action before the end of the session on 4 March. "A little group of willful men . . . ," fumed Wilson, "have rendered the great Government of the United States helpless and contemptible."[51] Although the administration was able to find authority in old statutes to arm the ships, the filibuster left a bitter sense of frustration and division on the eve of Wilson's second inaugural.

In his inaugural address on 5 March Wilson tried to transcend these divisions and to focus national attention on fundamental issues. Recognizing that the United States had been "deeply wronged upon the seas" and warning that "we may even be drawn on, by circumstances, not by our own purpose or desire, to a more active assertion of our rights," he nevertheless urged Americans not to lose sight of more important matters. Once again he outlined the peace terms he had suggested in his 22 January speech, declaring that Americans had become "citizens of the world" whose "fortunes as a nation are involved, whether we would have it so or not," and calling upon his fellow citizens to "dedicate ourselves to the great task to which we must now set our hand."[52] Amid the babble of competing voices there was little chance his recommendation would be heard or heeded.

On 12 March, a week after Wilson's inauguration, an unexpected revolution in Russia overthrew the czar and installed a democratic government. Wilson saw the revolution as part of a liberal tide that might sweep westward into Austria and Germany as well and told his cabinet that "if our entering the war would hasten and fix the movements in Russia and Germany, it would be a marked gain to the world and would tend to give additional justification for the whole struggle," but he was still unwilling to ask for a declaration of war.[53] Encouraged by House, he extended diplomatic recognition to the new Russian government on 22 March.

In the meantime, on 18 March came news that three American ships had been sunk in the war zone with the loss of fifteen American lives. Lansing declared that such acts amounted to "an announcement that a state of war exists," and House concluded that "we are already in the war" and might as well "throw all our resources against Germany."[54] Across the country newspapers clamored for war, but Wilson still hesitated. On 20 March he put the matter before the cabinet. In a long and dramatic meeting man after man spoke, each in his own style advising war. At last Wilson turned to Secretary of the Navy Josephus Daniels, a longtime friend of William Jennings Bryan and an ardent crusader for peace. "Well, Daniels?" said the president. Daniels's eyes filled with tears, his voice trembled, but he replied that he could see no alternative to war. Solemnly, Wilson adjourned the meeting without indicating what he intended to do, but just after it he spoke to Lansing and Burleson about summoning a special session of Congress on 2 April. Pressed by Lansing about his intentions, he replied with a smile, "Oh, I think I will sleep on it."[55] The next day he issued a proclamation calling the special session.

Despite the outward appearance of calm that so impressed Lansing in these days of crisis, Wilson displayed symptoms of considerable stress. For weeks after his inauguration he hardly appeared in his office at all, having a few papers sent to him for his signature, but letting most things pile up on his desk. Withdrawing even more than usual from his advisors, he spent his days golfing or motoring with Dr. Grayson, or reading, talking, and playing pool with his wife. Angry, frustrated reporters begged to be allowed to see him, but he spurned all requests. In the White House he was so testy with the staff that everyone walked on tiptoe and spoke only in whispers.

Of the message he was gradually drafting on his portable typewriter Wilson said little to anyone. Occasionally he asked someone about a particular point, but not a word of the draft was shown to the cabinet. Like everyone else, they had to wait to hear what he would say to Congress on the evening of 2 April.

The essence of his message was a call for a declaration of war. Recounting Germany's offenses in sober, careful tones, he drew the reluctant conclusion that its violations of American rights had "thrust upon" the nation the status of belligerent. Grimly, he asked for conscription of a half million men into the armed services, urged the extension of credit and cooperation to the Allies, and recommended that the war be paid for through taxation rather than borrowing. Americans, he declared, sought "no conquest, no dominion," nor did they feel any hostility to the German people. He promised the United States would "conduct our operations as belligerents without passion and ourselves observe with proud punctilio the principles of right and of fair play we profess to be fighting for." "We enter this war," he insisted, "only where we are clearly forced into it because there are no other means of defending our rights."[56]

Only occasionally did the president yield to the temptation to invoke great principles and stir emotions, but those few passages were then the most noted and are still the most memorable. Americans would fight, he proclaimed, "for the rights of nations great and small and the privilege of men everywhere to choose their way of life and of obedience. The world must be made safe for democracy." "We shall fight for the things we have always carried nearest our hearts," he concluded, "for democracy, for the right of those who submit to authority to have a voice in their own governments, for the rights and liberties of small nations, for a universal dominion of right."[57] Deeply stirred, the nation prepared for war, unsure whether it was embracing a crusade for democracy or a defense of neutral rights; for most people it was enough to bring an end to the long period of uncertainty and humiliation.

Largely overshadowed by the national anger at Germany's submarine warfare and by the launching of a crusade to make the world safe for democracy was Wilson's reiteration of a purpose that went beyond war. "I have exactly the same things in mind now that I had in mind

when I addressed the Senate on the twenty-second of January . . . ,"
he said; "our object now, as then, is to vindicate the principles of peace
and justice in the life of the world as against selfish and autocratic
power and to set up amongst the really free and self-governed peoples
of the world such a concert of purpose and of action as will henceforth
ensure the observance of those principles."[58] The obligation to maintain the world's order to which he so confidently committed the nation
would require a change in policy more radical than most of his audience
could imagine and the assumption of a burden that "was not to be put
down after a year or a decade."[59] When the president signed the declaration of war against Germany just after noon on 6 April 1917, Good
Friday, America truly entered the twentieth century.

10

WAR LEADER
1917–1918

"It is a fearful thing to lead this great peaceful people into war," said Wilson in his war message on 2 April 1917.[1] Because he knew just how difficult that task would be, he had explored every alternative to war, but even so, he could hardly have realized that April evening what problems and challenges lay ahead.

Wilson's first challenge as a war leader was to assure national unity, what he called "a single way of thinking."[2] He had reason to be concerned. America in 1917 was a nation of immigrants, with one of every six Americans foreign-born. In 1916 Wilson had warned that a "fire of pure passion" had to be kept burning under the "melting pot . . . in order that the mixture that comes out may be purged of its dross and may be the fine gold of untainted Americanism."[3] Like many Americans, the president feared that in wartime loyalties to European homelands might prove stronger than love of the United States.

Equally a matter of concern was the possible effect of war upon progressivism. Soon after the war began, Wilson told Secretary Daniels that he believed "every reform we have won will be lost if we go into this war."[4] Other reformers shared the same fear. Settlement house worker Lillian Wald spoke for many when she argued that war would be "inevitably disastrous to the humane instincts which had been asserting themselves in the social order."[5] Yet as war became likely, and as Wil-

son embraced first preparedness and then, ultimately, war, many reformers followed him, out of patriotism, personal loyalty, a desire to
influence wartime policy, and sometimes out of hope that war might
create a situation wherein "new sources of energy are tapped, when the
impossible becomes possible, when events outrun our calculations," as
Walter Lippmann wrote in 1917.[6] Among progressives, war created uncertainty and indecision that divided friends and agonized individuals.

Within the Republican party there was a strain of bellicosity
shared by progressives and conservatives that far outran Wilson's, and
that created a basis for a reunification of the wings of the party sun-
dered in 1912. In 1916 the Republican candidate Charles Evans
Hughes came within a few thousand votes of carrying California and
the election, while in the Senate the Democratic majority was reduced,
and in the House 216 Democrats faced 210 Republicans and 6 Indepen-
dents. So even was the division in the House and so bitter partisan feeling that Wilson had to delay his war message for several hours before
the House could organize itself with a Democratic Speaker. In this context, Wilson's hope for national unity would have been laughable had
the situation been less serious.

Europe's three years of war had burned away opposition to strong
governments that regulated every phase of life and coerced unity, but
in America danger was less obvious. Wilson, raised in the American
tradition that government was suspect, preferred voluntary methods to
unite Americans behind the common cause. Seeking national unity
and cooperation, the administration proposed to achieve it by arousing
patriotism rather than through coercion. As Wilson saw it, the nation
was "in danger of creating too much machinery," which could become
a permanent burden if the government expanded the bureaucracy to
run the war rather than relying on volunteers.[7]

The congressional debate that followed Wilson's war message revealed how little consensus there was in the country. Just as Wilson in
his speech seemed to offer as alternative justifications for war the issue
of neutral rights or the possibility of spreading democracy and justice,
the legislators who favored war were divided. Their opponents warned
against giving up isolationism and declared that many Americans would
die in a war that would benefit only the rich. While the number in
Congress willing to vote against war was small, their arguments and the
divisions among supporters of the war meant that Wilson did not have
the national unity he needed to be successful in organizing for war
along voluntaristic lines.

Central to the administration's commitment to enlisting the people voluntarily in the war effort was the creation by executive order on 14 April 1917 of the Committee on Public Information. The CPI was largely the result of work by journalists who feared rigorous censorship and argued even before the United States entered the war that the government could avoid censorship by managing the news, releasing a large amount of accurate but controlled information. A "censorship policy must be based on publicity, not suppression," wrote journalist George Creel to Secretary of the Navy Josephus Daniels on 28 March.[8] On 11 April Daniels forwarded to Wilson a memorandum from Creel recommending the formation of a special publicity committee made up of the secretaries of the army, navy, and state, with himself as civilian chairman, to "arouse ardor and enthusiasm," stimulate recruitment, expose corruption and praise patriotism in the confidence that "in the rush of generous feeling much that is evil and nagging will disappear." The "whole spirit" of the committee "must be one of absolute co-operation," Creel advised; "It must go upon the assumption that the press is eager and willing to do the handsome thing, and its attitude must be one of frankness, friendship and entire openness."[9]

"I like his memorandum very much," Wilson told Daniels, and Creel thus became the obvious man to head the CPI.[10] It was, as Creel said, "the world's greatest adventure in advertising," and Creel treated it as such.[11] Seventy-five thousand volunteer speakers known as "Four Minute Men" were organized to deliver more than seven and a half million patriotic speeches to more than 314 million people; a motion picture division distributed patriotic films; historians and other scholars were recruited to write pamphlets explaining the war's meaning; overseas branches spread America's message in Latin America and Europe.

The CPI's goal, in which it was brilliantly successful, was to arouse patriotism by depicting American and Allied motives as noble, while Germany was blamed for the war and portrayed as the epitome of autocratic repression. Unity, sacrifice, and service were the themes evoked by the CPI, and Woodrow Wilson was depicted as the world articulator of these ideals. As it turned out, the CPI oversold its case, arousing superpatriotism and persuading Americans that war could remake the world.

The Creel committee took advantage of a belief that had been at the heart of domestic progressivism; the faith that corruption would melt away before an informed and outraged citizenry. Convinced that at heart all Americans wanted the same things from their government,

Wilson's ultimate weapon in the fight for reform had always been to take his case to the people. Now he and the CPI took the same approach in appealing to what they believed was the unity of decent people everywhere behind basic war goals.

The difference between Wilson's earlier appeals to the people and the CPI's advertising campaign was that the CPI made a far more intense and sustained appeal to emotionalism than Wilson had. Few complained when the drive was to encourage enlistments, promote the sale of war bonds, or conserve food, but all too easily mass patriotism could slip over into "vigilantism . . . inflicted in the name of popular sovereignty and often connived at by officials sworn to uphold the law."[12] German-Americans, socialists, pacifists, or any dissenter who did not measure up to popular standards of "100% Americanism" became fair game for popular and official persecution.

Unofficially, "patriots beat victims, doused them in horse troughs, clipped their hair, tarred and feathered, painted them yellow, drove them out of town on rails."[13] At the official level, Postmaster General Burleson made enthusiastic use of the Espionage and Trading-with-the-Enemy Acts of 1917 and the Sedition Act of 1918 to take away mailing privileges from publications that seemed to him "to impugn the motives of the government and thus encourage insubordination."[14] Attorney General Thomas W. Gregory, before the war a strong advocate of progressive reforms and civil rights, unwittingly contributed to the repression. Locked in a bureaucratic struggle with Secretary of the Treasury McAdoo for control of federal police, Gregory granted to the private American Protective League quasi-police powers in order to supplement the limited resources of his Bureau of Investigation (later the FBI). By so doing, he could claim that he was protecting domestic security without calling upon the Treasury's Secret Service. Gregory had "inordinate faith in the motives" of volunteers like the APL, but the faith was misplaced.[15] Most APL zealots were far more interested in persecuting domestic radicals and labor organizers than in hunting spies, and they had no scruples about using illegal methods to achieve their goals. Once again, the administration's insistence on voluntarism produced unexpected and unwanted results.

Particularly shocking examples of the APL's distorted interpretation of "espionage" appeared in the West. There the radical union, the Industrial Workers of the World, became a special target of persecution. Federal agents and APL volunteers arrested and jailed nearly 200 IWW members, and in Bisbee, Arizona, in the summer of 1917 the sheriff and two thousand local patriots led by the APL rounded up 1,186 IWW miners, loaded them into boxcars, and shipped them into the desert to roast for two days with little food, water, or shelter. For mineowners and lumbermen the war came as a heaven-sent opportunity to smash a union that had dared to challenge labor exploitation in some of the most dangerous industries in America.

Elsewhere, socialists who argued that war benefited the rich and slaughtered the poor were attacked. Sixty-three-year-old Eugene V. Debs, perennial Socialist candidate for president, was sentenced to ten years in the Atlanta penitentiary for opposing the draft, and Victor Berger, twice elected to the House of Representatives from a Milwaukee district, was twice denied his seat by the House. Such attacks led to a bitter split among Socialists between the small prowar and large antiwar factions. In an effort to protect itself from repression, the party eventually expelled its most vehemently antiwar elements, who organized two tiny Communist parties, but most Socialists had trouble forgetting principle in the name of patriotism.

The Bolshevik Revolution of November 1917 gave impetus to the wartime fear of radicalism and enabled conservatives to carry it over into the postwar Red Scare of 1919–20. Fear of bolshevism, made more acute by a series of strikes and race riots in 1919, and given focus by a few bombings in the United States by extreme radicals, was seen to justify a crackdown by Gregory's successor, A. Mitchell Palmer, on all dissent. On 7 November 1919 federal agents arrested 250 members of the Union of Russian Workers, an anarchist group, and that inspired other federal and local officials to arrest other aliens thought to be radicals. A few months later, on 2 January 1920, police arrested four to five thousand members of the Communist party and Communist Labor party with the intent of deporting them. Many of the arrests, some involving breaking into homes without warrants, were flagrantly illegal, and as the hysteria subsided in the spring and summer of 1920, most of those arrested were released. Of the thousands arrested, only 840 were actually deported.

By the time of the Red Scare, Wilson was of course an invalid, so he may perhaps be forgiven his failure to restrain federal excesses, but the truth is that he defended civil liberties only halfheartedly even in 1917 and 1918. He urged upon Burleson "the utmost caution and liberality in all our censorship" and told Gregory that "the treatment of foreign language publications is giving me a great deal of anxiety these days," but when officials stood their ground, Wilson did not insist on tolerance.[16] To one critic, Wilson wrote that not only had Burleson's "statements been misunderstood but that he is inclined to be most conservative in the exercise of these great and dangerous powers."[17]

One reason for Wilson's failure to defend civil liberties more vigorously was that, as Burleson pointed out, legislation such as the Espionage Act and the Trading-with-the-Enemy Act clearly showed Congress's intent to suppress any opposition to the war effort. If Burleson and Gregory were sweeping in their interpretation of such offenses, they were no more so than Congress. The Sedition Act, passed in May 1918, prohibited "any disloyal, profane, scurrilous, or abusive language about the form of government of the United States, or the Constitution of the United States, or the flag of the United States, or the uniform of the Army or Navy," or even any language that reflected "contempt, scorn, contumely, or disrepute" on those institutions.[18] Extreme as that act was, the administration supported its passage (but did not enforce it) because it sidetracked an even more draconian bill that would have tried such offenses by military courts-martial. Even Burleson's, Gregory's, and Palmer's most bizarre and excessive actions reflected what seemed to be a widely shared public will. Believing, as he always had, that as a leader he should sense and interpret the public mood, Wilson could not help but feel great ambivalence about trying to stem the tide of public opinion. The dark side of the national unity he sought to build was repression of dissent, and it proved almost impossible to have one without the other.

Yet if there were ways in which the war thrust the nation toward conservatism, it also brought some victories for progressives. To a limited extent it promoted economic and social planning by the government, but more important to most reformers was the boost war gave to specific social reforms. Although as it turned out, "the social reforms of the war years were caused more by the emergency situation than by a reform consensus," a few proved lasting.[19] Of these, one of the most important was woman suffrage, to which Wilson had been cool even after the 1916 Democratic platform endorsed the idea, but to which he had gradually come around as a war measure because of "the marvelous heroism and splendid loyalty of our women, and the services they have rendered the nation."[20] In January 1918 the House passed a woman suffrage amendment with Wilson's active support, but the Senate did not respond to his efforts. There the amendment failed by two votes, despite a personal appeal by the president on 30 September. When the new, Republican-controlled Congress met on 19 May 1919, however,

Wilson again urged the passage of the suffrage amendment, and on 4 June he won one of his few victories in that Congress when the Senate passed it. Approved by the states, it went into effect on 26 August 1920, in time for women to help elect Warren G. Harding president.

Reformers also found in the war the opportunity to fulfill their longtime dream of prohibiting the sale of alcohol. Although Wilson did not drink himself, he was no prohibitionist, believing that at least beer and light wines should continue to be sold, mainly because he thought that complete prohibition would be unenforceable. With the beginning of the war, prohibitionists acquired a powerful new argument, that enough grain was turned into alcohol every year to feed seven and a half million people, as William Jennings Bryan put it. Using that argument, prohibitionists were able to ban the use of edible grains in the making of alcohol in 1917 and to send the Eighteenth Amendment to the states in December of the same year. Wilson believed that the Volstead Act, which established machinery to enforce the new amendment, could not be enforced and so vetoed it, but Congress overrode him, and Prohibition became law on 15 January 1920.

Other reforms adopted during the war proved to be ephemeral or illusory. The railroads were nationalized, but only for the duration of the war; child labor laws were struck down by the courts; efforts to broaden health insurance and worker compensation laws made little progress, although public health programs flourished, especially in the vicinity of military training camps.

The administration's friendly attitude toward labor carried over into the war to the extent that it paid generous wages on government contracts and defended the right of workers to organize, but it had no use for radical unions such as the IWW. When the administration organized a National War Labor Board in the spring of 1918 in an effort to reduce the number of strikes affecting the defense effort, it defended the right of organization and collective bargaining but directed that unions must "not use coercive measures of any kind to induce persons to join their organizations, nor to induce employers to bargain or deal therewith."[21] In the atmosphere thus created, really independent unions were discouraged, while company unions flourished, and the AF of L, which was willing to give up many rights in return for economic benefits, also did well. "I like to lay my mind alongside of a mind that knows how to pull in harness," said Wilson in praise of AF of L president Samuel Gompers in November 1917.[22]

In broad terms, the government's need for production, its willing-

177

ness to pay good wages for that production, and the labor shortage caused by the war meant pretty good times for the poorest paid and least skilled members of the work force. Despite a jump in consumer prices of 100 percent between 1914 and 1920, the great demand for unskilled labor kept wages advancing fast enough so that such workers benefited from full employment. Salaried and skilled workers did not do nearly so well, making relatively few gains in pay and losing heavily to inflation.

Just as the government was willing to pay docile workers generously, so a bountiful treasury was the engine that propelled the voluntarist war mobilization. In his war message in April 1917 Wilson promised that the war would be "sustained so far as may be equitable by taxation" in order to avert "the very serious hardships and evils which would be likely to arise out of the inflation which would be produced by vast loans," but that promise was an early war casualty.[23] McAdoo recommended that "fifty per cent of the cost of the War should be financed" by taxation,[24] but the political unpopularity of large tax increases and the astonishing costs of the war, which McAdoo estimated for fiscal 1919 first at $3.5 billion, then at $15 billion, and finally at $24 billion, quickly led the administration to what a historian of the subject calls "a victory of expediency over economics."[25]

The least obviously painful way of raising money was through borrowing, and the government made heavy use of this power, holding five major Liberty Loan drives, which raised $21.4 billion, and forty-eight short-term Treasury certificate sales, which were used to tide the government over pending the receipt of taxes. To lessen the burden of interest on future generations, McAdoo issued the Liberty loans at low interest rates—3½ to 4½ percent—but kept them attractive to investors by exempting their interest from taxes. Because of this tax advantage, many bonds were bought by banks and wealthy individuals, who sometimes borrowed to purchase them. Under the Federal Reserve system, such bonds when held by banks, or the promissory notes of individual borrowers, could serve as the basis for the issuance of Federal Reserve notes (i.e., paper money). Thus government bonds became the basis for a rapid and inflationary expansion of the amount of money in circulation. The money supply expanded by 75 percent between 1916 and 1920, and with few consumer goods available, inflation was inevitable. For the administration, that meant that war contracts could be paid in devalued dollars and the real costs of war disguised, at least for the time being, by inflation. No one meant to be deceitful, but cheap money inevitably appealed to hard-pressed officials.

Few people understood the complexities of war finance, and those who criticized the administration's course were often denounced as unpatriotic. Complicating the matter was the fact that Representative Claude Kitchin and Senator Robert M. La Follette, who led the congressional group seeking to pay at least half the war's cost through taxation, had voted against the war resolution. When Kitchin proposed an excess-profits tax on industry, businessmen howled in outrage, and the New York *Sun* implied that his secret aim was to interfere with the war effort. He had, wrote the *Sun*, "proceeded upon the assumption that the war would prove unpopular, and, rather frankly, he has endeavored to make it so."[26]

After his April 1917 war message Wilson took little part in the controversy over war finances until 27 May 1918 when he went before a joint session of Congress to try to rescue the tax bill from the partisan controversy that threatened to destroy it. "Enormous loans freely spent in the stimulation of industry . . . ," he argued, "produce inflations and extravagances which presently make the whole economic structure questionable." The solution, he declared, was "fair, equitably distributed taxation, of the widest incidence and drawing chiefly from the sources which would be likely to demoralize credit by their very abundance." In the interests of the nation, he urged Congress to face up to duty "without selfishness or fear of consequences. Politics is adjourned," he promised, and in the fall elections the voters would reward those "who go to the constituencies without explanations or excuses, with a plain record of duty faithfully and disinterestedly performed."[27]

The appeal was unrealistic. Politics certainly was not adjourned, and the vote on the tax bill was delayed until after the elections, by which time the Republicans were in control of Congress and the signing of the armistice had dramatically reduced tax needs for 1919. To a considerable degree, Wilson's failure to secure the tough tax policy for which he originally asked was a result of the administration's success in selling the idea that the war could be financed painlessly and even profitably for many Americans through borrowing. Expecting Congress to upset that comfortable assumption and to impose sacrifices on the voters in an election year was naive.

Nevertheless, the administration did not do badly in financing the war. It did not achieve its original goal of paying half the cost through taxation, but it did pay about one-third that way, and in the process it firmly established the income tax as the major source of federal revenue and the Federal Reserve System as a key element in controlling and directing the economy. Before the war almost 75 percent of federal revenues had come from the tariff and excise taxes; during and after the war about 75 percent of larger tax revenues came from income, corporate, and estate taxes, all of which bore more on the wealthy than on the poor. The national debt's increase from a billion dollars in 1915 to $24.3 billion in 1920 guaranteed that this shift in the form of taxation could not be reversed by the conservative Republican administrations of the 1920s. Given the stupendous and totally unprecedented costs of war, which shot federal expenditures up from under a billion dollars a year in 1916 to over $2 billion in 1917, to about $14 billion in 1918, and to about $19 billion in 1919, Wilson and McAdoo did as well as could be expected in balancing economic with political necessities.

Aside from the obvious political cost of drastic tax increases, there were two other reasons that the administration preferred to borrow rather than tax to pay for the war. One was that it depended upon the voluntary efforts of industry to organize war production, and heavy taxes on profits would have undermined business cooperation. The other reason was that Wilson, McAdoo, and Commerce secretary Redfield wanted American companies to build up production capacity and capital to take advantage of trade disruption and the withdrawal of European capital from Asia and Latin America during the war.

Neither the administration nor business leaders did much planning for economic and industrial mobilization before the war. Such planning as was done was by engineers like Howard E. Coffin, vice-president of the Hudson Motor Car Company, who had for many years urged standardization in industry, and who argued that through cooperation between businesses and between business and government, production could be made so efficient that war could be fought without reorienting the economy. At the urging of Coffin and others, in August 1916 Congress created a Council of National Defense with a Civilian Advisory Commission to plan for mobilization. Wilson stressed its voluntary nature when he announced the appointment of the commission members in October. "The organization of the Council . . . ," he said, "opens up a new and direct channel of communication and cooperation between business and scientific men and all departments of the Government" so that manufacturers would know "the part which they can and must play in a national emergency."[28]

Having no power, the council created regional councils that were to coordinate local industries in the event of war. That structure proved unworkable in practice, because factories needed to be organized according to the products they produced rather than where they were located. After April 1917, therefore, the activities of the council were supplanted by new agencies such as the Food Administration (August 1917), the Fuel Administration (August 1917), the Railroad Administration (December 1917), and the War Industries Board (July 1917). Run by "dollar-a-year" businessmen who volunteered their services, the new agencies also depended on voluntary methods but were organized along functional lines.

Typical of these agencies was the Food Administration, run by Herbert Hoover, a millionaire engineer who became an international hero by organizing a relief program for Belgium after the Germans invaded that unfortunate neutral country. When Hoover set up the Food Administration in the summer of 1917, the Allies were desperate for food and American farmers had had a very poor crop, with the result that wheat prices were skyrocketing and speculators getting rich. Hoover set out to increase production and to promote conservation by voluntary methods. He called upon Americans to observe "wheatless" and "meatless" days, launched an advertising campaign to promote conservation, created a government Grain Corporation capitalized at $150 million to guarantee farmers a minimum price of $2.20 a bushel for wheat, and persuaded Allied purchasing commissions that they should pay high prices for food to encourage production. The conservation campaign was the most visible aspect of his program and provided a reinforcement of the patriotic emotionalism evoked by the Creel committee, but in the long run the hope of profit was what lured most farmers into the increased production that was the key factor in solving the food crisis.

The Wilsons pitched in to do their part for the war effort. Edith Wilson signed a Food Administration pledge to conserve food and received a sticker to display in the White House window. In the yard she planted a "war garden" of vegetables, and Wilson captured headlines by arranging to have a flock of sheep graze on the White House lawns. When sheared, the sheep produced almost a hundred pounds of wool, which was auctioned off across the country and raised a hundred thousand dollars for the Red Cross. In the evenings the women of the household knitted socks and scarves, and the president held the yarn they rolled into balls.

Other aspects of mobilization were less successful than Hoover's Food Administration. Fuel Administrator Harry Garfield, a former Princeton professor, struggled during the winter of 1917–18 with a coal shortage caused partly by inadequate rail transportation. On 17 January 1918 Garfield was forced to order that all factories east of the Mississippi close for four days to make coal available for residential use. In the end Garfield solved the shortage by setting the price of coal at three dollars a ton, the price wanted by the industry. The administration had "stumbled badly" in rejecting that price when it was proposed by the coal operators in June 1917.[29]

In the same period during the autumn and winter of 1917–18 the War Industries Board, set up in July 1917 to coordinate manufacturing, floundered under a series of directors because Congress had decreed that no government official could contract for supplies from any company in which he had an interest, thus eliminating most of the "dollar-a-year men." Not until March 1918 did the agency begin to function efficiently under the leadership of Bernard Baruch, a wealthy Wall Street speculator who believed that the board should "encourage, under strict Government supervision, such cooperation and coordination in industry as should tend to increase production, eliminate waste, conserve natural resources, improve the quality of products, promote efficiency in operation, and thus reduce costs to the ultimate consumer."[30] Although the board did not have the power Baruch would have liked, it worked with producers during the spring of 1918 to set prices at levels that ensured profits and encouraged production. In so doing, it was at least tacitly violating the antitrust laws, but Attorney General Gregory consulted with Wilson about the matter, and they agreed to "let the cases go to sleep until the war was over."[31] Wilson refused, however, to give the board power over purchasing for the armed services along with responsibility for production. The interest of the military purchasing agents in keeping prices down exercised some check on inflation and on the growth of the cooperative relationship between government and industry that Baruch and other Wilsonian war managers wanted.

The chaos in economic mobilization during the early phases of American participation provided ammunition for a major attack on the administration. In April 1917 Republican Senator John W. Weeks of Massachusetts proposed the creation of a Joint Committee on the Conduct of the War. Remembering how a similar committee had tormented Lincoln during the Civil War, Wilson persuaded Democratic members of the rules committee to bury it, but Weeks revived it again in July, and it took all of Wilson's influence to deflect it. "I honestly think that it would be impossible for me to conduct the war with success if I am to be placed under daily espionage," he wrote to Senator Robert Owen.[32]

By early 1918, with war production still lagging, serious coal shortages, and frequent charges that military training was being bungled, it began to look as if a joint committee might be the least of Wilson's worries. Even Democrats were grumbling, and on 19 January Oregon Democratic Senator George E. Chamberlain introduced a bill that would have taken control over the war away from the president and vested it in a war cabinet of "three distinguished citizens of private ability."[33] Furious, Wilson replied that Chamberlain's proposal "sprang out of opposition to the administration's whole policy rather than out of any serious intention to reform its practice," which may have been true but did not solve the problem.[34] A counterattack was essential.

Early in February Burleson handed to Senator Lee S. Overman of North Carolina the draft of a bill that Overman introduced the next day. The Overman bill authorized the president "to make such redistribution of functions among executive agencies as he may deem necessary," to restructure, transfer, or alter existing agencies, and to create "any additional agency or agencies and to vest therein the performance of such functions as he may deem appropriate" for the duration of the war and one year thereafter.[35] The bill was a masterstroke, for it took up Republican charges that the administration had been weak and disorganized and used them to secure unprecedented powers for the president. "Senator after Senator has appealed to me most earnestly to 'cut the red tape,' " declared Wilson. "I am asking for the scissors."[36]

With critics temporarily silenced, the Overman bill passed Congress, and Wilson signed it on 20 May. By the time his opponents recovered, he had reclaimed control over the war. Yet victory brought a price. The same critics who had earlier attacked the administration for weakness and inefficiency now denounced the president as dictatorial, and more seriously, a rift had been created in the formerly close and harmonious relationship between the president and Congress. The charge of dictatorship was ridiculous, since Wilson made little use of the Overman Act, but in addition to the other strains and tensions accumulating during the war, the act became an element in the eventual defeat of the Treaty of Versailles.

In sum, the administration's mobilization policy combined a large amount of ballyhoo to arouse public support with guaranteed profits to producers to stimulate production. Under the circumstances, producers found it easy to be patriotic. Even the railroad companies, whose assets were nationalized in December 1917, were guaranteed a profit and the return of their improved lines within twenty-one months after the end of the war. Disgruntled railroad workers were pacified by a substantial pay raise, and the bill for improvements and higher wages was paid by raising shipping rates and drawing on general government revenues. Wartime prosperity and the requirement that money loaned to the Allied governments be spent in the United States prevented the American public from realizing that eventually someone was going to have to foot the bill for government borrowing, guaranteed profits, and artificially subsidized wages. Voluntarism was the external manifestation of mobilization, but guaranteed profit was the fuel that made the machine run. In subsequent years a rosy but false memory of the wartime experience would shape the voluntarist economic ideal of Herbert Hoover and other Republicans of the 1920s. During the Great Depression of the 1930s and World War II the voluntarist lessons of the First World War proved to have little relevance to a harder time.

Several members of the administration hoped to sustain wartime prosperity into the postwar period by expanding foreign trade and investment. The administration had of course been working in that direction before the war, and several of its members were eager to exploit Europe's misfortunes ruthlessly. "Unless we continue to develop our foreign trade," said Edward N. Hurley, head of the Shipping Board, "after the war we can have no enduring prosperity."[37]

In June 1916 the Allies held an economic conference in Paris in which they laid plans for a postwar economic union that would have discriminated against the United States. Alarmed by this threat, American business leaders abandoned their objections to a government-owned merchant marine, and in September Wilson signed the Shipping Act into law. It created a Shipping Board to own and operate a commercial fleet during the war and for five years after it, and it set up an Emergency Fleet Corporation to buy and build ships.

For almost a year after the passage of the Shipping Act until the appointment of Hurley in July 1917 the new American merchant marine existed mostly in imagination, although with the entrance of the United States into the war in April the need was desperate. In the month of April 1917 alone, German submarines sank almost a million tons of Allied shipping, more than the whole total of American merchant tonnage at that point. After war was declared, frantic efforts to increase American tonnage resulted in the confiscation of German ships interned in American ports and the requisitioning of 163 vessels being built in American shipyards for the British, as well as construction of new ships. Because American shipyards were small and antiquated, few American-built ships were put into use before the end of the war. Nevertheless, confiscation and construction enlarged the American merchant marine while that of Britain shrank because of sinkings; by the end of the war the American merchant fleet, miniscule before 1917, had become 40 percent the size of England's.

From Edward N. Hurley's point of view the war offered an opportunity to build for the future even more than for the present. "My whole thought is to get a fleet of large sized ships . . . so that we may be able to compete with Germany and England after the war," he said frankly.[38] Hurley and his allies in the administration tried to keep American ships off the dangerous trans-Atlantic routes, forcing the British to carry American supplies and troops, while American ships were sent to take over trade routes elsewhere in the world. Among the greatest successes of Hurley and his cohorts were the passage in 1918 of the Webb-Pomerene Act exempting business combinations in the export trade from antitrust laws and the passage in 1919 of the Edge Act permitting Federal Reserve member banks to combine in creating foreign investment corporations. Wilson supported both bills.

Nevertheless, Wilson's aims were far broader than Hurley's economic nationalism. He believed that the war, which had turned the United States from an international debtor into the world's greatest creditor, presented an opportunity to end, once and for all, economic conflict. As he explained in his Fourteen Points address on 8 January 1918, his goal was "the removal, so far as possible, of all economic barriers and the establishment of an equality of trade conditions among all the nations."[39] Confident that the United States would do well in such a world, but that others would benefit from a universal Open Door also, he rejected Hurley's economic nationalism, instructing the shipping chief "not to talk now or publicly plan the use we shall make of our shipping after the war, because while it is true, contrary to the English impression, that we do not intend to seek any unfair advantage of any kind or to shoulder anybody out, but merely to give the widest possible currency to our own goods, the impression made by past utterances has been that we, like the English, are planning to dominate everything and to oust everybody we can oust."[40] Wilson explained to House that by the end of the war Allied economic dependence on the United States would enable him to "force them to our way of thinking," but that for the present maintaining unity was essential.[41] With a major re-structuring of the world's economic relations in reach, the president re-fused to fritter away America's advantage on short-term, selfish goals.

Because the United States was so distant from the actual war, American war planning was dominated more by the president's vision of what might be achieved in the future than by fears of what could happen in the present. When, in response to criticism that the admin-istration lacked forceful leadership, Wilson on 20 March 1918 created a War Cabinet, its membership reflected his concerns. It included Sec-retary of the Treasury and Railroad Administrator McAdoo, Secretary of the Navy Daniels, Secretary of War Newton D. Baker, War Indus-tries Board chairman Bernard M. Baruch, Fuel Administrator Harry A. Garfield, Shipping Board chairman Hurley, War Trade Board chairman and chairman of the Democratic National Committee Vance G. Mc-Cormick, and Food Administrator Herbert Hoover. All except Baker and Garfield had been successful businessmen; all were devoted to Wil-son and, except for Hoover and Garfield, to the Democratic party; and all were examples of Wilson's Princeton ideal of men whose "character, integrity, social consciousness, and proud individualism would be com-bined with the efficiency and technical expertise of the modern social manager."[42] Meeting every Wednesday with this group, the president refined his emerging conception of a society and a world in which vol-untary cooperation could replace competition and conflict. Utopian though such an idea may seem, it appeared to be working within the American economy, and the members of the War Cabinet shared Wil-son's belief that it could be made to work in the world as well. His peace plans were born from the ideals of progressivism and this unique American wartime experience.

Strikingly absent from the War Cabinet were any military officers. Wilson's first secretary of war, Lindley M. Garrison, alarmed by what he saw as the president's unrealistic antimilitarism, had proposed the creation of an auxiliary force he called the Continental Army, but it was opposed by congressional friends of the National Guard, and Wil-son gave in to them. Garrison resigned early in 1916, convinced that the nation was not preparing adequately for war. His successor, Newton D. Baker, was no more militaristic than the president, and neither thought it desirable to give the military direct representation in the War Cabinet. Nevertheless, in the months after the declaration of war, the administration somehow managed to put together "a huge army of enormous fighting power" and get it to France in time to make a decisive difference. That achievement, concludes one historian, "is in re-trospect simply amazing, one of the great wonders of the present century."[43]

For the most part Wilson left the raising, equipping, training, and transportation of the American Expeditionary Force to the experts, but he made crucial decisions about the nature and uses of the force. One of the earliest and most important of these decisions was his commit-ment to conscription. As late as 25 January 1917 the president ex-pressed serious doubts about the wisdom of a draft, but when he asked Congress to declare war in April he strongly endorsed "the principle of universal liability to service," a draft.[44] Exactly when and why he changed his mind is not clear. To one correspondent he explained that he thought a draft would create a "conclusive impression of strength and determination" that might impress the enemy and reduce the like-lihood "that our men will have to be sacrificed in any great numbers." To another, he explained that an all-volunteer army too often, as had been the case with England and France, drew the best and brightest young men and did not provide for the rational "mobilization of all the productive and active forces of the nation and their development to the highest point of cooperation and efficiency."[45] No doubt the problem of how to deal with an especially embarrassing volunteer, Theodore Roosevelt, who wanted to lead a division to France, helped him decide that an all-conscript army would be a good idea. Ironically, even as the administration declined Roosevelt's offer and decided on conscription, it christened the draft the Selective *Service* system and ran it with vol-unteers staffing local boards, thus managing to place the implication of voluntarism on this least voluntary of operations. When the president signed the new law he issued a proclamation written by Baker declaring that the draft was "in no sense a conscription of the unwilling; it is, rather, selection from a nation which has volunteered in mass."[46] Hard though it may have been to take such patriotic hypocrisy seriously, Americans made the best of the draft, and eventually 24 million men registered for it, of whom just over 2.7 million were actually called. As Wilson had hoped, the draft was effective in getting men to fight and in keeping those vital to war production at home in their jobs.

Another important decision about the military in which the presi-dent shared was that American forces would not be integrated into existing Allied units but kept separate under their own commanders. That was particularly the desire of the AEF commander, General John J. Pershing, who argued that keeping American forces separate would strengthen America's position in peace negotiations and protect the Americans from British and French defeatism. Somewhat more tactfully, Wilson told the British that a separate American force would increase American support for the war while merging them into Allied units would play into the hands of critics who argued that the War Department was incompetent. "Nothing except sudden and manifest emergency," Wilson instructed Secretary of War Baker, should "be suffered to interfere with the building up of a great distinct American force at the front, acting under its own flag and its own officers."[47] The president, said House, was "determined that it shall be known to the world that this country is acting independently of our allies."[48]

Behind the president's reluctance to merge American forces with those of the Allies was a powerful desire to keep his hands free for the peace conference. In July 1917 he wrote House that "England and France *have not the same views with regard to peace that we have* by any means."[49] Whether or not Wilson knew at that point in detail about the secret treaties among the Allies in which they agreed on how to divide up the enemy's assets, he realized that securing the sort of "peace without victory" that he had in mind would be difficult. In January 1918, after the Russian Bolsheviks published the secret treaties, Wilson told British secret service agent Sir William Wiseman that the treaties had created widespread concern that the war was being waged "for some imperial or capitalist purpose." Some Americans might welcome imperialism, he added, but he had opposed it all his life, and he hoped "that no-one in England thinks that we are in this war for any material advantage."[50]

At the same time the president was hearing about the secret treaties, he sensed an opportunity to appeal to the European left for support of a better kind of peace. In England war weariness led to a major parliamentary debate about war aims on 6 November 1917, during which radicals from the Liberal and Labour parties attacked the government and urged a peace along the lines Wilson had proposed. Meanwhile, in France and Italy serious military reverses also aroused radical criticism of their governments' commitment to victory. Even in Germany, reported Walter Lippmann, who was secretary of The Inquiry, a group organized by House at Wilson's request to study peace issues, liberal opinion would welcome a negotiated settlement such as Wilson had been proposing. Lippmann was well informed about the internal condition of the Central Powers, and his memoranda had great influence on Wilson's thought. To the president the moment seemed ripe for an appeal to the people of Europe over the heads of their governments, the tactic he had made the hallmark of his domestic political leadership.

Adding urgency to the situation was a Russian challenge to the president's leadership of the left. In April 1917 Danish and Dutch socialist leaders proposed an international socialist meeting at Stockholm to discuss peace. Wilson was instantly on his guard. "I do not like the movement among the Socialists to confer about international affairs," he wrote to Lansing. "They are likely to make a deal of mischief, especially in connection with affairs in Russia."[51] Not long afterward that concern was borne out, when the Petrograd Soviet endorsed the proposed conference. Although the Allied governments were able to prevent the conference from meeting by denying passports to possible delegates, the chance remained that Russia could still emerge as the leader of a leftist peace movement. By late 1917, after the November Revolution brought the Bolsheviks to power in Russia, Wilson became concerned that the peace movement could be captured by radicals committed to world revolution.

In his annual message to Congress on 4 December 1917 Wilson urged that the peace initiative be recaptured from the Bolsheviks. "The fact that a wrong use had been made of a just idea is no reason why a right use should not be made of it," he said. "It ought to be brought under the patronage of its real friends."[52] A few days later he told House that he meant to formulate "a broad declaration of war aims that would unite the world against Germany, and would not only help the Russian situation, but would knit together the best and most unselfish opinion of the world."[53] In so arguing, he was as concerned about the dangers of European imperialism as of Russian radicalism, for which he had a good deal of sympathy. The American people, he warned the British ambassador, "would not engage in a war . . . except on American principles," and especially they "would not fight this war for private ends."[54]

With the idea of seizing leadership of the peace movement from the Bolsheviks and socialists on the left, and from the Allied leaders on the right, Wilson drafted a speech laying out his own peace program to be presented before Congress early in January 1918. The main basis of the speech was a memorandum prepared by Walter Lippmann, David Hunter Miller, and Sidney Mezes of The Inquiry, which was sent to the president about 22 December. The memorandum argued that American and Allied support for the war effort could be strengthened by proclaiming a liberal peace program, while the Central Powers would be undermined. Its authors assumed that such a proposal might bring the Central Powers to the bargaining table without an actual invasion of Germany, but it was clear they did not have in mind a peace among equals. No peace conference should be held, they recommended, without significant democratization of the governments of Germany and Austria-Hungary, and Germany must give up all territorial claims in the East and West. To make those terms palatable to the enemy, they recommended the inclusion of broader goals such as a general economic Open Door in the world, the negotiated settlement of German colonial claims, and the creation of an international organization to mediate disputes. At the peace conference, they emphasized, the United States must be ready to use its economic power to compel the Germans to accept these terms. "If the possibility of exclusion from economic opportunity is associated with a vision of a world co-operation realized, the double motive of fear and hope can be used upon the German people. *This is our strongest weapon.*"[55]

On 8 January 1918 Wilson went before a joint session of Congress to make his speech. In it he took the experts' advice to offer the carrot and wield the stick. To arouse unrest within the Central Powers, he recommended that the map of Europe be redrawn "along clearly recognizable lines of nationality" so that Russia, Belgium, and France would be evacuated, and Italy, the states of the Austro-Hungarian Empire, those of the Ottoman Empire, and Poland would be assured "political and economic independence." That amounted to an appeal to the nationalities of the enemy states to rise up and overthrow their governments. At the same time he made an offer to the governments of the Central Powers to provide freedom of the seas, removal "so far as possible" of international economic barriers, reduction of armaments, "a free, open-minded and absolutely impartial adjustment of all colonial claims," "open covenants of peace, openly arrived at," and the creation of "a general association of nations . . . for the purpose of affording mutual guarantees of political independence and territorial integrity to great and small states alike."[56] From such proposals the Germans might reasonably hope to secure access to markets and assurances of security.

The initial response to Wilson's Fourteen Points speech was encouraging. In Britain the radicals took new heart and put pressure on the government to announce its agreement, while in Germany a series of major strikes raised hopes that the government might fall and the left take over. On 24 January both the German and Austrian chancel-

lors made speeches directed to Wilson that seemed to open the possibility of progress.

Those first bright hopes soon dimmed. On 2 February the Allied
prime ministers, meeting in a Supreme War Council at Versailles, declared, "The only immediate task before them lay in the prosecution
with the utmost vigor . . . of the military effort."[57] A month later, on
3 March, the Germans answered in kind by imposing the harsh Treaty
of Brest-Litovsk on the Russians, and soon after that by opening a great
offensive on the western front. Yet even as the fighting resumed with
renewed savagery, the German left continued to be very much interested in the Fourteen Points, and even the German Foreign Office put
out tentative peace feelers to American agents based on the more appealing parts of the Fourteen Points for Germany. Wilson was unwilling
to negotiate on the basis of anything but the whole package, and in a
speech at Baltimore on 6 April he expressed his disappointment. "I
have sought to learn the objects Germany has in this war from the
mouths of her own statesmen . . . ," he said, and they had replied that
they sought only "dominion and the unhindered execution of their own
will."[58] The United States, he concluded sadly on 18 May, must not
"be diverted from the grim purpose of winning the war by any insincere
approaches upon the subject of peace. I can say with a clear conscience
that I have tested those intimations and have found them insincere."[59]

During the later spring and summer of 1918 American soldiers
poured into Europe in enormous numbers: 245,945 in May; 278,664 in
June; 306,350 in July; 285,974 in August; 257,457 in September. Ill-
trained and inexperienced, they were thrust into the lines before General Pershing thought they were ready, but the Germans would not
wait. Believing that the Allies had sunk into a defensive mentality,
Pershing favored a strategy of rapid mobility and tactics based upon individual riflemen, both of which were controversial then and afterward,
but the truth was that neither strategy nor tactics were decisive. What
counted was sheer numbers, a "seemingly inexhaustible flood of gleam-
ing youth in its first maturity of health and vigour . . . , burning to
reach the bloody field."[60] Overwhelmed, the German advance stopped,
then turned into slow retreat.

By the end of September German military leaders were convinced
that the situation was desperate. Wilson's Fourteen Points now offered
the best hope for salvaging something from the ruin, and so on 6 October, the new German chancellor, Prince Max of Baden, cousin of the

kaiser, sent a note to Wilson proposing an immediate armistice based on the Fourteen Points. The president was suspicious of the sincerity of the German offer, fearing that unless the German government was changed, the military would simply use an armistice to rebuild their position, which in fact was the intent of the German supreme command. "They have said that they agree to my terms," Wilson told Sir William Wiseman, "and if they were respectable people I should be obliged to meet them in a conference. Of course, we do not trust the present German Government; we can never trust them, and we do not want to discuss peace with them."[61]

Yet there were urgent reasons for both sides to want peace. The Germans were defeated, and Wilson told Wiseman that he was concerned about war weariness among the Allies, about the growth of bolshevism, and about the danger that if the war should continue, Americans would demand German destruction, leaving "nothing to build up from."[62] Wilson had to be tough enough to satisfy those in his own country who wanted Germany's annihilation, had to be sure that the German offers were sincere and that the German government would act honorably, and still had to avoid being so demanding as to cause a collapse of the German government and a possible Bolshevik revolution. Further complicating the situation was the attitude of British and French leaders, who were understandably mistrustful of any talks between Germany and the United States that excluded them and fearful that an armistice negotiated by Wilson on the basis of the Fourteen Points would deprive them of the fruits of victory.

Recognizing Wilson's dilemma, German leaders decided they must make whatever short-term sacrifices would be necessary to secure the long-term benefits of a Wilsonian peace. "We must concentrate our efforts on strengthening Wilson's position. By full compliance with his wishes, we can deny the Entente any pretext for persuading him to abandon his peace program," read a German Foreign Office memorandum.[63] Just how far the Germans had to go to satisfy Wilson was not, however, clear in Berlin.

Nor was it clear in Washington. Under enormous political pressure at home and from the Allies to impose absolute surrender on the Germans, Wilson was nevertheless reluctant to dictate to Germany the details of their internal political structure and fearful that if he pushed too far he would topple the country into revolution. On 23 October the president sent a note to the German government in which he tried to tread the indistinct path among these various perils. On the one hand he promised to convey the German peace offers to the Allies, but on the other he pointed out that the power of the military and the kaiser seemed unchanged and repeated that "the nations of the world do not and cannot trust the word of those who have hitherto been the masters of German policy."[64] Deliberately ambiguous, the note must be seen as reflecting Wilson's real mistrust of the German government and also as serving two interests not directly related to the armistice issue. One was to prevent the Allies from crushing Germany militarily, which would free them from military and economic dependence on the United States and weaken Wilson's power over peace terms. The other was to portray the president as tough on Germany in order to improve Democratic prospects in upcoming congressional elections.

Within Germany Wilson's note was read as a mandate for a change of government, and on 28 October the imperial constitution was altered to make Germany a constitutional monarchy. A few days later there was a massive naval mutiny, and Prince Max resigned as chancellor to be replaced by a Socialist government. On 6 November the new government sent peace emissaries to propose an armistice to Supreme Allied Commander Marshal Ferdinand Foch.

In the meantime, Colonel House had been putting pressure on Allied leaders to accept the Fourteen Points as a basis for an armistice. On 30 October he met with British prime minister Lloyd George and French premier Clemenceau in Paris and suggested that if the Allies did not accept the American terms, the United States might have to negotiate a separate peace. Reluctantly, the Allies gave in, rejecting only the freedom of the seas clause of the Fourteen Points and Wilson's subsequent proposal that reparations be kept to a minimum. When the kaiser abdicated on 9 November and fled to Holland, the final obstacle to an armistice was removed, and at 11:00 A.M. on 11 November 1918 the reign of death ended.

Although Wilson succeeded at last in securing both German and Allied agreement to base the armistice on the Fourteen Points, he had not done so easily, nor did the success of the Republicans in winning a solid majority in the House and a two-vote majority in the Senate in the 5 November elections promise easy going for a peace based on the Fourteen Points. Ironically, the administration's achievement in arousing patriotic enthusiasm for the war now made it harder to end it rationally.

George Creel, whose efforts were partly responsible for that situation, preferred to blame the problem on Burleson and Gregory, arguing that when the Post Office and Justice Department "were allowed to silence or intimidate" all the "radical, or liberal friends of your anti-imperialist war policy," until "there was no voice left to argue for your sort of peace," then only "the reactionary Republicans had a clean record of anti-Hun imperialistic patriotism."[65] Progressive Amos Pinchot put the matter more bluntly, saying that the president had put "his enemies in office and his friends in jail."[66] However one chose to interpret the problem, it was apparent that all-out support for the war was likely to translate into enthusiasm for total victory and a punitive peace, instead of into support for the liberal peace Wilson sought.

Republican leaders interpreted the election result as a repudiation of Wilson's war leadership, although they differed as to just what it meant. Henry Cabot Lodge, who would become chairman of the Foreign Relations Committee in the new Senate, attributed the Republican victory to "the dread deep down in the people's hearts of the establishment of a dictatorship," but Theodore Roosevelt argued just the opposite, that Wilson's weakness was the issue. "The Republicans made the fight on the unconditional surrender issue," he wrote, "and their victory serves notice on Germany that Foch will dictate the terms of the Armistice."[67]

More realistically, the election result probably had little to do with foreign policy; congressional races rarely turn on such issues. The normal pattern is for the party out of power to improve its standing in midterm elections, and for it to do so on the basis of local issues. In fact, the Democrats did somewhat better in 1918 than is usually the case, losing some western support because the guaranteed price of wheat was not as high as farmers would have liked and some urban votes because of the rising cost of living. Some liberals, disenchanted with the administration's stand on civil liberties or unhappy with its progress toward woman suffrage, also deserted, although it was hard to imagine the Republicans would be more liberal. A few voters may have been affected by the difference between the parties on peace terms, but probably not many.

Nevertheless, partisan differences about the peace were real, and leaders on both sides chose to interpret the election as a referendum on Wilson's policy. That was because Republican leaders like Lodge and Roosevelt had centered their attacks on the "peace without victory" idea, and Wilson, who had tried to stand above partisanship, allowed himself to be drawn into replying. His May 1918 "politics is adjourned"

194

remark had exploited a continuing frustration among Republicans, who recognized that sharp attacks on the administration might seem unpatriotic. "We must give no opening for the charge that we are drawing the party line and the cry that we are not loyal to the war," warned Lodge, but Republican leaders gradually realized that they could enjoy both partisanship and patriotism by accusing the administration of insufficient zeal in prosecuting the war.[68]

By October Democrats were urging Wilson to drop his nonpartisan stance and reply to these charges, and on 25 October he did, urging the voters to elect Democrats to assure "undivided support to the government under a unified leadership." The Republicans, he admitted, had "unquestionably been pro-war, but they have been anti-administration," attempting "to take the choice of policy and the conduct of the war out of my hands and put it under the control of instrumentalities of their own choosing." It was essential to maintain Democratic control, Wilson asserted, "not for my own sake or for the sake of a political party, but for the sake of the nation itself, that its inward unity of purpose may be evident to all the world."[69]

Inasmuch as Wilson had always asserted that his policy merely reflected the national will, his appeal had a certain logic, as well as wrapping Democratic aspirations in the flag. Republicans of course vigorously denied any Democratic monopoly on patriotism, and thus the publicly debated issue in the election became Wilson and his policy toward war and peace, even if that question was not of great importance to voters in most congressional districts. When the Republicans won, they inevitably claimed that the president had been repudiated, although in retrospect it is also plausible to argue that Wilson's appeal may have minimized Democratic losses. In any event, the identification of the peace issue with partisanship that took place during the election meant that party conflict would also play a central part in the Senate's treaty debate.

The 1918 election was symbolic of a dilemma that was inherent in the way the administration had chosen to fight the war. Seeking to minimize its impact on the economy and government, and to avoid making government a coercive and intrusive force in everyday life, Wilson had relied on arousing patriotism and enlisting the voluntary support of Americans behind his leadership. With the aid of George Creel's propaganda, the president emerged as the single voice and symbol of America's war goals, to a much greater extent than he had ever been able to stand as a symbol and voice for progressive reform. The weakness of that approach, however, was that man and policy became inseparable, so that defeat of one meant defeat of the other. When Wilson told Sir William Wiseman, just before he left for the peace conference at Paris, "I ask for nothing better than to lay my case before the American people," he could not imagine rejection, but the 1918 election was an ominous sign.[70]

11

FAILURE AND HOPE
1919–1924

On 18 November 1918 Wilson announced that he would lead the American delegation to the peace conference at Paris in December. Soon afterward he named as the other American delegates Colonel House, Secretary of State Robert Lansing, General Tasker H. Bliss, and Henry White, a career diplomat and the only Republican on the delegation. No member of the Republican-controlled Senate that had to approve the treaty was included, nor was any prominent Republican.

The president's decision was controversial at the time and remains so. Lansing believed that Wilson was "making one of the greatest mistakes of his career and imperiling his reputation," and other close friends and advisers like Tumulty and Dr. Grayson also opposed the decision.[1] Historians have generally shared this opinion, arguing that, as a recent study puts it, "had he remained at home, . . . he could have taken credit for accomplishments of his representatives, or disavowed inconvenient agreements."[2]

There were several reasons for Wilson's decision, some good, some not so good. One was personal. He wanted to be remembered as the author of a new international structure that could abolish war; such an achievement was worth taking chances for. Wilson really believed that he alone had a clear vision of "a world organized for justice and democracy," and that the other nations who had joined to defeat Germany

197

had far less noble aims.[3] "No one in America, or in Europe either, knows my mind and I am not willing to trust them to attempt to interpret it," he told House in October 1917.[4] To a great extent he was right.

It is hard to imagine who else could have led the American delegation if Wilson had not done so. For all the president's affection for House, and for all the Texan's experience in Europe, Wilson knew that House's limitation was an eagerness to say yes to whomever he was talking with. Moreover, Edith was jealous of the colonel and had been criticizing him subtly behind his back as "not a very *strong* character . . . , a weak vessel," which inevitably undermined Wilson's confidence in his friend.[5] Wilson himself derided Lansing as "the most unsatisfactory Secretary in the Cabinet," with "no imagination, no constructive ability, and but little real ability of any kind."[6] Henry Cabot Lodge, new Republican chairman of the Senate Foreign Relations Committee, was a bitter personal enemy whom Wilson dismissed as "narrow and partisan."[7] Former president Taft and another prominent Republican, Elihu Root, were early possibilities for the delegation, but Wilson seems to have suspected them of conspiring with the British "to formulate a plan for a league of nations" in advance of the conference, and they too were eliminated.[8] Thus for a variety of reasons, some petty and some sensible, Wilson was forced to the conclusion that he must go to Paris.

The most important reason for Wilson's decision was his conviction that his peace program reflected the deepest desire of people all over the world, and that, although other leaders might recognize that desire, everyone else was committed to other goals first and to his program only secondarily, if at all. Someone, he said at the University of Paris on 21 December 1918, must remind the peace conference delegates that "they are the servants of mankind, and if we do not heed the mandates of mankind we shall make ourselves the most conspicuous and deserved failures in the history of the world."[9]

Wilson was the most popular man in the world in that late autumn and early winter of 1918. When his ship, the *George Washington*, sailed from New York on 4 December 1918, the whistles of tugs and ferries drowned out all conversation, a blizzard of confetti inundated Manhattan, and naval fliers frightened many of the passengers by buzzing the ship. Obscured for the moment by the cheers were the mutterings of Theodore Roosevelt, who scoffed that the Fourteen Points ranged from "thoroughly mischievous" to merely "vague and ambiguous," and who declared that Wilson's duty in Europe should be to "stand by our allies."[10]

Europe's greeting to Wilson surpassed even the American send-off. On 14 December, the day after the president's arrival at Brest, two million Frenchmen lined the streets of Paris to pour out their hearts in welcome. Those standing along the parade route could measure the progress of the president, smiling and waving his top hat from an open carriage, by the cheers that rolled along in great waves. Forty years later a Frenchman who was there remembered the sense of hope the scene inspired: "His was the first great voice from outside Europe to resound in our minds, and through him, for the first time in centuries, a force from outside Europe contributed to the shaping of our destinies."[11] During the next month before the conference began on 12 January 1919 Wilson received ecstatic greetings in Italy and a more restrained welcome in England.

Whether Europeans were cheering Wilson's Fourteen Points, celebrating the end of the war, thanking Americans for their military help, or simply responding to a unique and exciting event was not clear. Being human, Wilson enjoyed the adulation, but he did not fool himself that securing the peace he wanted would be easy. The Allied leaders, he said, were "determined to get everything out of Germany that they can," and he warned that if worse came to worst, the United States might have to withdraw from the conference and make a separate peace.[12]

Although twenty-seven Allied and associated powers were represented at the peace conference, everyone soon agreed that full plenary sessions were too cumbersome. Accordingly, most negotiating was done either in the Council of Ten, consisting of Wilson, French premier Georges Clemenceau, British prime minister David Lloyd George, Italian premier Vittorio Orlando, their foreign ministers, and two Japanese delegates, or in the Council of Four, made up of Wilson, Clemenceau, Lloyd George, and Orlando (who was often absent). Working on the details of policies whose broad outlines were sketched in these forums were many commissions of experts, including members of the American Inquiry. Six plenary sessions ratified the work done by the various subgroups.

Everyone at the conference was conscious that unless they stabilized the European situation quickly, there was a danger that bolshevism (Russia was not invited to the conference) would spread westward into Europe. Herbert Hoover, whom Wilson had asked to undertake a relief program for the war-devastated areas, reported that suffering was intense and warned that food was a "fundamental necessity to prevent anarchy," which could destroy all hope of a stable peace.[13]

Yet despite their fear of revolution, there were higher priorities for the Allied leaders than order. The Italians wanted territory on their northern border and the Adriatic coast; the Japanese wanted island bases and a clear title to German concessions in China; the British were determined to protect their naval supremacy, and their Dominions sought territory; the French were dedicated to assuring their security against Germany. The seventy-eight-year-old French premier, Clemenceau, known as "the Tiger," was the most outspoken about what his nation wanted, but not necessarily the greediest. None of the Europeans except the British cared greatly about Wilson's prime concern, the creation of a league of nations.

The issue was joined symbolically when the first issue taken up by the conference was the disposition of Germany's colonies in Africa and the Pacific. Point 5 of the Fourteen Points had called for a "free, open-minded, and absolutely impartial adjustment of all colonial claims" with concern for the rights of the colonial and colonizing peoples.[14] Japan and the European Allies wanted to divide up the colonies, but Wilson wanted to hand them over to some of the smaller neutral nations like Holland or Sweden, who would guide them toward self-government under the oversight of the League of Nations. Everyone agreed that the colonies should not go back to the Germans, whether for economic or strategic reasons, or because the Germans were charged, even by German liberals, with being barbarous masters whose colonial soils were "manured by the blood of natives."[15] But there was a vast difference between Wilson's antiimperialist "mandate" plan and the outright partition advocated by the Allies. The battle was hard fought, and eventually a compromise was reached on the basis of a suggestion by South African general Jan Smuts, who proposed giving the colonies to the major powers under a mandate system. Thus it was obvious at the outset that Wilson would not be able to dictate the terms of peace.

One of Wilson's greatest disappointments at Paris, evident even at this early stage of the conference, was that America's war-born economic power did not translate effectively into diplomatic power. He had counted on the fact that the United States had become the greatest creditor in the world, with the Allies dependent on America for the very food that kept them alive, "to force them to our way of thinking."

"I want to go into the Peace Conference armed with as many weapons as my pockets will hold to compel justice," he told the cabinet in October.[16]

Unfortunately, from the president's point of view the war ended a little too soon to maximize the American economic grip on the Allies, and American wartime economic policies weakened what grip there was. When the war ended, a planned American merchant fleet was just beginning to be built and the British fleet, although shrunken by war, was still vastly superior—so much so that American leaders had to ask the British for transports to bring American soldiers home. Even more significantly, although the Allies were deeply indebted to the American government, the Americans had insisted that borrowed money be spent in the United States. That stimulated the American economy during the war, but when war ended, the Allies abruptly began canceling orders, thus revealing that American prosperity was partly in Europe's hands. Despite the extraordinary reversal of roles between creditor and debtor that had taken place during the war, the United States was caught up in a web of interdependence and was less dominant than its leaders imagined.

Perhaps suspecting that his hand was weaker than he had expected, Wilson made an all-out effort at the beginning of the conference to secure agreement on the creation of a league of nations. The original plan of the conference was to operate in two stages: a preliminary meeting to work out the military and some economic terms of the treaty; and then a second session, including the Germans, at which the league would be negotiated and final terms agreed upon. That plan had advantages from the American point of view because it would have allowed passions to cool and brought the leaders of the new German Weimar Republic, who favored a league, into the negotiations. But its disadvantages were more serious. As the colonial issue showed, there was a danger that a one-sided peace would be imposed on Germany, and Wilson was not sure he could prevent it. If that happened, a league might be needed at once to rectify injustices. Moreover, the two-stage conference might produce two treaties, one setting peace terms, the other establishing the league. Some of the Europeans might reject the second, and Wilson feared that the Republican-controlled Senate might do the same thing. Making use of all his prestige, Wilson secured agreement from a plenary session on 25 January 1919 that the league's constitution, or "covenant," as Wilson liked to call it, would be part of the treaty. "When that treaty comes back gentlemen on this side will find the Covenant not only in it, but so many threads of the treaty tied to the covenant that you cannot dissect the covenant from the treaty without destroying the whole vital structure," Wilson warned his American critics.[17]

Wilson had been thinking in general terms about an international organization ever since 1914, when he mentioned the idea to Stockton Axson as a possible feature of a postwar settlement, and when House suggested that a Pan-American treaty might become "a model for the European Nations when peace is at last brought about."[18] At that point Wilson had suggested that such an agreement include a mutual guarantee of territorial and political integrity, and control of all armaments manufacturing and sales by governments. He had dropped the second suggestion by 1918, but the other became the fundamental principle of his league.

The president was not alone in thinking along such lines. Liberals and peace advocates in Britain and the United States were uniting under the impetus of war in hopes of finding some way to prevent the catastrophe from reoccurring. Earlier in Wilson's administration Secretary of State Bryan had followed a slightly different path toward the same goal by proposing and negotiating a series of bilateral treaties that bound signatories to submit all disputes to international investigation before going to war. The theory of the Bryan treaties and that of the advocates of international organization was essentially the same: that, as Wilson said in Paris in December 1918, "just a little exposure will settle most questions."[19] Just as progressives in the United States commonly held that publicizing evils was a first, vital step toward reform, so the international reformers argued that investigation and discussion could prevent war.

Wilson shared the faith of peace advocates in international organization but did not share their enthusiasm for specific plans. Both in England and in the United States groups sprang up and drafted elaborate proposals. In May 1916 Wilson addressed the most important of the American groups, the League to Enforce Peace, of which William Howard Taft was president, and in so doing became the first world leader to endorse the principle of an international organization. The president did not, however, endorse the League to Enforce Peace's proposals. Rather he suggested that the United States join "any feasible association of nations" that might be organized to advance self-determination, respect for territorial and political integrity, and equality among large and small nations.[20] Subsequently, Wilson was cool to the specific program of the League to Enforce Peace and, according to Taft, "persistently blocked public conventions of the League on the ground that it would embarrass him."[21] Privately, Wilson complained about the "League to Enforce Peace butters-in."[22]

Peace advocates suspected Wilson of discouraging their efforts because he wanted all the glory for himself, and that may have had some truth, but he insisted that there were good reasons for postponing discussion of specifics. "The principle is easy to adhere to," he pointed out, "but the moment questions of organization are taken up all sorts of jealousies come to the front which ought not now to be added to other matters of delicacy."[23] Aside from possible danger if the issue got caught up in domestic politics, House suggested that any organization endorsed by only one of the belligerents would become just another military alliance with "each side bidding for neutral countries to join their particular group."[24]

Wilson was also concerned about whether Americans would be willing to join a league of nations, given their isolationist tradition. In a speech in New York in September 1918 he tried to explain that "only special and limited alliances entangle," while a "general alliance . . . will avoid entanglements and clear the air of the world for common understandings and the maintenance of common rights," but his point, even if valid, was so obscure that few in the audience could have been persuaded.[25] Sensibly if belatedly, the president seems to have been trying to build public support for the principle of international organization by being deliberately vague about the degree to which any such commitment would alter traditional American policy.

In private Wilson was a little more specific about a possible organization. As the result of an exchange with House during the summer of 1918 he drafted a possible league of nations covenant. It was a modest document of thirteen articles providing that ambassadors accredited to Holland should make up an organization that would guarantee territorial and political integrity, supervise arms reductions, and provide for the investigation and arbitration of disputes. Any member state violating the provisions of the covenant could be coerced by economic methods; any nonmember that went to war with a member could be the subject of economic or military sanctions. Aside from the addition of the mandate system, this rather sketchy proposal was what Wilson brought to the peace conference.

Students of the conference have often been puzzled by the president's seeming lack of detailed preparation for what he regarded as the most important issue to come before the meeting. His behavior in this case, however, was perfectly in keeping with his previous experience of political leadership, which had been remarkably successful. As with the Geran bill and other important legislation while he was governor, and as with the Federal Reserve Act, the tariff, and antitrust legislation while president, he clarified in his mind the basic principles he wanted to achieve and prepared to bargain on the details. In addition, Wilson was convinced that the league was something that all the people of the world wanted, and that in fighting for it he would have on his side "a great wind of moral force" so strong that "every man who opposes himself to that wind will go down in disgrace."[26] For critics such confidence was an example of Wilson's "Messiah complex"; for admirers it revealed a humble willingness to make himself the servant of the people.

If Wilson was ill-prepared, the results did not show it. Named chairman of a special League of Nations Commission, he worked closely and intensely with British league advocates to produce a draft within ten days. On Valentine's Day, 14 February 1919, he read the completed draft to a plenary session of the conference as snow swirled by outside the windows. "We felt that in a way this conference had intrusted to us the expression of one of its highest and most important purposes," he said, "to see to it that the concord of the world in the future with regard to the objects of justice should not be subject to doubt or uncertainty."[27]

The heart of the league covenant, as Wilson saw it, was article 10, which bound league members "to respect and preserve as against external aggression the territorial integrity and existing political independence of all" members. Articles 6–15 spelled out various methods of resolving disputes peacefully and obligated the members to exhaust those methods before considering war. If a nation rejected peaceful solutions or deliberately attacked another, article 16 provided that a unanimous council of the league could call upon members to apply economic or even military sanctions. Wilson explained on 14 February, "Armed force is in the background of this program, but it *is* in the background . . . ," as "the last resort, because this is intended as a constitution of peace, not as a league of war." The threat of force, he declared, was unimportant beside "the moral force of the public opinion of the world."[28]

With the league covenant literally in his overcoat pocket, Wilson left the conference and returned home to begin the task of winning national support for it and to deal with urgent domestic business largely neglected during his two-month absence. Just before leaving he sent a cable inviting members of the congressional foreign affairs committees to dine with him at the White House on 26 February. He had not wanted to meet with them, but House insisted he must make an effort to win the support of the Senate. The meeting was not a success. Some senators refused to come, and Lodge sat in stony silence, saying nothing, asking nothing.

At two minutes after midnight on 4 March, the day the session of Congress was to expire, Lodge rose in the Senate to read a "round robin" signed by thirty-seven senators and senators-elect expressing their opposition to the league "in the form now proposed."[29] Specifically, the signers (more than enough to defeat the treaty) objected to the lack of recognition of the Monroe Doctrine in the covenant, to the apparent right of the league to offer advice to members on internal matters, to the lack of any way to refuse a mandate, and to the absence of specific recognition of Congress's right to declare war. Furious, Wilson lashed back in an unfortunate speech in New York in which he said that the league would be so much a part of the treaty that the two could not be separated, and that "an overwhelming majority of the American people" would demand its ratification.[30] Then he sailed back to France, where he landed on 13 March.

He arrived to find the American position in disarray. The European leaders, noting Senate opposition to the league, were talking about dropping it from the treaty, while House and Lansing had, in his opinion, been far too willing to make concessions to European demands in his absence. Although he and House probably did not have the dramatic confrontation remembered later by Edith Wilson, there is no doubt that Wilson's faith in his friend was severely undermined and that he never trusted him as much again. "The Colonel," wrote Dr. Grayson, "while meaning good, gives out statements telling the correspondents not to take things too seriously, that a compromise can be made—and this news, or rather news of this kind, is very harmful to the President, as it gives the French the impression that the Colonel is speaking for the President, and then the French say the President is bluffing."[31] After Wilson returned to the United States, he never saw House again. As for Lansing, he had never had any faith in the league of nations idea, and he was freely telling his friends in Paris that article 10 simply meant that the injustices of the treaty would be perpetuated forever.

Without unified support from his own compatriots, Wilson's position at the conference was undermined. He was able to block the threat of dropping the league from the treaty by reminding the delegates that a full plenary session had voted on 25 January to include it, but on other issues he was forced to compromise. Having had time to reflect, he realized that defying the Senate would be suicidal, while correspondence with Taft and other prominent Republicans suggested that with modest changes "the ground [would] be completely cut from under the opponents of the League in the Senate."[32] Accordingly, he asked the conference to accept amendments to the covenant recognizing the Monroe Doctrine, exempting internal affairs from league oversight, providing a mechanism for withdrawal from the organization, and assuring the right to refuse a mandate. After some argument, the others agreed to these changes, but only at the price of American concessions on other issues.

One of the most important of the battles of this period had to do with reparations, German payments for the damage they had done in invading France and other countries. On 11 February 1918 Wilson had said that the peace must be made on the basis of "no annexations, no contributions, no punitive damages," and one of the Americans' most significant victories in negotiating the armistice had been to secure the inclusion of a promise that Germany would be asked to pay no more than for damages to civilians.[33]

Yet the issue did not disappear. Lloyd George and Clemenceau had both secured election and parliamentary victories in the autumn of 1918 on the strength of their promises to make Germany pay all war costs, and they dared not go back on their pledges. The British premier was particularly embarrassed by the issue, because, although he agreed with Wilson that heavy reparations would embitter the Germans and sow the seeds of future conflict, important members of his delegation were insistent on wringing the maximum out of the Germans, and he was also aware that unless the reparations bill was inflated at least by including the cost of pensions to veterans, the sacrifices and losses of the British dominions would go unrewarded.

After his return to Paris, Wilson realized that the reparations issue could destroy the conference and decided he must find a compromise. Through endless meetings he stood resolutely against Clemenceau's demands to fix the reparations bill at some enormous sum, but eventually he agreed to include pensions because he had come to believe that otherwise "England would not get what she was entitled to in proportion to the other countries."[34] He also accepted a British proposal to create an international reparations commission, upon which the United States would be represented, and which would set the total bill and annual payments. Agreement to the commission proposal reduced conflict over the issue at the conference, and Wilson hoped that a commission, meeting in a less emotional atmosphere, would set a reasonable reparations bill.

As it turned out, the British and French blundered badly in forcing a compromise on Wilson over reparations. The German government reluctantly made token payments during the 1920s, but the treaty's declaration that Germany was solely to blame for beginning the war (the justification for reparations) was a constant source of German bitterness. To force the Germans to pay, Britain and France would have had to use force, for which they lacked the will, and which would have cost more than they could hope to recover. They would have been wise to have followed Wilson's advice to avoid heavy claims, but political decisions are not always rational.

A second major battle of this same period resulted from France's obsession with security against Germany. It was not enough for the French that Germany should be disarmed; they wanted to occupy the left bank of the Rhine River or to create an independent Rhenish Republic, and to annex the Saar Valley as well. When the French argued that Germany had systematically ruined French coal mines in the Nord and that France was entitled to the Saar's coal in compensation. Wilson's American advisers were impressed, even though French takeovers of the Saar and Rhineland would put several million Germans under the French flag. The president rejected the experts' opinions. For him the crucial issue was self-determination, and on 6 April he ordered his ship, the *George Washington,* to Brest. The next day he told the conference that unless a satisfactory solution of the dispute were reached, he would return to America. "How can I talk to a fellow who thinks himself the first man in two thousand years to know anything about peace on earth?" exploded Clemenceau, but the French did not want to destroy the conference.[35]

Elated, Wilson told one of his advisers that "his gesture in ordering the G[eorge] W[ashington] was effective," but he recognized that the time had come to help the French save face.[36] He was "obliged to remain faithful to [the] Fourteen Points," he told Clemenceau, "but without inflexibility, and going as far as possible to meet your legitimate wishes."[37] Two weeks later the conferees agreed France would control the coal mines of the Saar for fifteen years, with the region as a whole to be administered by the League of Nations. At the end of the period, a plebiscite would determine whether it would be French or German. France would occupy the Rhineland for the same period, and the area would be demilitarized forever.

The Saar and Rhineland agreements sought to protect both the principle of self-determination and French security, but Clemenceau was not satisfied. "The League of Nations is offered to us as a means of providing the security we need," he said; "I accept this method; but if the League of Nations cannot enforce its orders with military sanctions, we must find this sanction some other way."[38] Wilson, of course, dis-agreed with this attitude, but when Lloyd George proposed that En-gland and the United States sign security treaties promising to send troops to France's aid in the event of unprovoked German aggression, the president agreed. Believing that the obligation thus incurred was no greater than that already specified by the League of Nations covenant, Wilson placed no emphasis on the security treaty. "All that I promised is to try to get it," he told Henry White, and after he submitted the treaty to the Senate on 29 July he let it die without any effort to defend it.[39] In his confidence that the league would be a panacea, Wilson un-derestimated French fears and German anger, but to have behaved dif-ferently would have required him to give up the whole basis of his peace program.

While Wilson struggled with the French, the Italians were gazing hungrily northward. Italy had entered the war in 1915 on the Allied side because the secret Treaty of London promised her Austro-Hunga-rian territory, and she now demanded Fiume, main seaport of the newly created state of Yugoslavia and the Dalmatian coast and islands, in ad-dition to the Brenner Pass area that Wilson had already promised Italy to provide a defensible northern border. Since Fiume was mainly Italian and the region around it predominantly Slav, the Italian request strained Wilson's concept of self-determination. Arguing sophistically that the aim of the Treaty of London had been to protect Italy against the Austro-Hungarian Empire and that the disintegration of that em-pire nullified the treaty, Wilson resisted Italian demands doggedly. Pre-mier Orlando, no intellectual match for Wilson, walked out of the conference in a huff, and on 23 April the president issued an appeal to the Italian people, asking them to overrule their leaders and to insist that peace be based upon the "clearly defined principles which should set up a new order of justice and right."[40]

When Wilson visited Italy he was given the most tumultuous welcome he received anywhere in Europe, but his Fiume statement turned January's adulation to fury in April. The British and French, who agreed privately with the president's position, stood silent and let him take the storm. More than a month later, after Orlando had returned to Paris, an agreement was reached that established Fiume as a free state under the league and arranged that the region's future would be settled after fifteen years by a referendum. But the scars of the Fiume battle remained. Wilson had been shown forcibly that his ideals were less universal than he had thought, while in the United States the Fiume settlement would be attacked as a significant departure from self-determination.

The Italian crisis also gave the Japanese an opportunity to press their interests. From the beginning of the conference the Japanese had made a determined effort to have a clause inserted in the covenant of the league recognizing racial equality. Western leaders, including Wilson, were profoundly embarrassed by this demand, which they recognized as just but politically impossible for them to accept. Wilson and House tried to find language that would satisfy the Japanese yet not alarm Australians or American senators, but the Japanese and Chinese, in agreement for once, refused to be fobbed off. At a meeting of the League of Nations Commission on 11 April the issue burst into the open when the Japanese introduced a racial equality amendment and demanded a vote. Wilson, in the chair, tried to dodge the issue but could not, and the vote was eleven to six in favor of the amendment. Nevertheless, Wilson ruled that since the commission was not unanimous, the amendment had failed. Technically, he was right, but at least two other amendments had been adopted by majority vote. When some delegates protested his high-handedness, Wilson replied that there were "too serious objections on the part of some of us" to have this amendment become part of the covenant.[41]

The Japanese had been in earnest about the racial equality clause, but when they failed to get it, the western nations' embarrassment strengthened the Japanese position on other issues. Secret treaties of 1917 had promised British and French support for the Japanese acquisition of Germany's concession in China's Shantung Province and had provided that German islands north of the equator would go to Japan, while those south of that line would become British. With the Italian walkout imperiling the conference and the rejection of the racial equality clause fresh in everyone's mind, the Japanese demanded that the provisions of 1915 and 1918 Sino-Japanese agreements according the

Japanese special privileges in Kiaochow and Shantung be validated in the peace treaty. Adding to the problem was the fact that the Japanese had occupied the territories in question for four years before the conference met.

Under the circumstances, Wilson's choices were limited, but with British support, he did the best he could. The German islands were divided up as promised, but as mandates, not as outright grants, and the Japanese agreed to keep the German concessions in Shantung but to return the province to Chinese control soon. Wilson concluded sadly that the agreement was "the best that could be accomplished out of a 'dirty past,' " and hoped that "through the mediation of the League of Nations all extraordinary foreign rights in China and all spheres of influence" could be terminated.[42] Several members of the American delegation thought that he had made a "terrible mistake" and had sacrificed China to Japan.[43] Their bitter criticisms became a focus of attack on the treaty.

Critics who charged that the Shantung provisions were a betrayal of self-determination were unfair, but other settlements were less satisfactory. These included the transfer of one hundred fifty thousand Austrian Germans in the Brenner Pass region to Italy and of several million German Bohemians to Czechoslovakia in the Sudetenland. For Irish nationalists the treaty's failure to address the Irish question was an even worse violation of principle. Elsewhere in Europe and the Middle East other violations occurred on a greater or lesser scale.

Focusing on the failures of self-determination, however, obscures Wilson's successes in creating the states of Poland, Yugoslavia, and Czechoslovakia, as well as protecting the Rhineland and Saar from French annexation, to mention only some of the more conspicuous achievements. Wilson himself had always denied that self-determination was an absolute principle, arguing in February 1918 that "well defined national aspirations" should "be accorded the utmost satisfaction that can be accorded them *without introducing new or perpetuating old elements of discord.*"[44] By admitting that other concerns had to limit self-determination, Wilson made his own task almost impossible. As one analyst has observed, his was an effort to "square the circle," but it was also the first serious attempt by a major world leader to provide a mechanism for the accommodation of nationalist aspirations within a stable international system.[45] Since nationalism commonly threatened the status quo, Wilson's attempt to turn it into orderly change was daring but unlikely to succeed. Conservatives attacked his failure to control the problem as if they could thereby block change itself, liberals blamed him for failing to achieve perfection, and the treaty was squeezed between the absolutes.

On 7 May 1919, the two-hundred page treaty was handed to the Germans. They objected strongly to a number of its provisions and during the next month and a half negotiated significant changes in reparations, in the terms governing the plebiscite to be held in the Saar region, and in the rules governing the French occupation of the Rhineland. They failed, however, to secure elimination of article 231, the "war guilt clause," or to fix a $25 billion limit on reparations. Wilson was seriously concerned about what might happen if Germany rejected the treaty, but he was angered when the Germans accused him of violating his own principles. Like the British and French, he blamed Germany, or at least German militarism, for the war, and he believed the Germans must prove they had changed. When the French adamantly opposed Germany's request for immediate membership in the League of Nations, Wilson reluctantly concurred. Thus in the end the last German objections were overridden, and on 28 June the sullen German delegates were marched into the Hall of Mirrors at the Palace of Versailles and compelled to sign the treaty.

After the ceremony, Wilson, Lloyd George, and Clemenceau strolled outside the palace to enjoy the sun that had broken through the clouds and was sparkling on the fountains, running for the first time since the war. Crowds who had been restrained by flimsy barriers broke through and mobbed them joyously until they were rescued by French troops. Once again at the end of the peace process the conferees were hailed as the voice of the people, but how different was the peace they had written from the one Wilson had imagined six months earlier!

Yet despite the faults of the treaty, which would be highlighted over the next months, it had notable virtues. It took the first tentative steps toward eliminating colonialism; it moderated the selfish demands of the victorious powers; it met many nationalist aspirations in central and eastern Europe; and it created a mechanism for the maintenance of international order that might have been workable if the nations had been willing to use it. Although Wilson freely admitted that "many of the results arrived at are far from ideal," he insisted that "on the whole we have been able to keep tolerably close to the lines laid down at the outset." At very least, he argued, the results were "much better than at one time I feared."[46] Given the radically conflicting aims of the negotiators, the treaty was as good as could have been hoped for.

Americans, only dimly aware of the problems facing Wilson in Paris and unaccustomed to such negotiations, had developed unrealistic expectations of what was possible. To some extent Wilson and George Creel, who had turned the war into a crusade, must bear blame for what happened, but they shared the illusions they created. The most crucial flaw of the treaty was neither its obligations on the United States, as nationalists charged, nor its failure to realize all the Fourteen Points, as idealists believed. Rather the treaty failed as any broad settlement would have failed, because it attempted to create a stable international order at a time when the world was being swept by ideological, economic, and political changes so profound that there was little hope of controlling and channeling them. The Fourteen Points expressed so many of the long-term interests of the western nations that they have remained beacons of western policy ever since, but in the rest of the world they aroused aspirations that could not be satisfied without radical changes. In the context of 1919, even a treaty reflecting the Fourteen Points perfectly, if such a thing had been possible, would have been trying to harness lightning.

Wilson arrived back in the United States on 8 July an exhausted man. He had worked harder and more continuously during the months in Paris than ever before in his life, taking part in meetings and conferences all day and until late at night. Within the American delegation he made every important decision and most of the minor ones as well. As time passed, he trusted even his closest aides, House and Lansing, less and less. In April he had been ill briefly, and his temperature went to 103°, but he refused to stop working. On top of everything else, he had to keep some contact with domestic affairs in the United States. Given his always frail health, it seems miraculous that he was able to survive all of this at the age of sixty-two. Inevitably, exhaustion sharpened his temper and distorted his judgment.

After landing in New York, Wilson made a brief speech at Carnegie Hall and then returned by train to Washington. Arriving in the late evening, he found a hundred thousand people gathered to greet him. As he rode back to the White House through the warm evening, Secretary Daniels's wife remarked that it was too bad that all the buildings and monuments were illuminated except the Capitol. "It never is," replied Wilson.[47]

Two days later, on 10 July, Wilson went before the Senate to present the treaty. The League of Nations, he declared, was "the hope of the world. . . . Shall we or any other free people hesitate to accept

212

this great duty? Dare we reject it and break the heart of the world?" Then he allowed a glimpse into his own heart. "The stage is set, the destiny disclosed," he declared. "It has come about by no plan of our conceiving, but by the hand of God who led us into this way. We cannot turn back. We can only go forward, with lifted eyes and freshened spirit, to follow the vision. It was of this that we dreamed at our birth. America shall in truth show the way. The light streams upon the path ahead, and nowhere else."[48]

Listening disapprovingly to the president's challenge was the chairman of the Senate Foreign Relations Committee, Henry Cabot Lodge. Lodge detested Wilson and his league. Although he had once and briefly been a member of the League to Enforce Peace, Lodge was a nationalist with little faith in international organizations. He had already said that he believed that article 10 of the league covenant would compel the United States to use "military or economic force" to "guarantee the territorial integrity of the far-flung British Empire . . . , of China or Japan, or of the French, Italian and Portuguese colonies in Africa." Lodge wanted no part of any such limitation on American freedom of action. At most, he was willing to accept "a League among the Nations with whom we have been associated in the war" to keep the peace, but he preferred to maintain complete American freedom in the hope that American practice would influence the world by example.[49]

In May and June, when Congress first met, American public opinion seemed strongly in favor of the league. Thirty-two state legislatures and thirty-three governors endorsed it, as did most newspapers. But as time went by, opposition began to gather. Republicans, smarting at the president's domination of the government during the war, were eager to put him in his place even if they did not oppose the treaty on principle. German-Americans thought the treaty was too hard on Germany; Italian-Americans were angry about Wilson's stand on Fiume; Irish-Americans were infuriated that the treaty failed to provide Irish independence. Editor William Randolph Hearst urged "one-hundred-per-cent-Americanism" and traditional isolationism.

Most serious from Wilson's point of view was the defection of many of his progressive supporters who were bitterly disillusioned by the treaty's departures from the perfection of the Fourteen Points. "Wilson is and was a thoroughly good man, an idealist, a clean man," wrote one, "yet like Parsifal 'ein reiner Tor' [a complete fool]."[50] In the Senate David I. Walsh of Massachusetts, the only new Democratic senator elected in 1918 and a professed Wilsonian until the autumn of 1919, reversed himself and came out against the treaty. "It is the complete absence of the high-minded sentiments we proclaimed during the war that has provoked the great opposition to this covenant and crushed the hopes of progressive, forward-looking men throughout the world," Walsh explained.[51] William C. Bullitt, a disillusioned former member of the American staff at Paris, told the Foreign Relations Committee that Secretary of State Lansing thought the treaty should be defeated because its "unjust clauses" were imposed on the world by the requirement that all changes necessitated a unanimous vote of the league council.[52] Lansing would not confirm that publicly, but he told colleagues that the treaty was "almost hopelessly bad" because article 10 would compel the United States "to guarantee all the mistakes of the treaty."[53]

During July and August Lodge held hearings in the Senate Foreign Relations Committee before which sixty witnesses appeared. A few were experts, but most represented minorities who disliked some aspect of the treaty. As this parade continued, Lodge, who at first hoped only to amend the treaty slightly, began to believe it could be reshaped radically or even defeated.

Wilson fought back in daily meetings with doubtful senators, and on 19 August he invited the members of the committee to the White House for a three-hour question-and-answer session and lunch. The meeting may have been the last real chance for compromise, and it was a failure. Believing he was winning and convinced that adoption of reservations or amendments would open the treaty to changes by other signatories, the president was stiff and imperious, and the senators, feeling they were being dictated to, made no effort to initiate a serious discussion of possible amendments or reservations. Wilson came out of the meeting believing the opposition was partisan and could be overcome by an appeal to the American people, as Tumulty had suggested months earlier.

Weak, gaunt, and visibly trembling, Wilson may already have suffered a minor stroke on 19 July. He knew that a major speaking trip would exhaust him and threaten his health, but he was determined to go. "I cannot put my personal safety, my health in the balance against my duty—I must go," he told Dr. Grayson, and on 3 September he left Washington for the West.[54]

The trip was an incredible ordeal. In twenty-two days the president delivered thirty-seven major speeches, speaking to as many as thirty thousand people at a time, all but once without the help of a loudspeaker. Before and after speeches he was carted about in parades and forced to shake hands endlessly. Almost at once he began to have splitting headaches, and at night he frequently slept sitting up on the train because of asthma that had afflicted him since his illness in April.

Wilson's speeches on the trip were seldom great, because he had prepared nothing before he left Washington and often had to speak several times a day, but they did what he wanted. They put before the people his answers to the objections being made by treaty opponents, and even more importantly, they penetrated the fog of quibbling about details to remind people of the great dream the League of Nations represented. By the time Wilson reached the Rockies he was attracting enormous, enthusiastic crowds and a groundswell of support for the treaty seemed to be building. Worried Republican leaders sent senators William E. Borah of Idaho and Hiram W. Johnson of California after the president to show that opponents of the treaty could whip up enthusiasm too.

After moving down the West Coast, Wilson's train swung back eastward, and on 25 September he reached Colorado, speaking twice that day, in Denver and Pueblo. The Pueblo speech was the high point of the trip, not because it was especially inspired, but because the audience was so enthusiastic, rising and cheering for ten minutes before the president even began to speak. In the speech Wilson said again what he had said so often before, that the peace treaty was not his personal work but that it represented "the thought of the people of the United States" and "the moral judgment of the United States."[55] The reception given his words, tired and ordinary though they were, seemed to show that his listeners approved.

That night Wilson came to the end of his strength. Exhausted but unable to sleep, he collapsed. Summoned by Dr. Grayson at four o'clock in the morning, Tumulty found the president seated, fully dressed, in his drawing room compartment. The left side of his face sagged, and when he tried to move, Tumulty realized the whole left side of his body was paralyzed. In an indistinct voice Wilson said, "I don't seem to realize it, but I seem to have gone to pieces. The doctor is right. I am not in condition to go on. I have never been in a condition like this, and I just feel as if I am going to pieces." Then, turning away, he stared out the window into the dark, tears rolling down his cheeks. Over his weak protest that Lodge would think him "a quitter," Tumulty, Grayson, and Edith Wilson canceled the rest of the trip and ordered the train back to Washington.[56]

215

By the time he reached the capital, the president had recovered enough to walk to an automobile, but the improvement was temporary. On the morning of 2 October Wilson suffered a massive stroke that paralyzed his left side, impaired his speech, made it difficult for him to swallow, and left him with only partial vision. No accurate report of his illness was released to the press until February 1920, and even within the administration few people knew what had really happened. On 6 October Grayson told cabinet members that Wilson had suffered "a nervous breakdown, indigestion, and a depleted nervous system."[57] When Lansing suggested that the Constitution provided that the vice-president should take over when the president was incapacitated, Grayson refused to sign a certificate to that effect, probably on Edith Wilson's orders. She was convinced that carrying through the treaty fight was literally a matter of life and death to Wilson, and that he would not survive a resignation. "I am not thinking of the country now, I am thinking of my husband," she said.[58]

For about six weeks Wilson lay in bed, paralyzed on the left side and with his kidneys functioning poorly. Except for a very brief ceremonial visit by the king and queen of the Belgians on 31 October, no one except doctors and family saw him until November. Not until late December was he able to work for even five or ten minutes at a time. Throughout the remainder of his term he was at least a semi-invalid, unable to stand, seeing poorly, incapable of concentrating for a sustained period.

Just as the stroke impaired Wilson's ability to concentrate, so it seemed to narrow and limit his mind, stripping away his political skills and ability to deal with complexities, bringing emotion very near the surface, and intensifying his deep-seated tendency to judge all issues as right or wrong. On such matters he could be clear and decisive, firing Lansing for his disloyalty on the treaty and for encouraging a movement toward intervention in Mexico, refusing to see House because he thought the colonel had given away too much in Paris. Unwittingly, Edith Wilson and Dr. Grayson contributed to his oversimplification of issues by shielding him from problems that might be complicated and unpleasant. Because, like many stroke victims, he denied the severity of his own illness, Wilson really believed that he was quite himself. By 1920 he was even talking about running for a third term to vindicate his stand on the league.

Edith Wilson's role in these months has long been a subject of curiosity and controversy. She referred to the period as her "stewardship" and denied that she ever made "a single decision regarding the disposition of public affairs."[59] That is nonsense. Probably she made the most critical decision of all, that the president should not resign; she screened all visitors, denying access to most; she winnowed papers sent to the president, returning most unseen and sending back a few with marginal notes to the effect that "the President directs . . . ," or "the President orders. . . ." Even assuming that these notes really came from Wilson, it is obvious that he knew little of what was happening in the country and in the administration. At very least, Mrs. Wilson shielded the president from bad news and put the most optimistic possible interpretation on everything.

Almost certainly Wilson's illness prevented him from winning at least a partial victory in the battle over the treaty. At the time he was stricken, there was evidence he was gaining public support for ratification of the treaty without amendments or reservations. The enormous popular response to his speaking tour showed that wartime idealism was not dead, and many senators were opposed to amendments that might compel renegotiation of the treaty. When the Republican majority on the Foreign Relations Committee proposed forty-five amendments, all were defeated by the full Senate. The president's illness demoralized and confused treaty supporters, but until that time the outcome was not inevitable.

Whether Wilson could have secured approval of the treaty without reservations, and whether he would have been willing to compromise on such reservations are more difficult questions. The fight was bitter, and Wilson, by now a seasoned politician, knew that a leader who offers to compromise before his back is to the wall will get less than one who holds out until the last moment. To House he declared, "I have found one can never get anything in this life that is worth while without fighting for it," and he told Lansing that the only way to defend the treaty was "to take the most militant and aggressive course."[60] Nevertheless, he had already shown a willingness to compromise, in securing amendments to the covenant after Lodge's "round robin," and in bargaining with the Allied leaders. On 18 July he told Sir William Wiseman confidentially that he might be "obliged, in order to secure a really satisfactory majority, to agree to some reservation defining or interpreting the language of one or more Clauses of the Covenant," but he was determined to exhaust every alternative before moving in that direction.[61] His leadership style had always been to make a case for perfection in presenting an issue to the public, but to compromise if necessary on anything other than principle. Up to the point of his stroke, the treaty fight was following that pattern.

The stroke, by stripping away his ability to discriminate between principle and detail, by destroying his more subtle intellectual abilities and thrusting him back onto the bedrock of religious morality, destroyed his sense of what and when to compromise. Shielded by Edith and Grayson from ugly reality, he saw no need to compromise, and thinking in simplistic terms of good versus evil, he was powerfully driven to avoid doing so. The statesman became the moralist, and as such he was no match for Lodge.

On 6 November 1919 Lodge, having been defeated in his effort to amend the treaty, set out to achieve the same thing by proposing fourteen "reservations" that would limit American obligations under the treaty but not require the approval of the other signatories. The idea of reservations appealed to many groups in the Senate, from "irreconcilables" who hoped to make the treaty unpalatable to its friends, to Republican "mild reservationists" who thought a few clarifications desirable. Wilson himself had earlier said that he did not object to "interpretations accompanying the act of ratification," provided such understandings did not "form part of the formal ratification itself," so it seemed possible even he might be brought to accept some variation of Lodge's proposals.[62] Although Lodge supported "strong reservations" intended to assure complete American freedom of action, compromise was not out of reach in early November.

On 7 November, and again on 17 November 1919, just before the treaty vote, the Democratic minority leader, Gilbert M. Hitchcock, was able to talk briefly to the president about strategy. Hitchcock believed that if Wilson would authorize him to offer interpretive reservations, the Republican "mild reservationists" could be brought to support the treaty, thus providing the two-thirds majority necessary for Senate approval. Wilson would not listen. "With the exception of interpretations, which would not alter the substance," he said, "I am not willing to make any compromise."[63] The confused condition of his mind was strikingly revealed when he drew a totally inappropriate analogy between South Carolina's attempt in 1832 to "nullify" the tariff and Lodge's effort to "nullify" the covenant. "Let Lodge compromise," he ordered Hitchcock.[64]

Two days later, on 19 November, the treaty was defeated. In the first of three votes, there were thirty-nine yeas and fifty-five nays, with thirty-five "reservationist" Republicans and four Democrats favoring the treaty with Lodge's reservations, and thirteen "irreconcilable" Republicans and forty-two Democrats opposed. A second vote later in the day was almost the same, forty-one to fifty-one, and a third attempt, by Democrats, to pass the treaty with no reservations, failed by thirty-eight to fifty-three. On no vote was there even a majority for the treaty, let alone the two-thirds needed for approval.

The heart of the controversy, for Wilson as for Lodge, was article 10 of the league covenant, which guaranteed the political and territorial integrity of members. Critics insisted that the league could require members to commit economic or military force to maintain these guarantees. Wilson's interpretation of the obligation was clear to him but obscure to almost everyone else. He pointed out that the council of the league could not recommend sanctions without a unanimous vote, thus giving the United States a veto, and he added that even if the council voted sanctions, "the unanimous vote of the council is only advice in any case. Each Government is free to reject it if it pleases." Thus it seemed clear that the United States could not be compelled to act against its will–but then Wilson went on to explain further. Article 10's guarantee, he said, was "a very grave and solemn moral obligation," not a mere "legal" obligation; in the case of a "moral" obligation, Congress would have to decide whether or not an issue involved America's moral values, whereas a "legal" obligation was automatic.[65] If that seemed to listeners to loosen still further America's obligations, Wilson did not mean it to. To him, a "moral" obligation was infinitely superior to a merely "legal" one. Where, then, did that leave the nation's alleged freedom of choice under article 10? In retrospect, it is unlikely that this problem would have been as serious as it seemed it might at the time, but since it was clear that to some extent the United States would have to give up its traditional freedom of action, exact shadings of meaning acquired enormous importance.

A few Americans were pleased at the defeat of the treaty, but a great many were shocked. Representatives of twenty-six national organizations, with over 20 million members, urged Lodge to find a way to support the treaty. Impressed, Lodge worked for a while with Democrats to draft acceptable reservations, but eventually his efforts were stopped by the irreconcilables, who accused him of selling out to the enemy. Democrats like Hitchcock and William Jennings Bryan, who also sought compromise, were brought up short by the president, who suggested that antileague senators resign and stand for reelection. After the absurdity of that idea was demonstrated to him, he proposed to make the presidential election "a great and solemn referendum" on the treaty.[66] He would entertain no hint of compromise. "I hear of reservationists and mild reservationists," he wrote to Hitchcock on 8 March, "but I cannot understand the difference between a nullifier and a mild nullifier."[67]

Yet despite the reluctance of either side to make any concession, the pressure of public opinion forced the Senate to bring the treaty to a vote once more on 19 March 1920. Twenty-one Democrats deserted the president to vote for approval with reservations, but twenty-three voted with the irreconcilables, and the treaty fell seven votes short of the necessary two-thirds majority, forty-nine to thirty-five. Wilson had already said that even if it had been approved, he would have refused to ratify it. "I feel like going to bed and staying there," he told Grayson after the vote, and after a silent but sleepless night he added, "Doctor, the devil is a busy man."[68]

Following the second defeat of the treaty, Wilson made a pathetic attempt to take his case to the people once more by trying to run for a third term. Since he could not even meet with the cabinet until April, a campaign was obviously out of the question, but Democrats who had not seen the president might have nominated him had Dr. Grayson not gone quietly behind the scenes to party leaders. Ultimately, the Democratic convention nominated Governor James M. Cox of Ohio on the forty-fourth ballot. William Gibbs McAdoo might have been a stronger candidate, but his father-in-law refused to endorse him.

During the campaign Wilson welcomed Cox and his running mate, Franklin D. Roosevelt, to the White House but seemed unable to grasp the likelihood of Democratic defeat. Josephus Daniels and Stockton Axson, who tried to prepare him for the coming disaster, could make no impression. The day after Republican Warren Harding was elected Axson came to the White House, expecting to find Wilson morbidly depressed, but instead the president was "as serene as in the moments of his own preceding victories." He assured Axson, "I have not lost faith in the American people. They have merely been temporarily deceived. They will realize their error in a little while."[69] Axson understood that his refusal to face reality was as much a symptom of his illness as the paralysis of his body.

On 4 March 1921 Wilson summoned the energy for his last official duty. Dressed in morning coat and gray trousers, he struggled to a car with President-elect Harding for the ride to the Capitol for his successor's inauguration. Unable to climb steps, he slipped in a side door and rode up to the President's Room in a freight elevator. There he signed the last bills passed by the expiring session of Congress and then, unable to walk to the reviewing stand for Harding's inauguration, quietly left. In the streets few people noticed his car drive away; they were watching Harding begin his inaugural address.

For the next three years Wilson lived in a house on S Street in Washington that had been presented to Edith by friends. He had hoped to build a house overlooking the Potomac, but there was not enough money, and the former president refused to capitalize on his office by publishing the memoirs or reissues of his books for which publishers asked. Briefly, he joined his last secretary of state, Bainbridge Colby, in a law practice, but he could not do the work, and more important, he rejected any case that involved the United States government, which of course was what the firm's clients wanted. After a year, realizing he was a drag on Colby, he withdrew from the firm.

At home in the S Street house the Wilsons lived quietly. When he was able, Wilson dictated answers to the letters that poured in and sometimes visited with a few old friends. In the evenings Edith read to him, or they watched a movie or went to a vaudeville performance. During the baseball season he sometimes was driven to Griffith Stadium, where his car was parked on the outfield grass so he could watch. As always, his favorite activity was motoring, and almost every day he went for long rides in the White House Pierce Arrow he had purchased from the government when he left office.

By the spring of 1922 Wilson seemed a little better. He received visits from a number of world leaders with whom he discussed the state of the world. In consultation with Brandeis and other Democrats he worked on drafting a liberal platform for the 1924 convention. He thought Harding "a fool of a President," but he was pleased when the administration convoked a disarmament conference in Washington.[70] With enormous labor, finding it almost impossible to concentrate, he tried to spell out for one last time his convictions about world affairs. Aided by Stockton Axson and Edith, to whom he sometimes dictated sentences in the middle of the night, he gradually pulled together a little article. "They kept after me to do this thing," he told Axson, "and I did it. I have done all I can. I don't want these people bothering me any more."[71] In August 1923 the article was published in the *Atlantic Monthly* under the title "The Road Away from Revolution."

Strangers welcomed the article as a sign of Wilson's recovery, but friends knew that, small as it was, it had been almost more than he could manage. Still, despite its brevity, it was a last eloquent plea for the sort of world Wilson had hoped the League of Nations would ensure, a world of orderly change. On one side, he warned, lay the perils of the Russian Revolution; on the other, more shocking to comfortable Americans of the 1920s, the threat of selfish capitalism. The road away from revolution must lead between the two dangers. It must lead toward a truly "Christian civilization" that would "include sympathy and helpfulness and a willingness to forego self-interest in order to promote the welfare, happiness, and contentment of others and of the community as a whole."[72]

By the autumn of 1923 Wilson and those around him realized that he was getting worse. Hoping to cheer him, Bernard Baruch's daughter Belle suggested he deliver an Armistice Day talk on the radio. Edith and Grayson doubted he could do it, but he insisted. On the evening of 10 November, despite a blinding headache, he stood before a microphone and struggled through his talk. Unable to read or to memorize it, he had to be prompted by Edith, but the talk was a kind of purge. The "memories of that happy triumph," he said, "are forever marred and embittered for us by the shameful fact that when the victory was won . . . , we turned our backs upon our associates and refused to bear any responsible part in the administration of peace . . . , and withdrew into a sullen and selfish isolation, which is deeply ignoble because manifestly cowardly and dishonorable." The nation could, however, still "retrieve the past" and "put self-interest away and once more formulate and act upon the highest ideals and purposes of international policy."[73] Thus in the end hope transcended bitterness.

Depressed and sure he had bungled the address, Wilson turned from the microphone and went to bed. Only the next day did he learn that some 3 million people had heard his words. Across S Street a large crowd of veterans gathered to applaud their commander in chief, and once again Wilson rose to the challenge. Going out onto the steps of the house he spoke a few words to the crowd, praising "the most ideal army that was ever thrown together," and then turned to go back in. But as a band began to play the hymn "How Firm a Foundation," he stopped and whispered to a friend to ask the crowd to be quiet. Then, in a louder, firmer voice than he had been able to summon for many months he said, "Just one word more; I cannot refrain from saying it.

I am not one of those that have the least anxiety about the triumph of the principles I have stood for. I have seen fools resist Providence before, and I have seen their destruction, as will come upon these again, utter destruction and contempt. That we shall prevail is as sure as that God reigns. Thank you."[74]

A few weeks later, on 28 December, the family celebrated Wilson's sixty-seventh birthday. Outside, when he went for his afternoon ride, he found a gift from his old friends, a black Rolls Royce with a thin, Princeton-orange stripe. He would have little time to enjoy it. In January he invited the members of the Democratic National Committee to the house and managed to shake hands with each, but he knew he was failing. When a visitor asked how he was, he quoted another president, "John Quincy Adams is all right, but the house he lives in is dilapidated, and it looks as if he would soon have to move out."[75]

On 28 January Wilson failed alarmingly, and Edith sent a telegram asking Dr. Grayson, who had left for a brief vacation, to come. He hurried back to find his patient holding on stubbornly. Grayson called in consultants, but as they were about to enter, Wilson looked up and whispered, "Be careful. Too many cooks spoil the broth." It was his last joke. His last words, according to Dr. Grayson, were the same as those with which he had started his political career in New Jersey fourteen years before: "I am ready."[76] He died at 11:15 on Sunday morning, 3 February 1924.

Opposite the house, on the other side of S Street, people had been gathering for three days and nights. Silently, they stood or knelt to pray in the February chill. Now, when Dr. Grayson appeared to read a bulletin that most could not hear and then wiped tears from his face, they understood. Three days later Wilson was buried in a small chapel of the new National Cathedral.

No man's life can be appraised in a sentence, his work summarized in a paragraph. Historians will argue about the nature and meaning of Wilson's achievements for many years, just as they will argue about the nature and meaning of his mistakes. The silent throng that stood on S Street that February morning as the church bells rang out in the city was not there because of any special achievement, however. They had come and stood and prayed because they knew that Woodrow Wilson was a rare and special statesman whose life was dedicated to the service of the people. His mission was incomplete, but he had done his best; others must go on. Confident that they would do so, he had expressed his faith and hope in moving words on the occasion of the signing of the tariff bill in 1913, and those words may well stand as his epitaph:

> So I feel tonight like a man who is lodging happily in the inn which lies half way along the journey and that in time, with a fresh impulse, we shall go the rest of the journey and sleep at the journey's end like men with a quiet conscience, knowing that we have served our fellow men and have, thereby, tried to serve God.[77]

CHRONOLOGY

28 December 1856	Thomas Woodrow Wilson born, Staunton, Virginia.
1858	Wilson family moves to Augusta, Georgia.
1870	Wilson family moves to Columbia, South Carolina.
1873–1874	Attends Davidson College.
1873	Wilson family moves to Wilmington, North Carolina.
1874–1875	Studies at home.
1875–1879	Attends the College of New Jersey at Princeton (later Princeton University); receives B.A. degree.
1879–December 1880	Attends University of Virginia Law School.
1881–1882	Completes study of law at home.
Summer 1882–Summer 1883	Practices law in Atlanta. Passes Georgia bar examination, October 1882.
April 1883	Meets Ellen Axson in Rome, Georgia.
14 September 1883	Engaged to Ellen Louise Axson.

1883–1885	Enrolled in the graduate program in history and political science at the Johns Hopkins University; Ph.D. 1886.
January 1885	*Congressional Government.*
24 June 1885	Marries Ellen Axson.
1885–1888	Teaches at Bryn Mawr College.
16 April 1886	Daughter Margaret Woodrow Wilson born.
28 August 1887	Daughter Jessie Woodrow Wilson born.
14 April 1888	Mother, Janet Woodrow Wilson, dies.
1888–1896	Guest lecturer at Johns Hopkins.
1888–1890	Teaches at Wesleyan University, Middletown, Connecticut.
16 October 1889	Daughter Eleanor Randolph Wilson born.
Autumn 1889	*The State: Elements of Historical and Practical Politics, A Sketch of Institutional History and Administration.*
1890–1902	Professor of jurisprudence and political economy at Princeton University.
1893	*Division and Reunion, 1829–1889.*
1896	*George Washington.*
ca. 27 May 1886	Possible cerebral stroke.
Summer 1896	First trip to Great Britain.
21 October 1896	Sesquicentennial address: "Princeton in the Nation's Service."
1898	Spanish-American War.
Summer 1899	Trip to Great Britain.
1902	Five-volume *History of the American People.*
9 June 1902	Elected president of Princeton.
21 January 1903	Father, Joseph Ruggles Wilson, dies.
May or June 1904	Partial paralysis of right arm.
December 1904–February 1905	Operation for intestinal hernia followed by phlebitis.
February 1906	George Harvey introduces Wilson to the

	Lotos Club as a possible presidential candidate.
28 May 1906	Possible stroke including temporary blindness in one eye.
July–August 1906	Trip to Great Britain.
January 1907	First trip to Bermuda.
November 1907	"Attack of neuritis" including temporary paralysis of right arm.
January 1908	Second trip to Bermuda.
Summer 1908	Trip to Great Britain.
1908	*Constitutional Government in the United States.*
1910–1913	Governor of New Jersey.
May 1911	William Bayard Hale, "Woodrow Wilson: Possible President," *World's Work.*
July 1911	Wilson campaign headquarters opens in New York City.
7 November 1911	New Jersey election restores Republican control of state legislature.
Autumn 1911	Meets Edward M. House.
2 July 1912	Democratic nominee for president.
5 November 1912	Elected president of the United States.
1 March 1913	Resigns as governor of New Jersey.
4 March 1913	Inaugurated as president.
3 October 1913	Signs Underwood Tariff.
25 November 1913	Jessie Wilson married to Frank Sayre.
23 December 1913	Signs Federal Reserve Act.
April–November 1914	Vera Cruz intervention.
7 May 1914	Eleanor Wilson married to William Gibbs McAdoo.
28 June 1914	Austrian Archduke Franz Ferdinand assassinated.
July–August 1914	World War I begins in Europe.
6 August 1914	Ellen Wilson dies.

26 September 1914	Signs Interstate Trade Commission Act.
15 October 1914	Signs Clayton Antitrust Act.
January 1915	Japanese deliver Twenty-One Demands to China.
4 February 1915	German announcement of "war zone" around British Isles in which submarine warfare will be conducted.
March 1915	Meets Edith Bolling Galt.
28 March 1915	American Leon C. Thrasher killed in submarine attack.
7 May 1915	*Lusitania* sunk, with the deaths of 1,201 passengers, including 128 Americans.
10 May 1915	"Too proud to fight" speech.
May 1915	Pan American Financial Conference.
July 1915–1941	American occupation of Haiti.
6 October 1915	Engagement to Edith Bolling Galt announced.
19 October 1915	De facto recognition of Mexican government.
4 November 1915	Calls for preparedness.
18 December 1915	Marries Edith Bolling Galt.
22 February 1916	House-Grey Memorandum signed.
9 March 1916	Pancho Villa raids Columbus, New Mexico.
15 March 1916–5 February 1917	Pershing expedition into Mexico.
24 March 1916	*Sussex* torpedoed.
4 May 1916	"*Sussex* Pledge."
May 1916–1924	American occupation of Dominican Republic.
16 August 1916	Council of National Defense created.
29 August 1916	Signs Jones Bill promising independence to Philippines.
1 September 1916	Signs Keating-Owen Child Labor Act.
7 September 1916	Signs Shipping Act creating Shipping Board and Emergency Fleet Corporation.

7 November 1916	Reelected president.
18 December 1916	Note asking belligerents to state peace terms.
6 January 1917	German Imperial Conference decides to begin unrestricted submarine warfare.
22 January 1917	"Peace without Victory" speech.
31 January 1917	German announcement of unrestricted submarine warfare.
3 February 1917	Diplomatic relations with Germany severed.
28 February 1917	Zimmermann Telegram published.
5 March 1917	Second inauguration.
12 March 1917	Russian Menshevik revolution.
2 April 1917	Requests declaration of war.
6 April 1917	War declared.
14 April 1917	Committee on Public Information created.
28 July 1917	War Industries Board created.
August 1917	Food and Fuel Administrations created.
September 1917	Inquiry established to plan for peace conference.
26 September 1917	De jure recognition of Mexican government.
2 November 1917	Lansing-Ishii Agreement.
November 1917	Bolshevik Revolution in Russia.
26 December 1917	Railroad Administration created and railroads nationalized.
8 January 1918	Fourteen Points address.
3 March 1918	Treaty of Brest-Litovsk signed between Germany and Soviet Union providing for separate peace.
20 March 1918	War Council created.
10 April 1918	Signs Webb-Pomerene Act.
16 May 1918	Signs Sedition Act.
20 May 1918	Signs Overman Act.

August 1918–1 April 1920	Siberian intervention.
5 November 1918	Congressional elections result in Republican control of Congress.
9 November 1918	German kaiser abdicates.
11 November 1918	Armistice ends World War I.
18 November 1918	Announces he will lead American delegation to Paris peace conference.
4 December 1918	Sails for Europe.
13 December 1918	Lands at Brest, France.
14 December 1918	Reception in Paris.
12 January 1919	First meeting of Council of Ten at Paris peace conference; first plenary session, 18 January.
14 February 1919	Presents draft of League of Nations charter to peace conference.
February–March 1919	In United States.
26 March 1919	Meeting with Congressional foreign affairs committees.
3 March 1919	Lodge's "Round Robin" indicates that more than one-third of senators oppose the treaty unless it is amended.
7 May 1919	Treaty given to Germans.
28 June 1919	Treaty of Versailles signed.
8 July 1919	Returns to United States.
10 July 1919	Treaty submitted to Senate.
19 August 1919	Meeting with Senate Foreign Relations Committee.
3–25 September	Speaking trip to West in support of treaty; trip abruptly canceled after stroke on 25 September.
2 October 1919	Paralytic stroke.
6 November 1919	Lodge's Fourteen Reservations proposed.
19 November 1919	Senate defeats treaty.
1919–1920	Red Scare.
15 January 1920	Prohibition (18th Amendment) becomes effective.

19 March 1920	Treaty defeated for second time.
26 August 1920	Woman suffrage (19th Amendment) becomes effective.
2 November 1920	Warren G. Harding elected president.
4 March 1921	Harding inaugurated.
August 1923	"The Road Away from Revolution" published in *Atlantic Monthly*.
10 November 1923	Armistice Day radio address.
3 February 1924	Dies at home on S Street, Washington.
6 February 1924	Burial in National Cathedral, Washington.

NOTES AND REFERENCES

1. YOUTH AND EDUCATION (1856–1886)

1. Janet Woodrow Wilson to Thomas Woodrow, 27 April 1857, in *The Papers of Woodrow Wilson* [hereafter PWW], ed. Arthur S. Link et al., vol. 1, *1856–1880* (Princeton, N.J.: Princeton University Press, 1966), 7.

2. Quoted in John M. Mulder, *Woodrow Wilson: The Years of Preparation* (Princeton, N.J.: Princeton University Press, 1978), 29.

3. Wilson to Ellen Axson, 19 April 1888, PWW, vol. 5, *1885–1888* (1968), 719.

4. Wilson to Ellen Axson, 12 October 1884, PWW, vol. 3, *1884–1885* (1967), 349.

5. Stockton Axson, Memoir, "Woodrow Wilson and His Father"; in the possession of Professor Arthur S. Link at The Papers of Woodrow Wilson, Princeton University and used with his permission.

6. Joseph Ruggles Wilson to Wilson, 5 June 1880, PWW, 1:658.

7. "A Christian Statesman," Wilmington *North Carolina Presbyterian*, 6 September 1876, PWW, 1:189.

8. Joseph Ruggles Wilson to Wilson, 26 July 1877, PWW, 1:287.

9. Wilson to Robert Bridges, 1 January 1881, PWW, vol. 2, *1881–1884* (1967), 10.

10. Wilson to Ellen Axson, 22 April 1884, PWW, 3:144.

11. Quoted in Arthur S. Link, *Wilson: The Road to the White House* (Princeton, N.J.: Princeton University Press, 1947), 3.

12. "Stray Thoughts from the South," unpub. article, ca. 22 February 1881, PWW, 2:29.

13. Marginal note on a letter to the editor in Philadelphia *American*, 5 February 1881, PWW, 2:19; "Stray Thoughts," 27, 28.

14. Address, Worcester, Mass., 30 January 1902, PWW, vol. 12, *1900–1902* (1972), 261.

15. Link, *Wilson: Road*, 10.

16. From "Southern Presbyterian," 6 November 1873, PWW, 1:33.

17. Janet Woodrow Wilson to Wilson, 20 May 1874, PWW, 1:50.

18. "The Personal Factor in Education," *Youth's Companion*, 12 September 1907, PWW, vol. 17, *1907–1908* (1974), 330.

19. Wilson to Ellen Axson, 30 October 1883, PWW, 2:500.

20. Wilson to Charles A. Talcott, 31 December 1879, PWW, 1:591.

21. Wilson to Robert Bridges, 24 May 1881, PWW, 2:68.

22. Wilson to Richard Heath Dabney, 11 May 1883, PWW, 2:350; Wilson to Robert Bridges, 28 October 1882, PWW, 2:148.

23. Wilson to Robert Bridges, 24 February 1881, PWW, 2:32.

24. Joseph Ruggles Wilson to Wilson, 13 February 1883, PWW, 2:303–4.

25. Wilson to Richard Heath Dabney, 11 May 1883, PWW, 2:351.

26. Wilson to Ellen Axson, 30 October 1883, PWW, 2:501.

27. Wilson to Ellen Axson, 11 October 1883, PWW, 2:468.

28. Wilson to Ellen Axson, 16 March 1884, PWW, 3:86.

29. Wilson to Ellen Axson, 18 September 1883, PWW, 2:428.

30. Wilson to Ellen Axson, 15 November 1883, PWW, 2:531.

31. Wilson to Robert Bridges, 12 October 1883, PWW, 2:472.

32. Wilson to Ellen Axson, 16 October 1883, PWW, 2:479–80.

33. Wilson to Richard Heath Dabney, 17 February 1884, PWW, 3:26.

34. From the minutes of the Seminary of Historical and Political Science, 9 May 1884, PWW, 3:172.

35. Wilson to Ellen Axson, 15 November 1883, PWW, 2:531.

36. Wilson to Ellen Axson, 12 February 1884, PWW, 3:19.

37. Quoted in Link, *Wilson: Road*, 15.

2. BUILDING AN ACADEMIC CAREER (1885–1902)

1. Ellen Axson to Wilson, 7 July 1884, 3:234–36.

2. Ellen Axson to Wilson, 28 March 1885, PWW, vol. 4, *1885* (1968), 428.

3. Wilson to Ellen Axson, 27, 30 November 1884, PWW, 3:490, 499.

4. Wilson to Ellen Axson, 6 December 1884, PWW, 3:517–18.

5. Wilson to Ellen Wilson, 12 May 1886, PWW, 5:216.

6. Wilson to Ellen Wilson, 28 October 1885, 25 January 1887, PWW, 5:38, 437.

7. Wilson, Journal, 20 October 1887, PWW, 5:619.

8. Wilson to Ellen Axson, 24 February 1885, PWW, 4:287.

9. Wilson to Charles Andrew Talcott, 14 November 1886, PWW, 5:389.

10. Wilson to Richard Heath Dabney, 16 May 1886, PWW, 5:726.

11. Wilson to Ellen Wilson, 19 April 1888, PWW, 5:719.

12. Henry Wilkinson Bragdon, *Woodrow Wilson: The Academic Years* (Cambridge, Mass.: Belknap Press, 1967), 164.

13. Ibid., 168.

14. Wilson to Ellen Wilson, 9 March 1889, PWW, vol. 6, *1888–1890* (1969), 139.

15. *The State*, PWW, 6:304, 305–8, 311.

16. *Division and Reunion, 1829–1889* (New York: Longmans, Green & Co., 1894), 299.

17. Attributed to Wilson by Bragdon, *Woodrow Wilson*, 190.

18. "Mere Literature," *Atlantic Monthly*, December 1893, PWW, vol. 8, *1892–1894* (1970), 246, 249, 250; Wilson to Caleb Thomas Winchester, 29 May 1893, PWW, 8:220.

19. "The Making of the Nation," *Atlantic Monthly*, July 1897, PWW, vol. 10, *1896–1898* (1971), 222.

20. Address on Robert E. Lee, University of North Carolina, 19 January 1909, PWW, vol. 18, *1908–1909* (1974), 639.

21. Wilson to Ellen Wilson, 4 February 1898, PWW, 10:375.

22. *A History of the American People*, 5 vols. (New York: Harper & Brothers, 1902), 5:267.

23. "The Making of the Nation," PWW, 10:233.

24. "On the Study of Politics, *New Princeton Review* 3 (March 1887), PWW, 5:395; *A History of the American People*, 5:300.

25. Preface to *Congressional Government* (Boston: Houghton Mifflin, 1900), xi.

26. Memorandum "What Ought We To Do," ca. 1 August 1898, PWW, 10:576.

27. Quoted in Link, *Wilson: Road*, 27.

28. "Democracy and Efficiency," *Atlantic Monthly*, March 1901, PWW, 12:19.

29. Quoted in Link, *Wilson: Road*, 28.

30. Address, Washington Association of New Jersey, 23 February 1903, PWW, vol. 14, *1902–1903* (1972), 366–67.

31. Quoted in Edwin A. Weinstein, *Woodrow Wilson: A Medical and Psychological Biography* (Princeton, N.J.: Princeton University Press, 1981), 149.

32. "Princeton in the Nation's Service," 21 October 1896, PWW, 10:30.

33. Ibid., 19, 20.

34. Wilson to Ellen Wilson, 6 August 1902, PWW, 14:57.

3. PRESIDENT OF PRINCETON (1902–1910)

1. Remarks at a Princeton smoker, Washington, 3 March 1913, PWW, vol. 27, *1913* (1978), 147.

2. Address, Saint Paul, 25 May 1911, PWW, vol. 23, *1911–1912* (1977), 88.

3. Lawrence R. Veysey, "The Academic Mind of Woodrow Wilson," *Mississippi Valley Historical Review* 49 (March 1963):623.

4. Quoted in ibid., 622.

5. "Princeton for the Nation's Service," 25 October 1902, PWW, 14:177.

6. Axson, Memoir, "Woodrow Wilson's Educational Career."

7. Ellen Wilson to Mary Eloise Hoyt, 15 December 1902, PWW, 14:294.

8. Address, Boston, 3 January 1903, PWW, 14:317.

9. Notes for address, Chicago, 26 November 1902, PWW, 14:223.

10. Report to the Board of Trustees, 8 December 1904, PWW, vol. 15, *1903–1905* (1973), 561–62.

11. Ibid., 566.

12. News report of address, Chicago, 29 November 1902, PWW, 14:227.

13. Wilson to Hamilton Holt, 7 June 1905, PWW, vol. 16, *1905–1907* (1975), 111.

14. Robert K. Root, "Wilson and the Preceptors," in *Woodrow Wilson: Some Princeton Memories,* ed. William Starr Myers (Princeton, N.J.: Princeton University Press, 1946), 14–15.

15. Axson, Memoir, "Woodrow Wilson's Educational Career"; Report of the Trustees' Curriculum Committee, ca. 11 June 1906, PWW, 16:421.

16. Wilson to Walter Hines Page, 26 September 1913, PWW, vol. 28, *1913* (1978), 328.

17. Frances Wright Saunders, *Ellen Axson Wilson: First Lady between Two Worlds* (Chapel Hill: University of North Carolina Press, 1985), 162.

18. Ellen Wilson to Mary Eloise Hoyt, 12 June 1906, PWW, 16:423.

19. Ibid.

20. Ellen Wilson to Florence Stevens Hoyt, 27 June 1906, PWW, 16:430.

21. Wilson to Ellen Wilson, 2 September 1906, PWW, 16:445.

22. Address, Washington Association of New Jersey, 23 February 1903, PWW, 14:375.

23. Quoted in Ray Stannard Baker, *Woodrow Wilson: Life and Letters,* vol. 1, *Princeton, 1890–1910* (Garden City, N.Y.: Doubleday, Page & Co., 1927), 220.

24. Report to trustees, 6 June 1907, PWW, 17:185–86.

25. Saunders, *Ellen Axson Wilson,* 182.

26. Henry B. Thompson to Cleveland H. Dodge, 10 September 1907, PWW, 17:379.

27. Winthrop More Daniels to John G. Hibben, 9 August 1907, PWW, 17:342–43.

28. Axson, Memoir, "Woodrow Wilson's Educational Career."

29. Wilson to Cleveland H. Dodge, 3 July 1907, PWW, 17:245.

30. Moses Pyne to Andrew Clerk Imbrie, 23 October 1907, PWW, 17:453–54.

31. Ibid., 453.

32. Wilson to Joseph McCarter Bowyer, 23 May 1908, PWW, 18:306.

33. Andrew F. West to Wilson, 29 November 1902, PWW, 14:246.

34. Andrew West, *The Proposed Graduate College of Princeton University* (1903), PWW, 14:361, n. 1. (order of phrases slightly altered).

35. Preface to West, *Graduate College,* 17 February 1903, PWW, 14:361.

36. Wilson, Resolution of Board of Trustees, ca. 20 October 1906, PWW, 16:467.

37. Andrew F. West to the Board of Trustees' Committee on the Graduate School, 13 May 1907, PWW, 16:143.

38. Wilson to the Board of Trustees' Committee on the Graduate School, ca. 30 May 1907, PWW, 16:167–68.

39. Moses Pyne to Wilson, 6 December 1907, PWW, 16:549–50.

40. Wilson to Ellen Wilson, 26 January 1908, PWW, vol. 17, *1907–1908* (1974), 607–8.

41. Ibid., 612–13.

42. Ca. 1 February 1908, PWW, 17:611.

43. Wilson to Ellen Wilson, 29 June, 1, 2, 10, 13 July 1908, PWW, 18:345, 349, 350, 357, 363.

44. Wilson to Ellen Wilson, 20 July 1908, PWW, 18:372.

45. Wilson to Mary Peck, 22 January 1911, PWW, vol. 22, *1910–1911* (1976), 364.

46. Mary Peck to Wilson, ca. 11 October 1915, PWW, vol. 35, *Oct. 1, 1915–Jan. 27, 1916* (1980), 53.

47. Wilson to Mary Peck, 24 October 1909, PWW, vol. 19, *1909–1910* (1975), 443.

48. Moses Pyne to Joseph Bernard O'Shea, 18 December 1909, PWW, 19:608–9.

49. Ibid., 620.

50. Wilson to Moses Pyne, 25 December 1909, PWW, 19:630.

51. Wilson to Cleveland Dodge, 27 December 1909, PWW, 19:631.

52. Editorial Note, "Wilson at the Meeting of the Board of Trustees of January 13, 1910," PWW, vol. 20, *1910* (1975), 8.

53. Ellen Wilson to Wilson, 28 February 1910, PWW, 20:189.

54. *Daily Princetonian*, 18 March 1910, PWW, 20:255.

55. Ibid., 522.

4. GOVERNOR OF NEW JERSEY (1910–1913)

1. Quoted in Arthur S. Link, "Woodrow Wilson in New Jersey," in *The Higher Realism of Woodrow Wilson and Other Essays* (Nashville, Tenn.: Vanderbilt University Press, 1971), 47.

2. Founder's Day Address, Vassar College, 3 May 1902; Memorandum on Leadership, 5 May 1902, PWW, 12:362, 365 (emphasis added).

3. Address, Virginia Society of New York, 30 November 1904, PWW, 15:547.

4. Wilson to James Calvin Hemphill, 26 January 1906, PWW, 16:288.

5. Wilson to Adrian Joline, 29 April 1907, PWW, 17:124.

6. Address, Virginia Society of New York, 30 November 1904, PWW, 15:548.

7. *Daily Princetonian*, 12 January 1906, PWW, 16:280.

8. Address on Thomas Jefferson, 13 April 1906, PWW, 16:361.

9. Ibid.

10. Address, Lotos Club, New York, 3 February 1906, PWW, 16:300.

11. Axson, Memoir, "Governorship of New Jersey."

12. Address, Chicago, 12 February 1909, PWW, 19:41.

13. Wilson to Mary Peck, 18 July 1909, PWW, 19:312.

14. Address, Princeton Alumni, Pittsburgh, 17 April 1910, PWW, 20:365.

15. David W. Hirst, *Woodrow Wilson, Reform Governor: A Documentary Narrative* (Princeton, N.J.: Van Nostrand, 1965), 8–9.

16. Axson, Memoir, "Woodrow Wilson's Educational Career."

17. Wilson to Cyrus Hall McCormick, 14 July 1910, PWW, 20:577.

18. Wilson to David Benton Jones, 27 June 1910, PWW, 20:543.

19. Axson, Memoir, "Governorship of New Jersey."

20. Quoted in William Bayard Hale, *Woodrow Wilson: The Story of His Life* (Garden City, N.Y.: Doubleday, Page & Co., 1912), 168–69.

21. *Newark Evening News*, 15 July 1910, PWW, 20:581.

22. George B. D. Harvey to Wilson, 9 September 1910, PWW, vol. 21, *1910* (1976), 88.

23. Quoted in Link, *Wilson: Road*, 166–67.

24. Axson, Memoir, "Governorship of New Jersey."

25. Acceptance Speech, Democratic State Convention, Trenton, N.J.,

15 September 1910, PWW, 21:91.

26. Address, Elizabeth, N.J., 28 October 1910, PWW, 21:461.

27. Ibid., 338–47.

28. Wilson to George L. Record, 24 October 1910, PWW, 21:411.

29. Hirst, *Woodrow Wilson*, 106.

30. George Harvey to Wilson, 25 October 1910; Joseph Patrick Tumulty and Mark A. Sullivan to Wilson, 25 October 1910, PWW, 21:433.

31. Address, Hackensack, N.J., 27 October 1910, PWW, 21:446.

32. Address, Passaic, N.J., 1 November 1910, PWW, 21:501.

33. Frederick Jackson Turner, telegram to Wilson, 9 November 1910, PWW, 21:602.

34. Quoted in Saunders, *Ellen Axson Wilson*, 212.

35. *Trenton Evening Times*, 26 August 1911, PWW, 23:301.

36. Wilson to George B. D. Harvey, 15 November 1910, PWW, 22:46.

37. Quoted in Hirst, *Woodrow Wilson*, 130.

38. *Newark Evening News*, 9 December 1910, PWW, 22:166.

39. Wilson to Mary Peck, 16 December 1910, PWW, 22:204.

40. Wilson to Mary Peck, 22 January 1911, PWW, 22:363.

41. Quoted in Link, *Wilson: Road*, 234.

42. *Philadelphia Record*, 26 January 1911, PWW, 22:367.

43. Address, New Jersey Legislature, Trenton, N.J., 17 January 1911, PWW, 22:350, 353, 354. (The last phrases are slightly rearranged in order.)

44. *Newark Evening News*, 15 February 1911, PWW, 22:432.

45. Address, West Hudson Board of Trade, Harrison, N.J., 28 February 1911, PWW, 22:459.

46. Address, Hoboken Board of Trade, 2 March 1911, PWW, 22:471–72.

47. *Trenton Evening Times*, 7 March 1911, PWW, 22:482.

48. Quoted in Link, *Wilson: Road*, 250.

49. *Trenton Evening News*, 21 March 1911; Wilson to Mary Peck, 26 March 1911, PWW, 22:512–13, 518.

50. Ibid., 518.

51. Quoted in Link, *Wilson: Road*, 257.

52. Quoted in ibid., 326–27.

53. PWW, 23:235 n. 1.

54. Address, Trenton, N.J., 9 October 1911, PWW, 23:426.

55. Wilson to Charles Henry Grasty, 10 November 1911, PWW, 23:546–47.

56. *New York Times*, 24 December 1911, PWW, 23:629.

57. Address, New Jersey Legislature, Trenton, N.J., 9 January 1912, PWW, vol. 24, *1912* (1977), 23, 20, 24, 21.

58. Wilson to Mary Peck, 1 April 1912, PWW, 24:271.

59. Trenton *True American*, 12 April 1912, PWW, 24:325.

60. Address, New Jersey Legislature, Trenton, N.J., 13 January 1913, PWW, 27:46.

61. *Newark Evening News*, 20 February 1913, PWW, 27:120.

62. *Newark Evening News*, 15 February 1911, PWW, 22:432.

5. PRESIDENTIAL CANDIDATE (1912)

1. Wilson to Richard Heath Dabney, 13 May 1912, PWW, 24:398.

2. Wilson to Mary Peck, 9 June 1912, PWW, 24:466.

3. Quoted in Link, *Wilson: Road*, 432.

4. Wilson to William Jennings Bryan, 22 June 1912, PWW, 24:493.

5. William Gibbs McAdoo, *Crowded Years* (Boston: Houghton Mifflin Co., 1931), 141.

6. Quoted in Link, *Wilson: Road*, 443.

7. Ellen Wilson, quoted in *New York Times*, 3 July 1912, PWW, 24:523.

8. McAdoo, *Crowded Years*, 155.

9. Quoted in Link, *Wilson: Road*, 462.

10. Marshall, *Recollection of Thomas R. Marshall, Vice-President and Hoosier Philosopher: A Hoosier Salad* (Indianapolis: Bobbs-Merrill Co., 1925), 233.

11. McAdoo, *Crowded Years*, 159, 158.

12. *New York Times*, 3 July 1912, PWW, 24:522.

13. Quoted in Saunders, *Ellen Axson Wilson*, 225, 226.

14. Wilson to Mary Hulbert, 25 August 1912, PWW, vol. 25, *1912* (1978), 56. (The order of the phrases has been changed. Mary dropped the name Peck when her divorce became final in July 1912.)

15. Quoted in Link, *Wilson: Road*, 474–75.

16. Acceptance Speech, Sea Girt, N.J., 7 August 1912, PWW, 25:8.

17. Ibid., 11, 13.

18. David Benton Jones to Wilson, 13 July 1912, PWW, 24:549.

19. Benjamin J. Klebaner, "Potential Competition and the American Antitrust Legislation of 1914," *Business History Review* 38 (Summer 1964):163–85.

20. Address, Buffalo, N.Y., 2 September 1912, PWW, 25:75.

21. *New York Times*, 29 August 1912, PWW, 25:58.

22. Address, Buffalo, N.Y., 2 September 1912, PWW, 25:73.

23. Ibid., 77.

24. Ibid., 78.

25. Ibid.

26. Address, New York Press Club, 9 September 1912, PWW, 25:124.

27. Address, San Francisco, 14 September 1912, *The Works of Theodore*

Roosevelt, ed. Herman Hagedorn, National ed. 20 vols. (New York: Charles Scribner's Sons, 1926), 17:310.

28. Address, Scranton, Pa., 23 September 1912, PWW, 25:224–25.

29. Address, Indianapolis, 3 October 1912, 25:327.

30. Message to Democratic Rallies, 2 November 1912, PWW, 25:501–2.

31. Address, West Chester, Pa., 28 October 1912, PWW, 25:463–64. (The order of phrases has been changed.)

32. Address, Long Branch, N.J., 2 November 1912, PWW, 25:505.

33. Address, West Chester, Pa., 28 October 1912, PWW, 25:466.

34. Address, Hartford, Conn., 25 September, 1912, PWW, 25:235.

35. Wilson to Louis D. Brandeis, 27 September 1912, PWW 25:272.

36. Address, Wilmington, Del., 17 October 1912, PWW, 25:427.

37. Message to Democratic Rallies, 2 November 1912; address, Kokomo, Ind., 4 October 1912, PWW, 25:502, 330.

38. Address, Peru, Ind., 4 October 1912, PWW, 25:333.

39. *A History of the American People,* 5:212–13.

40. Address, Carnegie Hall, New York, 19 October 1912; Wilson to Cyrus Adler, 21 October 1912, PWW, 25:441, 450.

41. Wilson to Oswald Garrison Villard, 23 August 1912, PWW, 25:53.

42. Address, Burlington, N.J., 30 October 1912, PWW, 25:490.

43. Axson, Memoir, "Observations Made While Examining Proof of Ray Stannard Baker's Book."

44. Axson, Memoir, "A Note on Mrs. Wilson's Influence on Her Husband's Tastes and Ideas."

45. Quoted in John Milton Cooper, Jr., *The Warrior and the Priest: Woodrow Wilson and Theodore Roosevelt* (Cambridge, Mass.: Harvard University Press, Belknap Press, 1983), 200.

46. Address, Princeton, N.J., 5 November 1912, PWW, 25:520–21.

6. ORGANIZING THE ADMINISTRATION (1913)

1. Edward M. House, Diary, 25 September 1912, PWW, 25:234.

2. House, Diary, 1 April 1913, PWW, 27:253.

3. Quoted in Link, *Wilson: The New Freedom* (Princeton, N.J.: Princeton University Press, 1965), 20.

4. House, Diary, 8 January 1913, PWW, 27:23.

5. Address, New York Southern Society, 17 December 1912, PWW, 25:602.

6. Ibid., 598.

7. Address, Commercial Club of Chicago, 11 January 1913, PWW, 27:31, 33, 34.

8. Ibid., 36.

9. Inaugural address, 4 March 1913, PWW, 27:151 (order of phrases changed).

10. House, Diary, 26 February 1913, quoted in Link, *Wilson: New Freedom*, 27.

11. House, Diary, 8 January 1913, PWW, 27:20.

12. H. Parker Willis to Carter Glass, 31 December 1912, PWW, 25:650.

13. *Newark Evening News*, 28 December 1912, PWW, 25:641 n. 1.

14. Address, Princeton, 1 March 1913, PWW, 27:143.

15. Wilson to Mary Hulbert, 2 March 1913, PWW, 27:146.

16. Quoted in Saunders, *Ellen Axson Wilson*, 233.

17. Joel Williamson, *The Crucible of Race: Black-White Relations in the American South since Emancipation* (New York: Oxford University Press, 1984), 368.

18. Wilson to Howard Allen Bridgman, 8 September 1913, PWW, 28:265.

19. Quoted in Williamson, *The Crucible of Race*, 381.

20. Transcript of meeting, 12 November 1914, PWW, vol. 31, *Sept. 6–December 31, 1914* (1979), 302.

21. J. Daniels to F. D. Roosevelt, 10 June 1933, PWW, 31:309 n. 2.

22. PWW, vol. 32, *Jan. 1–April 16, 1915* (1980), 267 n. 1.

23. E.g., Williamson, *The Crucible of Race*, 392.

24. House, Diary, 28 September 1914, in *The Intimate Papers of Colonel House*, ed. Charles Seymour, 4 vols. (Boston: Houghton Mifflin Co., 1926–1928), 1:121.

7. DOMESTIC REFORM (1913–1916)

1. Enclosed in John Reed to Joseph Patrick Tumulty, 30 June 1914, PWW, vol. 30, *May 6–Sept. 5, 1914* (1979), 232, 233.

2. Marshall E. Dimock, "Woodrow Wilson as Legislative Leader," *Journal of Politics* 19 (February 1957):12.

3. House, Diary, 14 November 1914, PWW, 31:319.

4. House, Diary, 14 February 1913, PWW, 27:113.

5. Cooper, *The Warrior and the Priest*, 229.

6. Address, U.S. Congress, 8 April 1913, PWW, 27:270, 271.

7. *New York World*, 10 April 1913, PWW, 27:278, 279.

8. Ibid., 472, 473.

9. *New York Times*, 27 May 1913, quoted in Link, *Wilson: New Freedom*, 187.

10. Press conference, 9 June 1913, PWW, 27:504.

11. PWW, 28:267.

12. 31 May 1913, quoted in Frank Burdick, "Woodrow Wilson and the Underwood Tariff," *Mid-America* 50 (October 1968):280.

13. 9 September 1913, PWW, 28:267.

14. 3 October 1913, PWW, 28:352.

15. Wilson to Mary Hulbert, 22 June 1913, PWW, 27:556.

16. Address, Commercial Club of Chicago, 11 January 1913, PWW, 27:33.

17. William Jennings Bryan and Mary Baird Bryan, *The Memoirs of William Jennings Bryan* (Chicago: John C. Winston Co., 1925), 370.

18. New York *Sun*, 21 June 1913, quoted in Link, *Wilson: New Freedom*, 216.

19. William Jennings Bryan to Carter Glass, 22 August 1913, quoted in Carter Glass, *An Adventure in Constructive Finance* (Garden City, N.Y.: Doubleday, Page & Co., 1927), 139.

20. Glass, *An Adventure*, 167.

21. PWW, vol. 29, *Dec. 2, 1913–May 5, 1914* (1979), 64, 65.

22. Address, Columbus, 20 September 1912, PWW, 25:203; Remarks upon signing the Federal Reserve Bill, 23 December 1913, PWW, 29:65.

23. Stephen B. Wood, *Constitutional Politics in the Progressive Era: Child Labor and the Law* (Chicago: University of Chicago Press, 1968), 27.

24. Wilson to Joseph Patrick Tumulty, 24 January 1914, PWW, 29:170.

25. A. J. McKelway to Wilson, 17 July 1916, PWW, vol. 37, *May 9–August 7, 1916* (1981), 430.

26. Address, U.S. Congress, 2 December 1913, PWW, 29:7.

27. Address, U.S. Congress, 20 January 1914, PWW, 29:154.

28. Ibid., 155.

29. Ibid., 157.

30. Daniel Davenport in the *Springfield Republican*, 11 October 1914, quoted in Link, *Wilson: New Freedom*, 433.

31. Wilson to Sen. Charles A. Culberson, 30 July 1914, PWW, 30:320.

32. House, Diary, 2 October 1914, PWW, 31:122.

33. House, Diary, 28 September 1914, PWW, 31:94.

34. James MacGregor Burns, *Presidential Government: The Crucible of Leadership* (Boston: Houghton Mifflin Co., 1966), 198.

35. Ibid., 201–2. (The order of phrases has been reversed.)

36. Arthur S. Link, *Wilson: Campaigns for Progressivism and Peace, 1916–1917* (Princeton, N.J.: Princeton University Press, 1965), 124.

8. LATIN AMERICAN AND ASIAN POLICY (1913–1920)

1. Message to Democratic Rallies, 2 November 1912, PWW, 25:502–3.

2. Address, Mary Baldwin Seminary, Staunton, Va., 28 December 1912, PWW, 25:629.

3. Quoted, Link, *Wilson: Road*, 27.

4. Address, Cincinnati, 26 October 1916, PWW, vol. 38, *Aug. 7–Nov. 19, 1916* (1982), 539.

5. Josephus Daniels, Diary, 11 March 1913, PWW, 27:169; Press release, 12 March 1913, PWW, 27:172.

6. Address, Commercial Club of Omaha, 5 October 1912, PWW, 25:341.

7. Address, Mobile, Ala., 27 October 1913, PWW, 28:450; Statement on Latin American policy, 12 March 1913, PWW, 27:172.

8. Address, Mobile, 27 October 1913, PWW, 28:451; House, Diary, 16 December 1914, PWW, 31:469.

9. Quoted in Frederick B. Pike, *Chile and the United States, 1880–1962: The Emergence of Chile's Social Crisis and the Challenge to United States Diplomacy* (Notre Dame, Ind.: University of Notre Dame Press, 1963), 144–45; Treaty draft, 16 December 1914, PWW, 31:471.

10. Wilson to Mary Peck, 28 February 1912, PWW, 24:218.

11. Statement, 12 March 1913, PWW, 27:172. (The order of phrases is reversed.)

12. Sir Cecil Spring Rice to Sir Edward Grey, 7 February 1914, PWW, 29:229; 6 February 1914, PWW, 29:228; 7 February 1914, PWW, 29:230.

13. Samuel G. Blythe, "Mexico: The Record of a Conversation with President Wilson," *Saturday Evening Post*, 23 May 1914, PWW, 29:521.

14. Wilson to William Jennings Bryan, 2 June 1915, PWW, vol. 33, *Apr. 17–July 21, 1915* (1980), 308.

15. Venustiano Carranza to Eliseo Arredondo, 23 April 1915, quoted in Mark T. Gilderhus, *Diplomacy and Revolution: U.S.-Mexican Relations under Wilson and Carranza* (Tucson: University of Arizona Press, 1977), 20.

16. Thomas Beaumont Hohler, Memorandum, 21 October 1915, PWW, 35:98.

17. Pancho Villa to Emiliano Zapata, 8 January 1916, quoted in Gilderhus, *Diplomacy and Revolution*, 34.

18. Robert Lansing, Memorandum, 9 March 1916, quoted in Gilderhus, *Diplomacy and Revolution*, 35.

19. Wilson to Edward M. House, 22 June 1916, PWW, vol. 37, *May 9–Aug. 7, 1916* (1981), 281.

20. Address, New York Press Club, 30 June 1916, PWW, 37:333, 333 n. 2.

21. Ambassador Page sent a paraphrase of the telegram to the State Department on 24 February 1917, 1:00 P.M., U.S. Department of State, *Papers Relating to the Foreign Relations of the United States, 1917, Supplement 1: The World War* (Washington: Government Printing Office, 1931), 147.

22. Chandler Anderson, Diary, 10 March, 8 March 1917, PWW, vol. 41, *Jan. 24–Apr. 6, 1917* (1983), 386, 365.

23. Anderson, Diary, 23 July 1917, quoted in Gilderhus, *Diplomacy and Revolution*, 70.

24. Robert Lansing to Henry P. Fletcher, 19 March 1918; Wilson, Address, Mexican newspaper editors, U.S. Department of State, *Papers Relating to Foreign Relations . . . 1918* (Washington: Government Printing Office, 1930), 706, 577; Gordon Auchincloss, Diary, 9 August 1918, quoted in Gilderhus, *Diplomacy and Revolution*, 85.

25. Edith Bolling Wilson, *My Memoir* (Indianapolis: Bobbs-Merrill Co., 1938), 299.

26. Richard L. Metcalfe, comp., *The Real Bryan, Being Extracts from the Speeches and Writings of 'A Well-Rounded Man'* (Des Moines, Ia.: Personal Help Publishing Co., 1908), 248–49.

27. Bryan to Wilson, 16 August 1913, PWW, 28:177.

28. Wilson to Bryan, 20 March 1914, PWW, 29:360.

29. Article 6 of the treaty draft, 16 June 1913, PWW, 27:529.

30. Wilson to Bryan, 19 June 1913, PWW, 27:552.

31. Bryan to Wilson, 27 March 1915; Wilson to Bryan, 31 March 1915, PWW, 32:440, 458.

32. Ibid.

33. Wilson to Robert Lansing, 4 August 1915, PWW, vol. 34, *July 21– Sept. 30, 1915* (1980), 78.

34. Bryan to various Dominican leaders, drafted 27 July 1914, sent 10 August 1914, PWW, 30:308–9.

35. Bryan to James M. Sullivan, 12 January 1915, U.S. Department of State, *Papers Relating to Foreign Relations . . . 1915* (Washington: Government Printing Office, 1924), 279.

36. Wilson to Robert Lansing, 26 November 1916, PWW, vol. 40, *Nov. 20, 1916–Jan. 23, 1917* (1982), 81.

37. Jerry Israel, *Progressivism and the Open Door: America and China, 1905–1921* (Pittsburgh: University of Pittsburgh Press, 1971), 121.

38. Paul S. Reinsch, *An American Diplomat in China* (Garden City, N.Y.: Doubleday, Page & Co., 1922), 63.

39. Press release, 18 March 1913, PWW, 27:193; Josephus Daniels, Diary, 12 March 1913, PWW, 27:175.

40. David F. Houston, *Eight Years with Wilson's Cabinet, 1913 to 1920, with a Personal Estimate of the President*, 2 vols. (Garden City, N.Y.: Doubleday, Page & Co., 1926), 1:49.

41. Press conference, 14 April 1913, PWW, 27:304.

42. U.S. Department of State, *Papers Relating to Foreign Relations . . . 1913* (Washington: Government Printing Office, 1920), 629.

43. Daniels, Diary, 16 May 1913, PWW, 27:445.

44. Bryan, *Memoirs*, 367.

45. "Democracy and Efficiency," *Atlantic Monthly*, March 1901, PWW,

12:18; To an unknown person, 15 August 1911, PWW, 23:267.

46. Quoted in Roy Watson Curry, *Woodrow Wilson and Far Eastern Policy, 1913–1921* (New York: Bookman Associates, 1957), 84.

47. Reinsch, *American Diplomat*, 135.

48. Viscount Grey of Fallodon, *Twenty-Five Years, 1892–1916*, 2 vols. (New York: Frederick A. Stokes Co., 1925), 2:104.

49. U.S. Department of State, *Papers Relating to Foreign Relations . . . 1914, Supplement* (Washington: Government Printing Office, 1928), 190.

50. State Department, *Foreign Relations . . . 1915*, 108.

51. Wilson to Bryan, 24 March 1915, PWW, 32:426.

52. E. T. Williams to Bryan, 13 April 1915, quoted in Arthur S. Link, *Wilson: The Struggle for Neutrality, 1914–1915* (Princeton: Princeton University Press, 1960), 291; Wilson to Bryan, 14 April 1915, PWW, 32:520–21.

53. Wilson to Bryan, 16 April 1915, PWW, 32:531.

54. Wilson to Bryan, 10 May 1915, PWW, 33:140.

55. State Department, *Foreign Relations . . . 1915*, 146.

56. Wilson to Robert Lansing, 21 June 1918, PWW, vol. 48, *May 13–July 17, 1918* (1985), 382.

57. Robert Lansing, Memorandum for Viscount Ishii, 6 July 1917, PWW, vol. 43, *June 25–Aug. 30, 1917* (1983), 82.

58. U.S. Department of State, *Papers Relating to Foreign Relations . . . 1917* (Washington: Government Printing Office, 1926), 265.

59. Reinsch to Lansing, 4 November 1917, PWW, vol. 44, *Aug. 21–Nov. 10, 1917* (1983), 510.

60. Wilson to Lansing, 7 November 1917; Lansing to Reinsch, 5 November 1917, 4:00 P.M., PWW, 44:530, 531.

61. Quoted in Betty Miller Unterberger, "Woodrow Wilson and the Russian Revolution," in *Woodrow Wilson and a Revolutionary World*, ed. Arthur S. Link (Chapel Hill: University of North Carolina Press, 1982), 51.

62. Fourteen Points address, 8 January 1918, PWW, vol. 45, *Nov. 11, 1917–Jan. 15, 1918* (1984), 537; Translation from the Mantoux Minutes of the Council of Four at the Paris Peace Conference, 27 March 1919, 3:30 P.M., PWW, vol. 56, *Mar. 17–Apr. 4, 1919* (used in galley proof through the courtesy of the editors).

63. Quoted in Unterberger, "Woodrow Wilson and the Russian Revolution," 72.

64. Wilson, *The State* (1898 ed.), 555.

9. WAR AND NEUTRALITY (1914–1917)

1 Cary T. Grayson, *Woodrow Wilson: An Intimate Memoir* (New York: Holt, Rinehart and Winston, 1960), 34.

2. Wilson to Mary Hulbert, 2 August 1914, PWW, 30:328.

3. Grayson, *Woodrow Wilson*, 35.

4. Link, *Wilson: New Freedom*, 463.

5. Wilson to Mary Hulbert, 23 August 1914, PWW, 30:437.

6. PWW, 30:264, 307.

7. Link, *Wilson: Struggle*, 7–8.

8. Address, 18 August 1914, PWW, 30:393–94.

9. House, Diary, 28 September 1914, PWW, 31: 95; Address, 18 August 1914, PWW, 30:394.

10. Memorandum of an interview with Wilson by Bruce Brougham, 14 December 1914, PWW, 31:459.

11. Kathleen Burk, *Britain, America and the Sinews of War, 1914–1918* (Boston: George Allen & Unwin, 1985), 5, 6.

12. Ibid., 5.

13. William Jennings Bryan to Wilson, 10 August 1914, PWW, 30:373, 372.

14. Robert Lansing, Memorandum of a conversation with Wilson, 23 October 1914, PWW, 31:219.

15. Robert Lansing to Wilson, 6 September 1915, PWW, 34:421.

16. John W. Coogan, *The End of Neutrality: The United States, Britain, and Maritime Rights, 1899–1915* (Ithaca: Cornell University Press, 1981), 16.

17. Ibid., 187.

18. Grey, *Twenty Five Years*, 2:107.

19. Draft of a note to Germany, 6 February 1915, PWW, 32:194–95. The term "unprecedented" was Wilson's insertion in Lansing's draft.

20. Wilson to Bryan, 3 April 1915, PWW, 32:468–69.

21. House, Diary, 7 May 1915, quoted in Link, *Wilson: Struggle*, 370.

22. Address, Philadelphia, 10 May 1915, PWW, 33:149.

23. Wilson to Bryan, 11 May 1915, PWW, 33:155.

24. Ibid., 156.

25. Address, Manhattan Club, New York, 4 November 1915, PWW, 35:169.

26. House, Draft to Sir Edward Grey, with corrections by Wilson, 17 October 1915, PWW, 35:81.

27. Text of House-Grey Memorandum, PWW, vol. 36, *Jan. 27–May 8, 1916* (1981), 180 n. 2; House, Diary, 6 March 1916, PWW, 36:262.

28. Lansing to Wilson, 21 December 1915, PWW, 35:374.

29. PWW, 36:496.

30. Lansing to Wilson, 6 May 1916, PWW, 36:620.

31. Ambassador James Gerard to Lansing, 3 May 1916, PWW, 36:614.

32. Draft of a note to Germany, 7 May 1916, PWW, 36:650.

33. Wilson to House, 23 July 1916, PWW, vol. 37, *May 9–Aug. 7, 1916* (1981), 467.

34. Wilson to House, 27 July 1916, PWW, 37:480.

35. A colloquy with a group of antipreparedness leaders, 8 May 1916, PWW, 36:645.

36. Lansing to Joseph Clark Grew in Berlin, 29 November 1916, PWW, 40:107.

37. Appeal to leaders of the belligerent nations, 18 December 1916, PWW, 40:274.

38. House to Wilson, 20 December 1916; House, Diary, 20 December 1916, PWW, 40:294, 305.

39. Walter Hines Page to Lansing, 22 December 1916, PWW, 40:319.

40. James Bryce to Wilson, 22 December 1916, PWW, 40:317.

41. Ibid., 306. Italics in original.

42. Lansing, Diary, 3 December 1916, PWW, 40:310 n. 1.

43. House, Diary, 3 January 1917, PWW, 40:403–4.

44. Address, U.S. Senate, 22 January 1917, PWW, 40:533–39. (The order of phrases differs from that in the speech.)

45. Constitutional Government in the United States, PWW, 18:161.

46. Address, 22 January, PWW, 40:534.

47. Quoted in John Milton Cooper, Jr., "The Command of Gold Reversed: American Loans to Britain, 1915–1917," Pacific Historical Review 45 (May 1976):228.

48. House, Diary, 1 February 1917, PWW, 41:87.

49. John Sharp Williams to Wilson, 3 February 1917, PWW, 41:108.

50. House, Diary, 1 February 1917, PWW, 41:87.

51. Statement to the press, 4 March 1917, PWW, 41:320.

52. Ibid., 333, 334, 335.

53. At cabinet meeting, 20 March 1917, Houston, Eight Years, 1:244.

54. Lansing to Wilson, 19 March 1917; House to Wilson, 19 March 1917, PWW, 41:425, 429.

55. Lansing, Memorandum on cabinet meeting, 20 March 1917, PWW, 41:442–43, 444.

56. Ibid., 519–27.

57. Ibid., 525, 526–27.

58. Ibid., 523.

59. Patrick Devlin, Too Proud to Fight: Woodrow Wilson's Neutrality. (New York: Oxford University Press, 1974), 687.

10. WAR LEADER (1917–1918)

1. Address, U.S. Congress, 2 April 1917, PWW, 41:526.

2. Wilson to Cleveland Dodge, 4 April 1917, PWW, 41:543.

3. Address, Charlotte, N.C., 20 May 1916, PWW, 37:81.

4. Quoted in Ray Stannard Baker, *Woodrow Wilson: Life and Letters*, vol. 5, *Neutrality, 1914–1915* (Garden City, N.Y.: Doubleday, Doran & Co., 1935), 77.

5. Quoted in David M. Kennedy, *Over Here: The First World War and American Society* (New York: Oxford University Press, 1980), 34.

6. Quoted in ibid., 39.

7. Wilson to Newton D. Baker, 11 April 1917, PWW, vol. 42, *April 7–June 23, 1917* (1983), 33.

8. Quoted in Stephen Vaughan, *Holding Fast the Inner Lines: Democracy, Nationalism, and the Committee on Public Information* (Chapel Hill: University of North Carolina Press, 1980), 17.

9. George Creel, Memorandum, ca. 11 April 1917, PWW, 42:39–40, 41.

10. Wilson to Josephus Daniels, 12 April 1917, PWW 42:43.

11. Quoted in Robert H. Ferrell, *Woodrow Wilson and World War I, 1917–1921* (New York: Harper & Row, 1985), 202.

12. Kennedy, *Over Here*, 74–75.

13. Ferrell, *Woodrow Wilson and World War I*, 204.

14. Quoted in Kennedy, *Over Here*, 76.

15. Joan M. Jensen, *The Price of Vigilance* (Chicago: Rand McNally, 1968), 34.

16. Wilson to Burleson, 11 October 1917; Wilson to Gregory, 19 October 1917, PWW, 44:358, 405.

17. Wilson to Herbert Croly, 22 October 1917, PWW, 44:420.

18. Quoted in Kennedy, *Over Here*, 80.

19. Allen F. Davis, "Welfare, Reform and World War I," *American Quarterly* 19 (Fall 1967):532.

20. Memorandum of interview with Wilson by the Duke of Devonshire, Governor General of Canada, enclosed in Wilson to Joseph Tumulty, 23 January 1918, PWW, vol. 46, *Jan. 16–Mar. 12, 1918* (1984), 81.

21. "Principles and Policies to Govern Relations between Workers and Employees [Employers] in War Industries for the Duration of the War," enclosed in William B. Wilson to Wilson, 4 April 1918, PWW, vol. 47, *Mar. 13–May 12, 1918* (1984), 250.

22. Address, AF of L, Buffalo, N.Y., 12 November 1917, PWW, 45:15.

23. Address, U.S. Congress, 2 April 1917, PWW, 41:522.

24. Quoted in Kennedy, *Over Here*, 107.

25. Charles Gilbert, *American Financing of World War I* (Westport, Conn.: Greenwood Publishing Co., 1970), 236.

26. Quoted in Kennedy, *Over Here*, 108–9.

27. Address, U.S. Congress, 27 May 1918, PWW, 48:163, 164.

28. Presidential Press Release, 10 October 1916, PWW, vol. 38, *Aug. 7–Nov. 19, 1916* (1982), 387–88.

29. Robert Cuff, "Harry Garfield, the Fuel Administration, and the Search for a Cooperative Order during World War I," *American Quarterly* 30 (Spring 1978):46.

30. Quoted in Kennedy, *Over Here,* 131.

31. Gregory quoted in ibid., 133.

32. Wilson to Robert Owen, 23 July 1917, PWW, 43:246.

33. Quoted in Kennedy, *Over Here,* 125.

34. Presidential Press Release, 21 January 1918, PWW, 46:56.

35. PWW, 47:94 n. 1.

36. Wilson to Lee S. Overman, 21 March 1918, PWW, 47:94.

37. Quoted in Jeffrey J. Safford, "Edward Hurley and American Shipping Policy: An Elaboration on Wilsonian Diplomacy, 1918–1919," *Historian* 35 (August 1973):570.

38. Quoted in ibid., 572.

39. Address, 8 January 1918, PWW, 45:537.

40. Wilson to Hurley, 29 August 1918, PWW, vol. 49, *July 18–Sept. 13, 1918* (1985), 374.

41. Wilson to House, 21 July 1917, ibid., PWW, 43:238.

42. Robert D. Cuff, "We Band of Brothers—Woodrow Wilson's War Managers," *Canadian Review of American Studies* 5 (Fall 1974):140.

43. Ferrell, *Woodrow Wilson and World War I,* 15.

44. Address, U.S. Congress, 2 April 1917, PWW, 41:522.

45. Wilson to Edward W. Pou, 13 April 1917; Wilson to Guy T. Helvering, 19 April 1917, PWW, 42:52, 97.

46. Proclamation, 18 May 1917, PWW, 42:181.

47. Sir William Wiseman to Arthur J. Balfour, 3 February 1918; Wilson to Newton Baker, 4 February 1918, PWW, 46:231, 237.

48. House, Diary, 16 September 1918, PWW, vol. 51, *Sept. 14–Nov. 8, 1918* (1985), 23.

49. Wilson to House, 21 July 1917, PWW, 43:238.

50. Sir William Wiseman, Memorandum of an interview with Wilson, 23 January 1918, PWW, 46:88.

51. Wilson to Lansing, 11 May 1917, PWW, 42:274.

52. Address, U.S. Congress, 4 December 1917, PWW, 45:196.

53. House, Diary, 18 December 1917, PWW, 45:323–24.

54. Cecil Spring Rice to Arthur J. Balfour, 4 January 1918, PWW, 45:456.

55. Ibid., 462.

56. Ibid., 536–38.

57. Quoted in Laurence W. Martin, *Peace without Victory: Woodrow Wilson and the British Liberals* (Port Washington, N.Y.: Kennikat Press, 1973), 164.

58. Address, Baltimore, 6 April 1918, PWW, 47:268.

59. Address, New York, 18 May 1918, PWW, 48:54.

60. Winston S. Churchill, *The World Crisis, 1911–1918*, 6 vols. (New York: Charles Scribner's Sons, 1927), 4:178.

61. Sir William Wiseman, Notes of an interview with Wilson, 16 October 1918, PWW, 51:347.

62. Ibid., 347–48.

63. Quoted in Klaus Schwabe, *Woodrow Wilson, Revolutionary Germany, and Peacemaking, 1918–1919: Missionary Diplomacy and the Realities of Power* (Chapel Hill: University of North Carolina Press, 1985), 57.

64. PWW, 51:419.

65. Creel to Wilson, 8 November 1918, PWW, 51:645. (The order of phrases is slightly changed.)

66. Quoted in Kennedy, *Over Here*, 89.

67. Quoted in ibid., 244–45.

68. Quoted in William Widenor, *Henry Cabot Lodge and the Search for an American Foreign Policy* (Berkeley: University of California Press, 1980), 279.

69. Address, 25 October 1918, PWW, 51:381–82.

70. Quoted in James D. Startt, "The Uneasy Partnership: Wilson and the Press at Paris," *Mid-America* 52 (January 1970):55.

11. FAILURE AND HOPE (1919–1924)

1. Lansing, Memorandum, 18 November 1918, PWW, vol. 53, *Nov. 9, 1918–Jan. 11, 1919* (1986), 128.

2. Ferrell, *Woodrow Wilson and World War I*, 137.

3. Statement on the draft law, 6 April 1917, PWW, 41:551.

4. House, Diary, 13 October 1917, PWW, 44:378.

5. Edith Bolling Galt to Wilson, 26 August 1915, PWW, 34:338.

6. House, Diary, 28 March 1917, PWW, 41:497.

7. House, Diary, 27 January 1918, PWW, 46:116.

8. House to Wilson, 8 March 1918, PWW, 46:575.

9. Address, University of Paris, 21 December 1918, in *The Public Papers of Woodrow Wilson*, ed. Ray Stannard Baker and William E. Dodd, 6 vols. (New York: Harper, 1925–27), vol. 1, *War and Peace; Presidential Messages, Addresses and Public Papers, 1917–1924* (1927), 330.

10. Statement, 2 December 1918, PWW, 53:315 n. 4.

11. Bertrand de Jouvenel, "Woodrow Wilson," *Confluence* 5 (1956):320.

12. Cary Grayson, Diary, 8 December 1918, PWW, 53:336–37.

13. Herbert Hoover to Wilson, 20 December 1918, PWW, 53:453.

14. Address, U.S. Congress, 8 January 1918, PWW, 45:537.

15. Quoted in Thomas A. Bailey, *Woodrow Wilson and the Lost Peace* (New York: Macmillan Co., 1944), 165.

16. Wilson to House, 21 July 1917, PWW, 43:238; Josephus Daniels, Diary, 17 October 1918, PWW, 51:372.

17. Address, Metropolitan Opera House, New York, 4 March 1919, Baker and Dodd, *Public Papers*, 1:451.

18. House, Diary, 16 December 1914, PWW, 31:469.

19. Address, University of Paris, 21 December 1918, Baker and Dodd, *Public Papers*, 1:330.

20. Address, Washington, League to Enforce Peace, 27 May 1916, PWW, 37:116.

21. Quoted in Leon E. Boothe, "Anglo-American Pro-League Groups Lead Wilson, 1915–1918," *Mid-America* 51 (April 1969):100.

22. Wilson to House, 20 March 1918, PWW, 47:85.

23. Wilson to Theodore Marburg, 8 March 1918, PWW, 46:572.

24. House to Wilson, 8 March 1918, PWW, 46:575.

25. Address, New York, 27 September 1918, PWW, 51:131.

26. Address, University of Paris, 21 December 1918, Baker and Dodd, *Public Papers*, 1:330.

27. Ibid., 423.

28. Ibid., 426, 425.

29. Quoted in Ferrell, *Woodrow Wilson and World War I*, 166.

30. Address, New York, 4 March 1919, Baker and Dodd, *Public Papers*, 1:444.

31. Quoted in Dimitri D. Lazo, "A Question of Loyalty: Robert Lansing and the Treaty of Versailles," *Diplomatic History* 9 (Winter 1985):42.

32. William H. Taft to Wilson, 18 March 1919, PWW, 56 (galley proofs).

33. Address, U.S. Congress, 11 February 1918, PWW, 46:321.

34. Vance McCormick, Diary, 1 April 1919, PWW, 56.

35. Quoted in Bailey, *Lost Peace*, 221.

36. Ray Stannard Baker, Diary, 8 April 1919, quoted in Inga Floto, *Colonel House in Paris: A Study of American Policy at the Paris Peace Conference 1919* (Princeton: Princeton University Press, 1980), 207.

37. Paul Mantoux, Notes of the Meeting of the Council of Four, 9 April, 1919, 3:30 P.M., PWW, vol. 57, *April 5–22, 1919* (used in typescript by courtesy of the editors of *The Papers of Woodrow Wilson*).

38. Quoted in Lloyd E. Ambrosius, "Wilson, Clemenceau and the German Problem at the Paris Peace Conference of 1919," *Rocky Mountain Social Science Journal* 12 (April 1975):75.

39. Quoted in ibid., 77.

40. 23 April 1919, Baker and Dodd, *Public Papers*, 1:465.

41. Quoted in Paul Gordon Lauren,"Human Rights in History: Diplomacy and Racial Equality at the Paris Peace Conference," *Diplomatic History* 2 (Summer 1978): 272.

42. Grayson Diary, 30 April 1919, PWW, vol. 58, *April 23–May 9, 1919* (used in typescript by courtesy of the editors of *The Papers of Woodrow Wilson*); Wilson to Tumulty, 30 April 1919, Baker and Dodd, *Public Papers*, 1:474–75.

43. Ray Stannard Baker, Diary, 1 May 1919, PWW, 58 (typescript).

44. Draft of Address to a Joint Session of Congress, ca. 8 February 1918, PWW, 46:296. Emphasis added.

45. Michla Pomerance, "The United States and Self-Determination: Perspectives on the Wilsonian Conception," *American Journal of International Law* 70 (January 1976):23.

46. Wilson to George Davis Herron, 28 April 1919, PWW, 58 (typescript).

47. Quoted in Ferrell, *Woodrow Wilson and World War I*, 167.

48. Address, U.S. Senate, 10 July 1919, Baker and Dodd, *Public Papers*, 1:548, 551–52.

49. Quoted in Widenor, *Henry Cabot Lodge*, 316, 319.

50. Carl A. Schenck to Austin F. Cary, 4 January 1921, in " 'Different Men from What We Were': Postwar Letters of Carl A. Schenck and Austin F. Cary," ed. David A. Clary, *Journal of Forest History* 22 (October 1978):233.

51. David I. Walsh, 9 October 1919; quoted in John H. Flannagan, Jr., "The Disillusionment of a Progressive: U.S. Senator David I. Walsh and the League of Nations Issue, 1918–1920," *New England Quarterly* 41 (December 1968):491.

52. William C. Bullitt, 12 September 1919; quoted in Lazo, "A Question of Loyalty," 44.

53. Baker, Diary, 19 May 1919, PWW, vol. 59, *May 10–May 31, 1919* (used in typescript by courtesy of the editors of *The Papers of Woodrow Wilson*).

54. Grayson, *Woodrow Wilson*, 95.

55. Address, Pueblo, Colo., 25 September 1919, Baker and Dodd, *Public Papers*, 2:410.

56. Quoted from Grayson Diary in Ferrell, *Woodrow Wilson and World War I*, 169.

57. Quoted in Weinstein, *Woodrow Wilson*, 360.

58. Grayson, *Woodrow Wilson*, 53.

59. Edith Bolling Wilson, *My Memoir*, 56.

60. House, Diary, 29 June 1919, PWW, 61, *June 19, 1919–July 22, 1919* (typescript); Wilson to Lansing, 24 May 1919, PWW, 59 (typescript).

61. Wiseman to Arthur Balfour, 18 July 1919, PWW, 61.

62. Address, Foreign Relations Committee, 19 August 1919, Baker and Dodd, *Public Papers*, 1:579.

63. Grayson, *Woodrow Wilson*, 103.

64. Quoted in Weinstein, *Woodrow Wilson*, 362.

65. Address, Foreign Relations Committee, 19 August 1919, Baker and Dodd, *Public Papers*, 1:578–79.

66. Jackson Day message, 8 January 1920, Baker and Dodd, *Public Papers,* 2:455.

67. Quoted in Judith L. Weaver, "Edith Bolling Wilson as First Lady: A Study in the Power of Personality, 1919–1920," *Presidential Studies Quarterly* 15 (Winter 1985):69.

68. Grayson, *Woodrow Wilson,* 106.

69. Quoted in Weinstein, *Woodrow Wilson,* 369.

70. Quoted in Arthur Walworth, *Woodrow Wilson,* 2d ed., rev., 2 vols. (Baltimore: Penguin Books, 1969), 2:414.

71. Quoted in ibid., 418.

72. "The Road Away from Revolution," *Atlantic Monthly,* August 1923, Baker and Dodd, *Public Papers,* 2:538.

73. Armistice Day address, 10 November 1923, Baker and Dodd, *Public Papers,* 2:540–41.

74. Quoted in Gene Smith, *When the Cheering Stopped: The Last Years of Woodrow Wilson* (New York: William Morrow & Co., 1964), 231–32.

75. Quoted in ibid., 234.

76. Grayson, *Woodrow Wilson,* 139.

77. 3 October 1913, PWW, 28:352.

BIBLIOGRAPHIC ESSAY

Primary Sources

Until recently, the main primary sources for a biography of Wilson were the Wilson Papers in the Library of Congress. Now, however, *The Papers of Woodrow Wilson*, edited by Arthur S. Link, David Hirst, and others (Princeton, N.J.: Princeton University Press, 1966–), with almost sixty volumes in print, provides an unparalleled wealth of materials including not only Wilson's personal papers but also collateral records such as extracts from diaries and documents selected from many foreign archives. An older collection, still useful for the latter part of Wilson's career, is Ray Stannard Baker and William E. Dodd, eds., *The Public Papers of Woodrow Wilson*, 6 vols. (New York and London: Harper, 1925–27).

Wilson's most important books are: *Congressional Government: A Study in American Politics* (Boston: Houghton Mifflin, 1885); *The State: Elements of Historical and Practical Politics: A Sketch of Institutional History and Administration* (Boston: Heath, 1889); *Division and Reunion, 1829–1889* (New York and London: Longmans, Green & Co., 1893); *A History of the American People*, 5 vols. (New York and London: Harper, 1902); and *Constitutional Government in the United States* (New York: Columbia University Press, 1908). Among his many popular and scholarly articles should be noted: "Cabinet Government in the United States," *International Review* 7 (August 1879):146–63; "Committee or Cabinet Government?" *Overland Monthly*, 2d ser. 3 (January 1884):17–33; "The Study of Administration," *Political Science Quarterly* 2 (July 1887):197–222; "The Making of the Nation," *Atlantic Monthly*, July 1897, 1–14: "The Reconstruction of the Southern States," *Atlantic Monthly*, January 1901, 1–15;

"Politics (1857–1907)," *Atlantic Monthly*, November 1907, 635–46; "The Road Away from Revolution," *Atlantic Monthly*, August 1923, 145–46.

Biographies

Arthur S. Link, *Wilson*, 5 vols. (Princeton: Princeton University Press, 1947–65) is definitive for the period to 1917. Ray Stannard Baker, *Woodrow Wilson: Life and Letters*, 8 vols. (Garden City, N.Y.: Doubleday, Page, 1927–39), while entirely uncritical and supplanted in most areas by Link and other biographers, is still valuable because of Baker's personal acquaintance with Wilson, the Wilson family, and members of Wilson's administration. Arthur Walworth's two-volume biography, *Woodrow Wilson*, 2d ed., rev. (Baltimore: Penguin, 1969), lacks annotation and has some factual errors but is readable. Good one-volume biographies of Wilson are surprisingly few in number. The most notable is John Morton Blum, *Woodrow Wilson and the Politics of Morality* (Boston: Little, Brown, 1956), which criticizes Wilson sharply for moralizing issues. Others include John A. Garraty's delightful *Woodrow Wilson: A Great Life in Brief* (New York: Knopf, 1956), and Arthur S. Link, *Woodrow Wilson: A Brief Biography* (Cleveland: World, 1963). Both need to be supplemented by reference to more recent primary and secondary materials. An older biography of note is William Bayard Hale's campaign biography, *Woodrow Wilson: The Story of His Life* (Garden City, N.Y.: Doubleday, Page & Co., 1912), for which Wilson personally supplied material on his childhood.

The most significant recent studies of Wilson are: John Milton Cooper, Jr., *The Warrior and the Priest: Woodrow Wilson and Theodore Roosevelt* (Cambridge, Mass.: Harvard University Press, Belknap Press, 1983), a remarkable dual and comparative biography of the two great progressive leaders; and Edwin A. Weinstein, *Woodrow Wilson: A Medical and Psychological Biography* (Princeton, N.J.: Princeton University Press, 1981), which supplants Sigmund Freud and William C. Bullitt's psychologically and historically discredited *Thomas Woodrow Wilson, Twenty-Eighth President of the United States: A Psychological Study* (Boston: Houghton Mifflin, 1967). Weinstein stresses the importance of what he believes were a series of strokes on Wilson's personality and behavior at crucial points of his career. His interpretation has been challenged vigorously by Alexander L. George and Juliette L. George in several places, including *Political Science Quarterly* 96 (Winter 1981–82):662–63, and *Journal of American History* 71 (June 1984):198–212, and differs sharply from that put forward by the Georges in their own book, *Woodrow Wilson and Colonel House: A Personality Study* (New York: John Day, 1956), which emphasizes psychological rather than physical reasons for Wilson's political problems. An argument similar to the Georges' is also presented by James David Barber, *The Presidential Character: Predicting Performance in the White House* (Englewood Cliffs, N.J.: Prentice-Hall, 1972), chaps. 2–4.

Wilson's Pre-1912 Career

Best among the studies of the pre-1912 period is John M. Mulder, *Woodrow Wilson: The Years of Preparation* (Princeton, N.J.: Princeton University Press, 1978). Mulder's article, "Joseph Ruggles Wilson: Southern Presbyterian Patriarch," *Journal of Presbyterian History* 52 (Fall 1974):245–71, challenges those who have seen Wilson as dominated by his father. Henry Wilkinson Bragdon, *Woodrow Wilson: The Academic Years* (Cambridge, Mass.: Harvard University Press, Belknap Press, 1967), is charming but sometimes unreliable, and George C. Osborn, *Woodrow Wilson: The Early Years* (Baton Rouge: Louisiana State University Press, 1968), is more superficial and less reliable than either Mulder or Bragdon.

Laurence R. Veysey, "The Academic Mind of Woodrow Wilson," *Mississippi Valley Historical Review* 49 (March 1963):613–34, offers a penetrating analysis of Wilson's leadership at Princeton and places his reforms there into the context of American education at the time. Marcia G. Synnott's essay "Woodrow Wilson" in the *Dictionary of Literary Biography*, vol. 47, *American Historians, 1866–1912*, ed. Clyde N. Wilson (Detroit: Gale/Bruccoli-Clark, 1986), 343–57, provides both an excellent brief biography and perceptive assessment of Wilson's achievements as a historian. Several essays by Arthur S. Link, conveniently collected in *The Higher Realism of Woodrow Wilson and Other Essays* (Nashville: Vanderbilt University Press, 1971), explore the importance of religion and his southern heritage on the development of Wilson's thought. William Diamond, *The Economic Thought of Woodrow Wilson* (Baltimore: Johns Hopkins University Press, 1943) is standard. William Bayard Hale, *The Story of a Style* (New York: B. W. Huebsch, 1920), is a psychoanalytic analysis by a disillusioned admirer, but it offers interesting and useful insights.

Wilson's remarkable wife, who exercised great influence on him, has long needed a biographer and has finally found one in Frances Wright Saunders. Her book *Ellen Axson Wilson: First Lady between Two Worlds* (Chapel Hill: University of North Carolina Press, 1985) is sympathetic and readable but underestimates Ellen's political influence on her husband. Family memoirs include Eleanor R. W. McAdoo, *The Woodrow Wilsons* (Boston: Houghton Mifflin, 1931) and Margaret Axson Elliott, *My Aunt Louisa and Woodrow Wilson* (Chapel Hill: University of North Carolina Press, 1944).

Wilson's political apprenticeship as governor of New Jersey is covered in James Kerney, *The Political Education of Woodrow Wilson* (New York and London: Century, 1926) and David W. Hirst, *Woodrow Wilson, Reform Governor: A Documentary Narrative* (Princeton, N.J.: Van Nostrand, 1965). Background on the development of the progressive movement in New Jersey is in Ransom E. Noble, Jr., *New Jersey Progressivism before Wilson* (Princeton, N.J.: Princeton University Press, 1946).

Elections and Domestic Legislation, 1912–1916

For the first Wilson administration, the five volumes of Arthur S. Link's *Wilson* are indispensable. His *Woodrow Wilson and the Progressive Era, 1910–1917,* rev. ed. (New York: Harper, 1963) covers the same period much more briefly. Memoirs and biographies of major figures in the administration are cited in Notes and References.

A number of specialized books and articles help to clarify particular issues of the administration. Robert H. Wiebe, *Businessmen and Reform: A Study of the Progressive Movement* (Cambridge, Mass.: Harvard University Press, 1962) stresses the business leadership of the progressive movement and helps to explain its conservative nature. Other influences on Wilson's policy are explored in Marshall E. Dimock, "Woodrow Wilson as Legislative Leader," *Journal of Politics* 19 (February 1957):3–19; Richard M. Abrams, "Woodrow Wilson and the Southern Congressmen, 1913–1916," *Journal of Southern History* 22 (November 1956):417–37; Arthur S. Link, "The South and the New Freedom: An Interpretation," *American Scholar* 20 (Summer 1951):314–24. A particularly controversial issue is the expansion of segregation in the federal bureaucracy. The most thorough recent study of this issue is Joel Williamson, *The Crucible of Race: Black-White Relations in the American South since Emancipation* (New York: Oxford University Press, 1984).

An excellent article pointing out that the Underwood Tariff was less revolutionary in its impact than often thought is Frank Burdick, "Woodrow Wilson and the Underwood Tariff," *Mid-America* 50 (October 1969):272–90. On the antitrust legislation of 1914, a good place to start is with Melvin I. Urofsky, "Wilson, Brandeis and the Trust Issue, 1912–1914," *Mid-America* 49 (January 1967):3–28; Benjamin J. Klebaner, "Potential Competition and the American Antitrust Legislation of 1914," *Business History Review* 38 (Summer 1964): 163–85; and G. Cullom Davis, "The Transformation of the Federal Trade Commission, 1914–1929," *Mississippi Valley Historical Review* 49 (December 1962):437–55. Closely related to antitrust issues were questions about organized labor and child labor. These are sketched in Robert K. Murray, "Public Opinion, Labor, and the Clayton Act," *Historian* 21 (May 1959):255–70; John S. Smith, "Organized Labor and Government in the Wilson Era, 1913–1921: Some Conclusions," *Labor History* 3 (Fall 1962):265–86; Walter I. Trattner, "The First Federal Child Labor Act (1916)," *Social Science Quarterly* 50 (Dec. 1969):507–24; Stephen B. Wood, *Constitutional Politics in the Progressive Era: Child Labor and the Law* (Chicago and London: University of Chicago Press, 1968). The evolution of the Federal Reserve Act can be traced in Carter Glass, *An Adventure in Constructive Finance* (Garden City, N.Y.: Doubleday, Page, 1927) and H. Parker Willis, *The Federal Reserve System* (1923; reprint ed., Salem, N.H.: Ayer, 1975). A challenging thesis about the broad implications of banking reform is offered by James Livingston, *Origins of the Federal*

Reserve System: Money, Class, and Corporate Capitalism, 1890–1913 (Ithaca and London: Cornell University Press, 1986). On the woman suffrage movement and its triumph, see Lois W. Banner, *Women in Modern America: A Brief History* (New York: Harcourt Brace Jovanovich, 1974), and Eleanor Flexner, *Century of Struggle: The Woman's Rights Movement in the United States* (Cambridge, Mass.: Harvard University Press, Belknap Press, 1959). For Prohibition, see James H. Timberlake, *Prohibition and the Progressive Movement, 1900–1920* (New York: Atheneum, 1970).

Foreign Policy Issues Other Than World War I

Specific issues of the period 1913–17 are covered in considerable detail in volumes 2–5 of Link's *Wilson*. For Link's broad interpretation of Wilson's policy, see *Woodrow Wilson: Revolution, War, and Peace* (Arlington Heights, Ill.: AHM, 1979), a revised and rewritten version of his earlier *Wilson the Diplomatist: A Look at His Major Foreign Policies* (1957). Useful essays on Wilsonian policies by various scholars are in *Woodrow Wilson and a Revolutionary World, 1913–1921*, ed. Arthur S. Link (Chapel Hill: University of North Carolina Press, 1982).

Other broad interpretations include N. Gordon Levin, Jr., *Woodrow Wilson and World Politics: America's Response to War and Revolution* (London and New York: Oxford University Press, 1968), which argues that Wilson sought to create a "liberal-capitalist" world order, reminding us that there was a very practical side to Wilsonian idealism. Older but still valuable is Harley Notter, *The Origins of the Foreign Policy of Woodrow Wilson* (Baltimore: Johns Hopkins University Press, 1937). Frederick S. Calhoun, *Power and Principle: Armed Intervention in Wilsonian Foreign Policy* (Kent, Ohio: Kent State University Press, 1986) examines seven uses of armed force by Wilson and concludes that he employed force effectively as a diplomatic tool. Burton I. Kaufman, in *Efficiency and Expansion: Foreign Trade Organization in the Wilson Administration, 1913–1921* (Westport, Conn.: Greenwood, 1974), and "The Organizational Dimension of United States Economic Foreign Policy, 1900–1920," *Business History Review* 46 (Spring 1972):17–44, demonstrates the importance Wilson and his advisors placed upon economic expansion and documents the steps they took to advance American interests. A similar argument is made somewhat more stridently by Carl P. Parrini, *Heir to Empire: United States Economic Diplomacy, 1916–1923* (Pittsburgh: University of Pittsburgh Press, 1969). For a thesis that Wilson was the creator of an American "open door empire," see William Appleman Williams, *The Tragedy of American Diplomacy*, rev. ed. (New York: Delta, 1962). A recent variant of this argument is Lloyd C. Gardner, *Safe for Democracy: The Anglo-American Response to Revolution, 1913–1923* (New York: Oxford University Press, 1984). An excellent review article that points out the many different concerns affecting Wilsonian diplomacy is Samuel F. Wells, Jr., "New Perspectives of Wilsonian Diplomacy: The Secular Evangelism of American Political Economy," *Perspectives in American History* 6 (1972):389–419.

The best overviews of Wilsonian policy in Mexico are Mark T. Gilderhus, *Diplomacy and Revolution: U.S.-Mexican Relations under Wilson and Carranza* (Tucson: University of Arizona Press, 1977), and P. Edward Haley, *Revolution and Intervention: The Diplomacy of Taft and Wilson with Mexico, 1910–1917* (Cambridge, Mass.: MIT Press, 1970). On specific aspects of the policy, see Kendrick A. Clements, "Woodrow Wilson's Mexican Policy, 1913–1915," *Diplomatic History* 4 (Spring 1980):113–36; Robert E. Quirk, *An Affair of Honor: Woodrow Wilson and the Occupation of Veracruz* (Lexington: University of Kentucky Press, 1962); Friedrich Katz, *The Secret War in Mexico: Europe, the United States, and the Mexican Revolution* (Chicago: University of Chicago Press, 1981); Robert Freeman Smith, *The United States and Revolutionary Nationalism in Mexico, 1916–1932* (Chicago: University of Chicago Press, 1972); Clifford W. Trow, "Woodrow Wilson and the Mexican Interventionist Movement of 1919," *Journal of American History* 58 (June 1971):46–72.

American intervention in Haiti is well covered in Hans Schmidt, *The United States Occupation of Haiti, 1915–1934* (New Brunswick, N.J.: Rutgers University Press, 1971), and David Healy, *Gunboat Diplomacy in the Wilson Era: The U.S. Navy in Haiti, 1915–1916* (Madison: University of Wisconsin Press, 1976). For the Dominican Republic, see Bruce J. Calder, *The Impact of Intervention: The Dominican Republic during the U.S. Occupation of 1916–1924* (Austin: University of Texas Press, 1984).

For East Asian relations, see Tien-yi Li, *Woodrow Wilson's China Policy, 1913–1917* (Kansas City: University of Kansas Press, 1952), and Roy Watson Curry, *Woodrow Wilson and Far Eastern Policy, 1913–1921* (New York: Bookman Associates, 1957). Jerry Israel, *Progressivism and the Open Door: America and China, 1905–1921* (Pittsburgh: University of Pittsburgh Press, 1971) suggests that Americans were guilty of both cultural and economic imperialism. Helpful in understanding the balance between economic and other interests in Wilson's China policy is Eugene P. Trani, "Woodrow Wilson, China, and the Missionaries, 1913–1921," *Journal of Presbyterian History* 49 (Winter 1971):328–51.

World War I and After

The period of World War I during which the United States remained neutral (1914–17) is brilliantly analyzed in volumes 3–5 of Link's biography of Wilson. Patrick Devlin, *Too Proud to Fight: Woodrow Wilson's Neutrality* (New York: Oxford University Press, 1974), is a splendid account of the period and a perceptive portrait of Wilson that sheds light on many other issues as well. John Milton Cooper, Jr., *The Vanity of Power: American Isolationism and the First World War, 1914–1917* (Westport, Conn.: Greenwood, 1969), and Kendrick A. Clements, *William Jennings Bryan, Missionary Isolationist* (Knoxville: University of Tennessee Press, 1982), discuss the evolution of isolationism during the war. On economic issues, see Kathleen Burk, *Britain, America and the Sinews of War, 1914–1918* (Boston: George Allen and Unwin, 1985); and John W. Coogan, *The End of Neutrality: The United States, Britain, and Maritime Rights, 1899–1915* (Ithaca and London: Cornell University Press, 1981). Edward Buehrig, *Woodrow Wilson and the Balance of Power* (Bloomington: Indiana University Press, 1955), was one of the first to argue that Wilson had a realistic understanding of the importance of a European balance of power to the United States. Ernest May, *The World War and American Isolation, 1914–1917* (Cambridge, Mass.: Harvard University Press, 1959), based on multiarchival research, remains one of the best overviews.

Strikingly different from each other in style and emphasis, but equally authoritative and charming are David M. Kennedy, *Over Here: The First World War and American Society* (New York: Oxford University Press, 1980) and Robert H. Ferrell, *Woodrow Wilson and World War I, 1917–1921* (New York: Harper and Row, 1985). Readers who want to understand the war and the peace that followed should start with these.

Diplomatic issues and homefront problems were more important to Wilson personally than military problems. They are explored in many excellent studies of various issues, of which the following are only a sampling: David F. Trask, *Captains and Cabinets: Anglo-American Naval Relations, 1917–1918* (Columbia: University of Missouri Press, 1973); David F. Trask, *The United States in the Supreme War Council: American War Aims and Inter-Allied Strategy, 1917–1918* (Middletown, Conn.: Wesleyan University Press, 1961); Wilton B. Fowler, *British-American Relations, 1917–1918: The Role of Sir William Wiseman* (Princeton, N.J.: Princeton University Press, 1969); Jeffrey J. Safford, *Wilsonian Maritime Diplomacy, 1913–1921* (New Brunswick, N.J.: Rutgers University Press, 1978); Laurence W. Martin, *Peace without Victory: Woodrow Wilson and the British Liberals* (Port Washington, N.Y.: Kennikat, 1973); Robert D. Cuff, *The War Industries Board: Business-Government Relations during World War I* (Baltimore: Johns Hopkins University Press, 1973); Charles Gilbert, *American Financing of World War I* (Westport, Conn.: Greenwood, 1970); Stephen Vaughan, *Holding Fast the Inner Lines: Democracy, Nationalism, and the Committee on Public Information* (Chapel Hill: University of North Carolina Press, 1980); Seward W. Livermore, *Politics is Adjourned: Woodrow Wilson and the War Congress, 1916–1918* (Middletown, Conn.: Wesleyan University Press, 1966).

The armistice and peace conference have also produced a flood of historical material, of which some of the best books are: Peter Rowland, *David Lloyd*

George: A Biography (New York: Macmillan, 1975); Melvyn P. Leffler, *The Elusive Quest: America's Pursuit of European Stability and French Security, 1919–1933* (Chapel Hill: University of North Carolina Press, 1979); Klaus Schwabe, *Woodrow Wilson, Revolutionary Germany, and Peacemaking, 1918–1919; Missionary Diplomacy and the Realities of Power* (Chapel Hill: University of North Carolina Press, 1985); A. Lentin, *Lloyd George, Woodrow Wilson and the Guilt of Germany: An Essay in the Pre-History of Appeasement* (Baton Rouge: Louisiana State University Press, 1984); Charles Seymour, *American Diplomacy during the World War* (Baltimore: Johns Hopkins University Press, 1934); Arthur Walworth, *America's Moment, 1918: American Diplomacy at the End of World War I* (New York: Norton, 1977), and *Wilson and His Peacemakers: American Diplomacy at the Paris Peace Conference, 1919* (New York: Norton, 1986); Inga Floto, *Colonel House in Paris: A Study in American Policy at the Paris Peace Conference, 1919* (Princeton, N.J.: Princeton University Press, 1981); Thomas A. Bailey, *Woodrow Wilson and the Lost Peace* (New York: Macmillan Co., 1944); Lawrence W. Gelfand, *The Inquiry: American Preparations for Peace, 1917–1919* (New Haven: Yale University Press, 1963); Charles L. Mee, Jr., *The End of Order: Versailles, 1919* (New York: Dutton, 1980); Arno J. Mayer, *Political Origins of the New Diplomacy, 1917–1918* (New York: Vintage, 1970), and *Politics and Diplomacy of Peacemaking: Containment and Counterrevolution at Versailles, 1918–1919* (New York: Vintage, 1969); Seth P. Tillman, *Anglo-American Relations at the Paris Peace Conference of 1919* (Princeton, N.J.: Princeton University Press, 1961); Thomas J. Knock, "Woodrow Wilson and the Origins of the League of Nations" (Ph.D. diss., Princeton University, 1982).

Worthy of special note is the famous attack on the peace and Wilsonian diplomacy by John Maynard Keynes, *The Economic Consequences of the Peace* (New York: Harcourt, Brace & Howe, 1920). Keynes, a member of the British delegation in Paris, was critical of the treaty while it was being drafted and predicted that it would lead to conflict and disaster. Many years later Étienne Mantoux, in *The Carthaginian Peace: Or, the Economic Consequences of Mr. Keynes* (New York: Scribner's, 1952), demonstrated that Keynes's criticisms were intemperate and excessive. See also the biography of Keynes by Robert Skidelsky, *John Maynard Keynes: Hopes Betrayed, 1883–1920*, vol. 1 (New York: Viking, 1986).

On the Russian issue, see Peter G. Filene, *Americans and the Soviet Experiment, 1917–1933* (Cambridge, Mass.: Harvard University Press, 1967); George F. Kennan, *Soviet-American Relations, 1917–1920*, 2 vols. (Princeton, N.J.: Princeton University Press, 1956, 1958), and "Russia and the Versailles Conference," *American Scholar* 30 (Winter 1960–61):13–42; John M. Thompson, *Russia, Bolshevism, and the Versailles Peace* (Princeton, N.J.: Princeton University Press, 1967); Betty M. Unterberger, *America's Siberian Expedition, 1918–1920* (Durham: Duke University Press, 1956). In contrast to the prevailing view among historians that Wilson authorized intervention only reluctantly in response to Allied pressures, see William Appleman Williams, "The American Intervention in Russia, 1917–1920," *Studies on the Left* 3 (Fall 1963):24–48. A good summary and analysis of the various interpretations of intervention is Carl J. Richard, " 'The Shadow of a Plan': The Rationale behind Wilson's 1918 Siberian Intervention," *Historian* 49 (November 1986):64–84.

A lively controversy over the reasons for Wilson's self-defeating behavior during the treaty fight continues to rage. Edwin Weinstein's *Woodrow Wilson: A Medical and Psychological Biography* cited above strengthened the case for those who believe that had he been well, Wilson would have found a workable compromise and secured the ratification of the treaty. The Georges, both in their book and in subsequent articles, have disagreed vigorously. So too does Lloyd E. Ambrosius, whose forthcoming *Woodrow Wilson and the American Diplomatic Tradition: The Treaty Fight in Perspective,* appeared too late to be consulted in the preparation of this book, but who was kind enough to send me a copy of a paper prepared for the 1986 conference of the Society for the Historians of American Foreign Relations, "Woodrow Wilson's Health and the Treaty Fight." Another book by a physician that deals with the subject but appeared too late for me to use is Bert E. Park, *Fit to Lead? The Impact of Illness on World Leaders* (Philadelphia: University of Pennsylvania Press, 1986). For another view critical of Wilson, though not of his ideals, see Thomas A. Bailey, *Woodrow Wilson and the Great Betrayal* (New York: Macmillan Co., 1945). Four articles by Kurt Wimer are helpful in understanding Wilson's frame of mind and ideas during the struggle: "Woodrow Wilson's Plans to Enter the League of Nations through an Executive Agreement," *Western Political Quarterly* 11 (December 1958):800–812; "Woodrow Wilson's Plan for a Vote of Confidence," *Pennsylvania History* 28 (July 1961):279–93; "Woodrow Wilson and a Third Nomination," *Pennsylvania History* 29 (April 1962):193–211; and "Woodrow Wilson Tries Conciliation: An Effort That Failed," *Historian* 25 (August 1963):419–38.

Extremism in the defense of liberty during and after the war is catalogued in Robert K. Murray, *Red Scare: A Study in National Hysteria, 1919–1920* (Minneapolis: University of Minnesota Press, 1955); Burl Noggle, *Into the Twenties: The United States from Armistice to Normalcy* (Urbana: University of Illinois Press, 1974); H. C. Peterson and Gilbert C. Fite, *Opponents of War, 1917–1918* (Seattle: University of Washington Press, 1968). Some of the racist excesses of the period are covered in Elliott M. Rudwick, *Race Riot at East St. Louis, July 2, 1917* (Carbondale: Southern Illinois University Press, 1964); William M. Tuttle, Jr., *Race Riot: Chicago in the Red Summer of 1919* (New York: Atheneum, 1970); Robert L. Zangrando, *The NAACP Crusade against Lynching, 1909–1950* (Philadelphia: Temple University Press, 1980).

Wilson's final years and death can be traced in the delightful book by Gene Smith, *When the Cheering Stopped: The Last Years of Woodrow Wilson* (New York: Morrow, 1964). For the election of 1920, see Wesley M. Bagby,

The Road to Normalcy: The Presidential Campaign and Election of 1920 (Baltimore: Johns Hopkins University Press, 1962). The president's health is discussed in Weinstein's medical biography, and with great discretion, by Wilson's doctor, in Cary T. Grayson, *Woodrow Wilson: An Intimate Memoir* (New York: Holt, Rinehart & Winston, 1960). Wilson's second wife, Edith Bolling Galt, was vitally important to him and exercised considerable control over public policy during his last years in office. Among the books about her are her own not-very-accurate recollections, *My Memoir* (Indianapolis: Bobbs-Merrill, 1938) and Ishbel Ross, *Power with Grace: The Life of Mrs. Woodrow Wilson* (New York: Putnam's, 1975).

INDEX

ABOUT THE AUTHOR

Kendrick A. Clements is professor of history at the University of South Carolina. He is the author of *William Jennings Bryan, Missionary Isolationist* (1982) and the editor of *James F. Byrnes and the Origins of the Cold War* (1982). Other publications include articles on diplomatic and environmental history in the *American Historical Review*, *Diplomatic History*, *Pacific Historical Review*, and other journals.